# COOK ISLANDS COMPANION

---

## THE VISITOR'S GUIDE TO
## RAROTONGA
## AND THE OUTER ISLANDS
2nd Edition

---

### ELLIOT SMITH

*PACIFIC PUBLISHING COMPANY*
*ALBANY, CALIFORNIA*

# COOK ISLANDS COMPANION

## THE VISITOR'S GUIDE TO RAROTONGA AND THE OUTER ISLANDS

2nd Edition

*Published by*
Pacific Publishing Co.
735 San Carlos Avenue
Albany, California
94706 USA
Tel (510) 525-1441
Fax (510) 525-1275

**An Invitation**
Readers are invited to send comments about hotels, restaurants and services you've used in the Cook Islands. Comments about this edition of *Cook Islands Companion* are also welcomed. Please write to:

Elliot Smith
Cook Islands Companion
Pacific Publishing Co.
735 San Carlos Avenue
Albany, California
94706 USA

First edition:     1991
Second edition:    1994


Copyright © 1994 by Elliot R. Smith


**Library of Congress Cataloging in Publication Data**:
Smith, Elliot R.
Cook Islands Companion---
    The Visitor's Guide to Rarotonga and the Outer Islands (2nd ed.)
Bibliography: p. 167
Includes index
1. Cook Islands---Description and travel.
2. Rarotonga---Description and travel.
3. South Pacific---Description and travel.
4. Travel---Cook Islands
ISBN 0-9629622-6-0

## About the Author

Born and raised in New York, Elliot Smith received his B.A. in 1969 and M.Ed. in 1972. He served as Dean of the New College of Modern Education, University of Buffalo, from 1970 to 1975, when he moved to San Francisco.

He traveled and wrote about the South Pacific for two years, then became a lawyer in 1980. Boredom soon set in, so in his spare time he built a house from the ground up, appeared on *Jeopardy*, and did more travel writing. In 1990 he was appointed a part-time Judge of the California State Bar Court, where he presides over lawyer misconduct trials several months a year.

When not on the bench, Judge Smith raises funds for charitable projects in the Cook Islands. In recognition of his years of service to the country, he was awarded honorary citizenship in 1993. He spends a few months each year in the Cooks, at his little beach house in Titikaveka, Rarotonga.

## From the Author

This book began in 1977, when I was on the first flight from Hawaii to the Cook Islands---a place no one in the US had ever heard of. We travel writers had thoughts of sleep, but not so the Cook Islanders, including Premier Albert Henry. They were playing ukuleles and singing and dancing in the aisles.

Just about everyone on Rarotonga met us at the airport, and we were treated as honored guests. Needless to say we had a great time, made lots of friends, and met all sorts of characters.

There have been many trips since then, and I now live there part-time. My friends in the US always ask me "Why do you go there? What's there to do? Where should we stay? How much does it cost?" and on and on and on. I wrote this book to answer their questions and, hopefully, yours as well.

## Acknowledgements

Special thanks in this second edition to Chris Wong, Metua Ngarupe, and the staff of the Cook Islands Tourist Authority; Ewan Smith and Air Rarotonga; Brendan Akamu and Polynesian Airlines; Lawrance Bailey, John Akerauara, Trisha Thompson, Teina Bishop, Chris Story, Elaine Gragg, John Talent, Ruth Mawson, Joy and Bob Smith, John Turner, Linda Rabideau, Alan Jakes, Michael Smith and Scot Simpson.

Thanks also to our small group of advertisers, who helped us keep the *Companion*'s price the same as it was in 1991, despite higher printing costs. If you use their services, a mention of their ad might help again in the future.

## And A Request

Your opinions and experiences can help the Cooks remain a great place to visit. Whether it's praise, problems or suggestions, please write to the Tourist Authority, the Cook Islands News, and us.

PHOTO CREDITS---Cover photo by Lawrance Bailey, at Muri Beach with Jeannine Tuavera (Miss Cook Islands/Dancer of the Year) and Danny Mataroa (Tumutevarovaro Dance Troupe), also Plates 9, 20, 24, 30; Cook Islands News: 151; Cook Islands Tourist Authority: 17, 19, 69, 137, 139, Plates 3, 13; Stephen Glatt: 29, 33, 53, Plates 7, 12, 14, 16; Donna Nagy: 63; Polynesian Airlines: 36; Ewan Smith/Air Rarotonga: 145, 153, Plates 1, 2, 5, 6, 23, 35, 37, 40; Rick Welland: 157, 160, Plates 36, 38; all other photos by the author.

DRAWINGS---Title page by Rick Welland. Historical drawings from William Gill (1856) and William Wyatt Gill (1876, 1885). Other sketches courtesy Cook Islands Library and Museum.

MEASUREMENTS

1 meter = 3.3 feet/1.1 yds.
1 kilometer = 5/8 mile
1 mile = 1.6 kilometers
1 nautical mile = 1.15 statute miles
Text uses statute (land) miles.
Airlines use nautical miles.

1 liter = 1.1 US quarts
3.8 liters = 1 US gallon

1 kilogram = 2.2 pounds
1 pound = 454 grams

Celsius to Fahrenheit: x 1.8 + 32
Fahrenheit to Celsius: - 32 x .55

15°C = 59°F
20°C = 68°F
25°C = 77°F
30°C = 86°F
35°C = 95°F

CURRENCY CONVERSION:
US $1 = NZ$1.67 / NZ$1 = US 60c
Can$1 = NZ$1.33 / NZ$1 = Can 75c
Aus$1 = NZ$1.18 / NZ$1 = Aus 85c

Conversion rates change daily. Major banks, or the business section of major newspapers, can supply the latest rates.

PRICES: All were accurate at publication, based on information supplied by airlines, hotels, etc. Readers should, however, verify prices prior to all purchases.

# TABLE OF CONTENTS

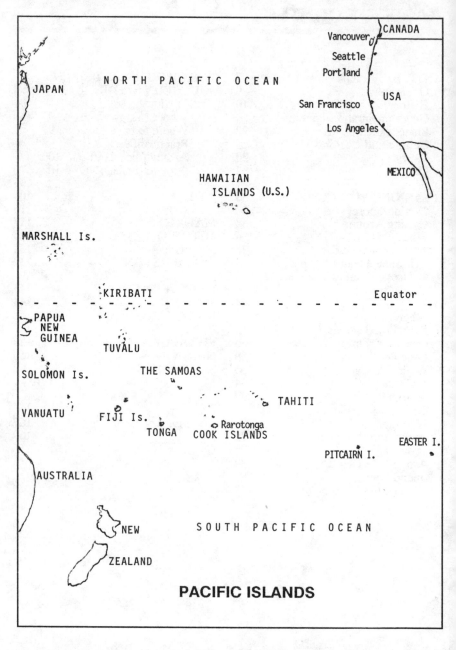

**PACIFIC ISLANDS**

*Rarotonga: A classic high island, with surrounding lagoon and islets*

# INTRODUCTION

Paradise has been found, alive and well, hidden deep in the exotic South Pacific. The Cook Islands, as they are more commonly known, lie 700 miles west of Tahiti. The main island of Rarotonga is a ten-hour flight from Los Angeles. It's well worth the trip.

These fifteen sun-drenched islands have been blessed by nature. They offer pristine white sand beaches, palm-fringed lagoons with colorful coral reefs, and perfumed flowers that overwhelm the senses. The climate is warm and temperate, and cool shore breezes provide natural air-conditioning.

Rarotonga is a compact paradise, only 20 miles around, and you're never far from anywhere else on the island.

There are excellent beachfront resorts, cozy cottages, and motels and hostels that can meet almost any budget. Fine restaurants offer a variety of dining choices, and recreational activities abound both in the water and on the land. Local nightlife features spectacular Polynesian dance shows, with audience participation encouraged.

The fondest memories of most visitors, however, are of the friendliness and hospitality of the islanders. The genuine warmth and generosity of the English-speaking *Maoris* clearly put Rarotonga and her sisters a cut above other vacation destinations.

Often compared to Hawaii of the 1950's, the Cooks offer a comfortable

COOK
ISLANDS

respite from the ill-effects of civilization. The pace of life is slow, the worries of the world far away. It's a place to kick back and relax, forget your troubles, and enjoy the good life in an idyllic island setting.

Visitors invariably have a great time, and most can't wait to return. Whether it's swimming, snorkeling, exploring the outer islands or just plain relaxing, the Cooks offer most tourists what they're looking for---unless it's traffic, noise, or other urban problems, which have yet to reach this little slice of paradise.

## GEOGRAPHY

The Cook Islands sit in the middle of the South Pacific, in storybook **Polynesia** (Latin for "many islands"). Also in this cultural grouping are Hawaii to the north, Tahiti to the east, and Samoa and Tonga to the west.

With a land area totalling only 93 square miles, the country is smaller than many cities. Yet the 15 islands are spread over an area one-fourth the size of the continental United States.

There are two natural geographic divisions. The islands of the **Southern Group**, which includes Rarotonga, are generally larger and more populous. The more remote **Northern Group** islands are mostly small coral atolls, with islets surrounding a large lagoon.

### Southern Group

Like Tahiti and Hawaii, **Rarotonga** is a so-called "high island," formed when an underwater volcano pushed its peak above sea level millions of years ago. The volcano is long-dormant, having eroded into mountain ridges flanked by lush valleys and a fertile coastal plain. Fronting much of the coast is a beautiful lagoon (Plate 6), with white sand beaches and swaying palms.

| | Area (sq.mi) | Pop. | Type |
|---|---|---|---|
| **SOUTHERN GROUP** | | | |
| Rarotonga | 26 | 10,918 | High/lagoon |
| Aitutaki | 7 | 2,366 | Lagoon/hills |
| Atiu | 10 | 1,003 | Makatea |
| Mauke | 7 | 639 | Makatea |
| Mitiaro | 9 | 249 | Makatea |
| Mangaia | 20 | 1,105 | Makatea |
| Palmerston | 0.8 | 49 | Lagoon |
| Manuae | 2.4 | 0 | Lagoon |
| Takutea | 0.5 | 0 | Sand Cay |
| **NORTHERN GROUP** | | | |
| Manihiki | 2.1 | 666 | Lagoon |
| Rakahanga | 1.6 | 262 | Lagoon |
| Penrhyn | 4 | 503 | Lagoon |
| Pukapuka | 1.9 | 780 | Lagoon |
| Nassau | 0.5 | 103 | Sand Cay |
| Suwarrow | 0.2 | 10 | Lagoon |
| **TOTAL:** | 93 sq.mi. | 18,652 pop. | |

Over half the country's population lives on Rarotonga, in neat and tidy villages that dot the main coastal road. The center of commerce is the north coast village of Avarua, two miles east of the modern international airport.

**Aitutaki**, a 45-minute flight north, is a high island where much of the central mountain dropped into the sea, creating a spectacularly large lagoon next to the remaining hills. Reminiscent of famed Bora Bora in French Polynesia, Aitutaki has beautiful beaches and coral reefs, with small *motus* (islets) circling the lagoon (Plates 20, 21). It's a must for snorkelers and divers, and its beauty makes it a popular second destination.

**Atiu, Mauke, Mitiaro** and **Mangaia** (Plates 27, 28, 31-34) were high islands that slowly sank to sea level, developed large coral reefs around them, and then were thrust back upward by underwater volcanic activity. Their central hills are now surrounded by a ring of high and dry dead coral, called *makatea*, often a mile wide, and always razor-sharp. There's no lagoon for swimming on these unique islands, but the beaches themselves are quite nice, and you can splash around in tiny "bathtub beaches" (reef holes) and sea caves.

Also a short flight from Rarotonga, they offer caves and inland areas to explore, and a chance to experience a more traditional culture. The few visitors to these non-commercial islands are welcomed with a hospitality rarely seen in most tourist destinations.

The three remaining southern islands are only accessible by sea. The lagoon atoll of **Manuae** is owned by the people of Aitutaki, while **Takutea** is a tiny sand cay owned by the people of Atiu. Both islands are uninhabited. **Palmerston**, a lagoon atoll populated by the descendants of one English settler and his three native wives, lies over 300 miles west of Rarotonga, and is sometimes mistakenly considered part of the Northern Group due to its location and coral atoll formation. Few tourists visit these three tiny islands.

### Northern Group

The remote lagoon atolls of the north, more than 700 miles from Rarotonga, are the classic tropical islands everyone wants to be stranded upon. With exotic names like **Manihiki**, **Pukapuka** and **Rakahanga**---and less romantic ones like **Penrhyn** and **Suwarrow**---their little palm-clad *motus* surround large lagoons and seem even more of a paradise than Rarotonga. Even little **Nassau**, without a lagoon, is covered with palm trees from head to toe.

There are pros and cons to these petite paradises. Most rise only a few feet above sea level, and whole villages can be destroyed by once-in-a-decade hurricanes. Fresh water is limited, and the sandy soil supports only coconut palms and subsistence crops.

The crystal-clear lagoons, however, teem with tropical fish, and in some cases, pearl oysters. The beaches, of course, are magnificent! Famous as well for their traditional lifestyles, these are once-in-a-lifetime destinations for a few lucky travelers (Plates 35-38, 40).

### HISTORY

For a small group of islands, the Cooks have had an amazing assortment of colorful characters and unique incidents in their history. The polygamy and cannibalism of the early days were replaced by the strict moral ordinances of the missionaries, and the islands later attracted a melange of traders, sailors, whalers and beachcombers. Somehow out of this cultural legacy emerged a small independent nation, which blends democratic institutions with the best of its traditional culture.

### Polynesian Discoverers

The first settlers were Polynesians, who arrived about 800 AD from Raiatea, in what is now French Polynesia. Sailing for weeks in great double-hulled canoes with large pandanus-leaf sails, these colonizers were the last wave of the great Polynesian Migration, which moved east from Asia beginning 1500 BC. Other Polynesians discovered Hawaii and Tahiti, explaining the similarity of cultures today.

Early explorers navigated by using familiar stars as course headings. Directional clues were gathered from the color and temperature of the water, and islands beyond the horizon were located by the haze resulting from waves crashing on their reefs. Frigatebirds, which instinctively head for land, were taken on these long voyages and then released far out at sea. When one headed in a direction other than home, the voyagers followed, releasing more birds until a new island was finally sighted.

### Early Legends

There is no written record of the early culture, but oral narratives were passed from generation to generation, often in the form of songs and dances. These tales include the name of **Toi**, a famous chief of the 11th century, who built the first coral road around Rarotonga. Lying inland, near the original villages, this ancient road---the *ara metua*---is still in use today.

In the 13th century another wave of Polynesians arrived, including the great chiefs **Tangiia** and **Karika**, who joined forces to conquer the earlier inhabitants. Many place names on Rarotonga still reflect incidents of that era, lending some credibility to these oral histories.

### Early Culture and Customs

After these early wars, Rarotonga was divided into three districts, each controlled by a high chief, the *ariki*. On the north was **Avarua**, bordered by **Puaikura** on the west; **Takitumu** covered the east and south. These are still recognized as the main divisions of the island, although land ownership has gotten complicated by tribal intermarriage.

The ariki were powerful rulers, seen by their subjects as having a supernatural power called *mana*. They had the power to divide lands, settle disputes, and punish thieves and other criminals. Each district had a central *koutu* (court) where the ariki would make his rulings known. The title of ariki usually passed to a male descendant, although this was a preference, not a necessity. The first female ariki was invested in the 1850's, and ariki today are women as often as men.

*Traditional thatched hut of woven palm leaves*

*Cook Islands native---1777*

Districts were divided into 400-acre sections called *tapere*, each home to about 200 members of an extended family. These were ruled by chiefs called *mataiapo*, with the help of sub-chiefs, *rangatira*. Each tapere had a central meeting place, and a sacred religious ground, a *marae*. Many *marae* can still be seen along the *ara metua*.

Native religion played an important role in daily life, and the priests---the *ta'unga*---had their own *mana*, almost as strong as that of the ariki. On behalf of an ariki, a priest could declare certain acts or places *tapu* (forbidden), and those who violated *tapu* were often clubbed to death. Priestly titles of the ta'unga were hereditary.

The ancient religion had many gods, and each *marae* was usually devoted to its own god. Many gods were symbolized by wood and stone carvings, and the most famous, the phallic male god *Tangaroa*, lives on today in carvings, coins, and government publications.

Elaborate religious ceremonies accompanied birth, maturity, marriage and death, as well as the frequent warfare. Before the missionaries arrived in the 1820's the tribes engaged in numerous battles, accompanied by a unique cultural ritual---cannibalism.

Cannibalism was evident in all the Southern Cooks, but it was essentially a by-product of warfare. The men fought over food, women, land, and petty affronts of all kinds. Successful warriors would eat their victims as a form of revenge. Women and children were spared, and anyone dying of natural causes was likewise off the menu.

Barbecuing was a favorite method of preparation, and a "long spear, inserted at the fundament, ran through the body, appearing again with the neck" reported early missionary W. W. Gill. The body was slowly singed over the fire to remove the hair and cuticles. The intestines were then washed and cooked separately, and, like the thighs, were considered delicacies.

Polygamy was also common, and women were virtually the slaves of their husbands. Women had to plant crops, fish in the lagoon, gather firewood, cook, clean, make clothing, and raise the children. Men had to fight wars, and catch fish in the ocean.

Both sexes dressed to attract their opposites. Men wore their hair long, often tied up in a topknot, and their arms were tattooed between the elbow and shoulder. Both sexes wore ear ornaments, necklaces, and flower wreaths. Men's clothing consisted of wrap-around loin cloths (*maro*) made of bark, and unmarried women wore bark cloth skirts cut just above the knee. After

*Maninitori—The traditional wedding march of royal brides and grooms on Mangaia*

marriage these were exchanged for skirts that reached just below the knee.

A unique custom on Mangaia was the **maninitori**, the wedding ceremony of the first-born of high-ranking families. The bridegroom walked to his father-in-law's house on his prone in-laws' backs, and months later the roles were reversed for the bride's walk.

Aside from periods of warfare and occasional famine, daily life was free from most hardship. Plantations needed tending only one day out of three, and the lagoon and ocean supplied ample fish. There was much time for social pleasures, including music, dancing, and drinking *kava*, a mildly narcotic drink made from the root of the *piper methysticum* plant (a type of pepper).

**European Explorers**

Pukapuka was the first island sighted by Europeans, by Spain's **Captain Alvaro de Mendana** on August 20, 1595. On March 2, 1606, **Captain Pedro Fernandez de Quiros**---Mendana's Chief Pilot in 1595---stopped at Rakahanga for provisions, on his way from the silver mines of Peru to the Philippines.

Quiros was impressed by the 70' double-hulled sailing vessels used for inter-island travel, and described the islanders as "the most beautiful white and elegant people, especially the women, who, if properly dressed, would have advantages over our Spanish women." From then on Rakahanga was known as *Isla de Gente Hermosa* (Island of Beautiful People).

There was no further European contact for over 150 years, until the voyages of **Captain James Cook**, for whom the group was eventually named. The English sent Cook to find *Terra Australia Incognitus*, the "Unknown Southern Continent," which cartographers thought must exist to counterbalance the continents of the northern hemisphere. One office-bound mapmaker, Alexander Dalrymple, tried to convince the Admiralty that he, not the experienced Cook, should lead the expeditions. Had he succeeded, you might be visiting the Dalrymple Islands!

On September 23, 1773, on his second of three Pacific voyages, Cook sighted Manuae. He named it Harvey's Isle, after a Lord of the Admiralty. This was modified to Hervey's Island, and was applied to the entire Southern Group until 1824, when the Russian cartographer von Krusenstern changed the name to honor Cook, who had been killed in Hawaii in 1779. Many maps still show Manuae as "Hervey's Island."

Cook also discovered Palmerston, Takutea, Mangaia and Atiu, and his observations were similar to those of Quiros. He thought "some of the men rather handsome" and his crew that went ashore thought the women modest, as "nature presented us with her productions in the fullest perfection, unbiased in sentiment by custom, or unrestrained in manner by art."

Despite being the namesake of the group, Captain Cook---and most European explorers---had little direct effect on the local culture. His diaries indicate he personally went ashore only on uninhabited Palmerston, collecting coconuts and swamp grass. Cook's real contributions to Pacific history were his detailed maps of the area, which were given broad distribution in Europe.

Earlier maps of trade routes had been kept secret, and shown only to a small group of international merchants.

Some locals feel the country should not be named after a European explorer who "discovered" islands already inhabited. (This could be said of Bolivia and the United States of America.) One suggested name is *'Avaiki*, the traditional Polynesian spiritland.

Cook's maps opened the Pacific to a new wave of European exploration, which included the ill-fated voyage of **Captain Bligh** in the *Bounty*, seeking breadfruit from Tahiti to feed slaves in the Caribbean.

He sighted Aitutaki after leaving Tahiti in 1789, a few weeks before the infamous mutiny led by **Fletcher Christian**. Bligh and a dozen men were cast adrift in a longboat, and they miraculously reached safety in the Dutch East Indies after a 3000-mile voyage. Bligh returned to England, and the British Navy came looking for the mutineers.

*Captain James Cook*

Christian and his men searched far and wide for a safe haven. They sighted Rarotonga in late 1789, but didn't come ashore. They did trade some oranges with the natives, however, and the current orange industry dates from those seeds. The mutineers eventually settled on tiny Pitcairn Island, 1200 miles southeast of Tahiti, and some descendants ended up in the Cook Islands.

Rarotonga's official discovery by Europeans is generally credited to **Captain Philip Goodenough** in the *Cumberland*, in 1814. He was seeking valuable sandalwood trees, but Rarotonga had none. He instead loaded up yellow dye-wood (*nono*) for sale in Australia, where it proved worthless.

Goodenough's few months on Rarotonga were marked by bloody clashes with the locals, caused by his crew's theft of food, *nono* wood and women, not necessarily in that order. This first sustained visit by Europeans is not fondly recounted in local history books.

Several months later, what is now called Suwarrow was sighted by the Russian **Captain Lazarev** in the *Suvarov*, who named the uninhabited island after his ship. Had he followed up on this claim, there is little doubt the Cook Islands would have figured more prominently in Cold War politics!

By 1823, when Mauke and Mitiaro were visited by the English missionary **John Williams**, all the islands had been re-discovered by Europeans. As the age of European discovery ended, the age of radical social change began, due in large part to Williams and his fellow missionaries.

**The Missionary Period**
Formed in 1797, the **London Missionary Society (LMS)** was one of many religious groups hoping to find converts

*Tepou, an early Rarotongan chief*

in the newly-discovered lands of the Pacific. The LMS sent teachers to Tahiti and Raiatea, and converted many locals. Some became missionaries and were sent to other islands, including the nearby "Hervey" (Cook) Islands.

**Papeiha**, a native missionary from Raiatea, was placed on Aitutaki by John Williams on October 26, 1821, a date commemorated as the national holiday of Gospel Day. Two years later Williams placed other Polynesian missionaries on Atiu, Mauke and Mitiaro, and relocated Papeiha to Rarotonga.

Within a few years Papeiha had converted much of Rarotonga, and practices such as cannibalism, infanticide and idol worship were abandoned. More modest forms of dress were adopted, and violent warfare subsided.

Williams returned in 1827 with missionary **Charles Pitman**, and they were soon followed by **Aaron Buzacott** and **William Gill**, among others. These European missionaries consolidated the work of their successful Polynesian brethren, and also brought massive social changes to the islands.

Mission houses and chapels were built on the coast, and Christian families had to leave their inland villages and move to these new settlements. Missionaries introduced the technique of building with burnt coral, and traditional huts were replaced by limestone houses. Clothing changed from bark cloth to cotton, and new crops were introduced to help avoid the frequent famines.

Basic laws were passed regarding theft, land use, and trespass, and formal courts with judges were established in cooperation with the ariki. Warfare and violence were prohibited for settling disputes, and some measure of political stability was achieved between the tribes. The church also directed that women be given a greater role in the community, and for the first time women were allowed to become ariki.

Missionaries created a written alphabet and vocabulary based on Rarotongan, and mission schools were established. Many islanders became missionaries, including **Maretu**, who served on Mangaia and other islands.

Not content with mere order and stability, however, the European missionaries also had strict "moral ordinances" enacted. *Kava* drinking and sensual dancing were prohibited, as was tattooing and the use of flowers and oils on the body. An eight o'clock curfew was instituted, and men had to cut their long hair and topknots. Polygamy was outlawed, and a man could only keep the wife that bore his first child.

Some typical acts prohibited by these "Blue Laws" included the following:

"(a) Consulting a sorcerer;
(b) Being pregnant as an unmarried woman;
(c) Card-playing;
(d) Placing one's arm round a woman, even though the offender have no torch in the other hand;
(e) Trading with an European without permission;
(f) Tattooing or being tattooed;
(g) Going from one village to another on a Sabbath;
(h) Taking an unmarried woman inland;
(i) Crying over a dead woman, even though not related to her."

To enforce these moral ordinances a large police force was created, staffed only by church members. At times fully one-third of all adult males were policemen, living on the fines they collected from those that did not toe the line. Church membership was essential to anyone wanting influence in the community, and all social activity eventually became centered around the church.

The prohibitions were in effect for over fifty years, until replaced by British law and religious freedom. Nonetheless, the church today remains a strong social, cultural, and political institution, and current law retains some of the flavor, if not the specific substance, of those early moral ordinances.

### Disease and Blackbirders

Along with the increased trade of this era came European diseases, to which the locals had little immunity. Epidemics of dysentery, whooping cough, influenza, mumps and measles were common from 1830 to 1880, and the population of Rarotonga dropped from 7000 to less than 2000. Since then it has slowly increased to over 10,000, and more than 30,000 Cook Islanders live in New Zealand.

*Early Cook Islands family at home*

Also contributing to depopulation, especially on the small atolls of the north, were raids in the 1860's by Peruvian slave traders, known as "blackbirders." About 140 Pukapukans were essentially kidnapped under false pretenses, and on Penrhyn the slavers took 412 out of a population of only 500. The islanders believed they were going to temporary jobs on nearby islands, but what they got was a life of slavery in the mines of South America, and few ever saw home again.

This ugly chapter in history ended a few years later after intervention by the French and British navies, but not before thousands of Pacific islanders had been sold into slavery.

**The Father of Palmerston**

As of 1863, the tiny atoll of Palmerston had not been affected by missionaries, diseases, or blackbirders, since it was totally uninhabited. Into this void stepped the legendary **William Marsters**, an Englishman who settled there with his three native wives and raised three separate families, each in its own tiny village.

He divided his prolific energy among the three branches, helping to create a lineage that now numbers in the thousands. Virtually the entire population of Palmerston is named Marsters, and you'll find Marsters on most islands in the country. See the Palmerston chapter for more on this unique slice of history.

## British Protectorate

In addition to their obvious lack of influence on Mr. Marsters, the missionaries' power began to wane on the other islands in the late 1800's. Merchants and whalers visited in greater numbers, and Mrs. Buzacott noted that men "of some wealth and little religious principle" were beginning to reside on Rarotonga.

Beer brewed from oranges ("bush beer") became popular among locals, and the influence of planters and European traders also increased. Cotton, coffee, copra and fruit were exported to Tahiti and New Zealand, and France and Britain both became interested in this small group of islands.

In 1888 there were less than a dozen foreigners living on Rarotonga, most of them of British extraction. One afternoon they learned from the captain of an arriving vessel that a French warship was coming from Tahiti to claim Rarotonga for the French. They convinced the *ariki* of the Avarua district, **Makea Takau**, that Rarotonga's "independence" would be better protected by Great Britain than France.

She reluctantly agreed, and a British flag was hastily sewn together from scraps of cloth. When the French warship appeared on the horizon the next morning the Union Jack was quickly run up a makeshift flagpole. The French captain sighted the British colors, and immediately turned his ship to the north. Had Makea Takau not agreed to British protection the previous evening, you'd be visiting a French colony, rather than an English-speaking independent country.

After Rarotonga accepted British protection the other islands soon followed, although Aitutaki was actually annexed by the British since they hoped to use the large lagoon as a major shipping center in the South Pacific.

During this short protectorate period the missionary laws were replaced by British law, and the moral conduct ordinances were mostly repealed. The islands were opened to other religions, and the Seventh Day Adventists and Catholics arrived in the 1890's.

The British governed via New Zealand, but after several years local sentiment favored a more formal relationship with the latter.

## New Zealand Administration

The Cooks were annexed by New Zealand on June 11, 1901. The next sixty-four years of colonial rule have been described as "benign," with modest improvements in health, education, agriculture and overseas trade.

Of some significance, however, was the colonial government's removal of almost all power from the *ariki* and other native chiefs, who were replaced by New Zealand administrators. The resulting lack of experience in self-government has been cited as one cause of the alleged nepotism and misuse of power following the gaining of independence in 1965.

Cook Islanders fought alongside New Zealanders in both World Wars, and in World War II about 1000 American servicemen were stationed on both Aitutaki and Penrhyn, with predictable effects on the future gene pool. The war in the Pacific, however, did not reach the Cook Islands.

## The Hermit of Suwarrow

It was during this period that **Tom Neale**, the modern Robinson Crusoe, moved to uninhabited Suwarrow. Arriving in 1952, he spent 15 of the next 25 years living alone on this small tropical atoll. Tom's story is included in the Suwarrow chapter, and in his auto-biographical *An Island to Oneself.*

### Independence

The country attained independence on August 4, 1965, in the form of internal self-governance in association with New Zealand. The original agreement gave New Zealand responsibility for defense and foreign affairs, but the latter has now been assumed by the local government. Cook Islanders are New Zealand citizens and carry New Zealand passports, and these legal ties have prevented the Cooks from gaining admission to the United Nations.

The early years after independence are a soap opera of politics, much of it revolving around the controversial and charismatic Albert Henry, the "George Washington" of the Cook Islands.

### Politics---The National Pastime

Born to an influential Aitutaki family, **Albert Royle Henry** (1907-1981) was educated in New Zealand, and later became a key figure in the independence movement. His dedication to the cause resulted in his election as the first Premier of the Cook Islands in 1965. He was knighted by Queen Elizabeth II in 1974, and Sir Albert was firmly in control of the destiny of his young country. That is, however, until the nation was rocked by its own version of the "Watergate" scandal, this one revolving around the national elections of 1978.

Thinking the race too close for comfort, Henry arranged to borrow NZ$300,000 in public funds from the government-owned Philatelic (stamp) Bureau. He then chartered planes to fly in 400 Cook Islanders residing in New Zealand, who, in turn, voted for his Cook Islands Party (absentee voting was

Rarotongan Mataiapo and the
New Zealand Governor-General

not allowed). The CIP won the close election, and Henry was again chosen Premier.

The details of the scheme became public, and the opposition Democratic Party filed a lawsuit contesting the "fly-in" voters. On July 24, 1978, the court ruled Henry had used public funds and bribery to win votes. The CIP fly-in votes were invalidated, and the Democrats were declared the winners.

Henry's reign was over. To add insult to injury, the Queen soon stripped him of his knighthood.

Albert Royle Henry died January 1, 1981, and his period in power is still the topic of heated debates. He is, however, kindly remembered by most locals as the man that led them to independence. Mourners lined the 20-mile coastal road during his funeral procession, and his impressive grave in Avarua is still well-maintained by his many admirers.

After the 1978 court decision Democratic Party leader **Dr. Tom Davis** became the Premier. Davis had worked as a research doctor with the US space program before returning home to join the political fray. During his term an overseas seat was added to Parliament, in part to prevent the fly-in voter problem. The Premier was renamed the Prime Minister, and a Bill of Rights was added to the Constitution.

In 1983 the CIP returned to power, and **Geoffrey Henry**, a cousin of Albert Henry, became Prime Minister. Due to a constitutional technicality another election was held in late 1983, and Tom Davis regained his position. He lost it, however, in 1987, on a "no-confidence" vote by his own party, and **Dr. Pupuke Robati** became Prime Minister. Geoffrey Henry returned as Prime Minister when the CIP won the 1989 election, and again after the CIP's 1994 victory.

Politics is a favorite topic of conversation, and mini-scandals seem to be alleged against whatever group is in power. Few are proven, however, and the overall political stability of the country has rarely been questioned.

### The Year Of The Fires

Even paradise occasionally has its problems. In 1992 a series of devastating arson fires destroyed a church, two restaurants, several businesses, and virtually the entire central government complex---including the Post Office, Courthouse, Ministers' Offices, and main telephone exchange.

The country had a communications blackout for almost two weeks, and the telephone system took several months to repair. Most locals simply took it in stride. As one friend commented: "We actually enjoyed doing business in person, rather than over the phone. Friends would stop by, rather than telephone. Maybe we should just get rid of the phones on our own!"

The damaged colonial-era buildings were razed, and the vacant section near the traffic circle is now in the hands of the planning department.

This main conflagration was set by two drunks who wanted to postpone their trial for allegedly stealing a pair of running shoes. They apparently succeeded, but now they'll have a dozen years in prison to consider the merits of their actions.

### GOVERNMENT AND ECONOMY

The country has a parliamentary system similar to Britain, Australia and New Zealand. The 25 elected members choose the Prime Minister, who serves as head of government. Elections are held at least every five years. Parliament meets February/March and July to September, at a minimum. Visitors may observe the proceedings (no shorts or jeans) at the Parliament Building, near the airport.

Political parties are active, and include the Cook Islands Party, Democratic Party and Alliance Party.

On Rarotonga, the House of Ariki is composed of the traditional high chiefs of the island. This respected body has little legal power, but is consulted on matters affecting land, customs and tradition. The Koutu Nui (Great Court) is comprised of chiefs and sub-chiefs (mataiapo and rangatira), and also has influence in these areas.

The Queen of England is the symbolic head of government, and the Queen's Representative is usually a local dignitary, chosen by the Cook Islands government.

An elected Island Council, and a Government Representative appointed by the Prime Minister, govern local affairs on each island.

## International Relations
The Cooks maintain strong ties to New Zealand, which provides defense and some assistance in foreign affairs. Cook Islanders are New Zealand citizens, but not vice-versa. Complete independence is available, but most locals feel the benefits of the current relationship outweigh its disadvantages.

The Cooks are active in regional organizations such as the South Pacific Forum, which coordinates programs on fisheries, shipping and similar concerns.

A Treaty of Friendship was signed with France, which controls neighboring Tahiti and French Polynesia. Fisheries, education, solar power assistance, and cultural exchanges are areas of cooperation. The controversial nuclear testing in French Polynesia was not a subject of the treaty, although Cook Islanders have been vocal opponents in the past. A seismic monitoring station on Rarotonga is one of the few such facilities in the South Pacific.

The Greenhouse Effect is of some concern to islanders. Caused in part by carbon dioxide produced by the burning of fossil fuels, scientists theorize that, as the heat from the sun becomes trapped, the glaciers and polar ice caps will begin to melt. This may cause the sea level to rise, and the low-lying atolls of the north would become submerged. The Cooks would lose half its islands, so the locals' concern is not surprising.

Relations with the US are now quite good, but they had been mildly strained by US claims to several northern atolls,

based on the self-serving US "Guano Act" of 1858. Despite the fact no guano (bird dung) was ever mined, the islands had been claimed as US possessions. All claims were relinquished in 1983, and US tuna boats were subsequently licensed to operate in the Cooks' Exclusive Economic Zone (EEZ).

## Economy
The economy is based on agriculture and tourism. Papayas and other tropical produce are major exports, along with clothing, soaps, perfumes and pearls.

Colorful stamps and unusual coins bring in revenue, and fees paid by tuna boats bring in hard currency. The country is also an offshore "tax haven" used by international corporations, and registration fees generate income for the government and local business.

Imports include manufactured goods and fuel. Of some note is the fact that Japanese canned fish is also imported. Most trade is with New Zealand, which takes 80% of exports and supplies 60% of imports. Cook Islanders living in New Zealand send home over US$3 million annually to relatives, and New Zealand supplies US$5 million a year to help balance the national budget.

Agricultural exports are hampered by high shipping costs and irregular schedules. Insect infestation of crops has, so far, been extremely low, and your plane may be fumigated on arrival as part of these safeguards.

If the Asian driftnetters don't clean out the ocean, the Cooks could develop a profitable tuna fishing industry. Their large EEZ comes from the fact that the 200-mile limit applies to even the tiniest atolls, so the economic clout of this small but widely-scattered country is potentially enormous. The ocean floor has manganese, cobalt and other precious metals, but exploration is expensive, and little research has been done.

The pearl industry, centered on the northern atolls of Manihiki and Penrhyn, is rapidly becoming a big moneymaker. Recent auctions of black pearls brought in over US$2 million, and the industry is growing rapidly.

Start-up costs are high, however, and a bank loan is usually required. Penrhyn is probably the only place in the world where the bank manager is required to have a scuba diving certificate!

## Tourism

The largest source of income is tourism, which developed after the runway extension in 1973 enabled jets to land. Visitor numbers increased in the late 1970's after the completion of the Rarotongan Resort and the expansion of the Edgewater. Aitutaki and other outer islands are becoming more popular, bringing needed revenue to these areas.

The 50,000 tourists visiting annually add US$15 million to the economy. A third are from New Zealand and Australia, and a like percentage arrives from Europe. North America adds about 12,000 visitors a year, and this is rapidly increasing as air links grow, and first-time visitors return.

## PLANTS AND ANIMALS

The ubiquitous coconut palm has a million uses. The husk fibers make brooms, brushes and rope, and the husk itself is fuel for cooking. Coconut smoke is a good mosquito repellent.

The green coconut has a clear, sweet liquid for drinking, and meat of the older nut is a tasty treat. It can also be grated and squeezed for sauces.

A main export is dried coconut meat, called copra. It's squeezed for oil, which is used in soaps, body lotions, candles, and medicines. The copra meal is used for animal food. A typical coconut palm can produce a hundred nuts a year.

In the center of a sprouted coconut is a sweet, spongy food called *uto*, which can be baked or eaten as is. This dessert treat is also called "coconut marshmallow" on many islands.

Palm leaves are woven into traditional roofs, fans, baskets, and mats. The young inner fiber of the coconut tree---called *rito*---is woven into highly-prized hats. The trunk can be used in construction and furniture, although few houses in the Cooks use coconut timber.

Pandanus is a hardy and useful tree, and one of the few that grows in the sandy soil of the northern atolls, and the harsh *makatea* of the raised atolls. The leaves are woven into beautiful hats and baskets, and also provide long-lasting roofing material.

The hard casuarina (ironwood) is used for furniture and tools, and is planted along the shore to prevent erosion. The barringtonia's seed pod (*ora*) was powdered and used as a fish poison in earlier days. The beautiful flamboyant, or flame tree, blossoms bright red flowers from November to February, adding a splash of color to the holiday season. These have been "trimmed" in many places, although many think "butchered" is a more accurate word.

The leaves of the yellow-flowered hibiscus (*au*) are used to cover earthovens (*umu*) in traditional feasts, and the flower is used in medicines. The fibers are braided into rope, and the inner bark is used for "hula" skirts. Soak it in the lagoon for a white skirt, dry it on shore for a brown one. Cut it just above the knee for men, and just above the ankle for women.

Two sticks of *au* can be rubbed together to start a fire. I kid you not! A native craftsman named Piri Puruto does it in his show. Don't miss it!

Fragrant tropical flowers are everywhere, and include *tiare* (gardenia), *pitate* (jasmine), plumeria, and the amber-petalled jewel called *tipani* (frangipani). *Tipani* is the intoxicatingly-sweet flower used in leis (*'eis*). All the above are used in scented oils and soaps, so you can take home a little of Mother Nature's private garden.

The leaves of the rare *maire* plant are blended with coconut oil to treat insect bites and sunburn. *Maire* is grown mostly on Mauke, but the medicinal oil is available on Rarotonga, and exported in large quantities to Hawaii.

Tropical fruits grow in abundance, and papayas and bananas are year-round treats. Pineapples, oranges and watermelons are plentiful, and mangoes drop at your feet as you hike inland in December and January. Starchy root crops include taro, yams and arrowroot. Breadfruit and avocados grow everywhere, and the latter are so plentiful they are fed to pigs.

Vanilla is grown on some islands, and excellent coffee is produced on Atiu. Rarotonga's valleys are home to a wide variety of ferns, creepers and climbers, and some evergreens and hardwoods. Valuable sandalwood trees are not found on Rarotonga, although a few survive on Mitiaro.

Very few animals are native to the Cooks, but these include a rare fruit bat found on Rarotonga and Mangaia. These are now quite scarce, and may be put on the endangered species list.

Mostly what you'll see are dogs, cats, chickens, goats and lots and lots of pigs, the traditional centerpiece of most island feasts.

*Sweet, chiffon-like* uto *is found in the nut of sprouted coconuts*

## Pet Pigs?

While on a jungle trek on Atiu, I was quite surprised when my guide stopped in the middle of nowhere, asked us to be quiet for a moment, and then whistled loudly a few times. Suddenly a dozen little piglets scampered from the lush undergrowth, and began begging for food like Pavlov's dogs! Pigs are treated *almost* like pets on many islands, especially on Aitutaki, which prohibits dogs (as does Mauke). Maybe the new pet pig craze in California has its roots in the Cook Islands!

You may also notice a little lizard, called a gecko, clinging to ceilings or walls. Locally called a *moko*, it's a harmless creature found throughout the

Pacific. Be glad when you see them---they love to eat mosquitoes!

Some locals have horses, but the days of equestrian transportation ended with the arrival of the first Honda motorbike. You'll occasionally see horses in rural areas, but few are used in the fields any longer.

The Cooks have no snakes or poisonous insects, so hikers have no worries on this score. Mosquitoes (*namu*) are common inland, but none are malarial.

## Birds

Only ten native species of land birds live in the islands, but six of these are found nowhere else in the world. The rare *kopeka*, a small swift that makes unique clicking sounds to navigate, is limited to a few caves on Atiu.

The Rarotonga Flycatcher (*kakerori*), found in the high mountain forests, is one of the world's rarest birds. In 1990 only 30 birds remained, with nestlings being preyed upon by the European ship rat. The Conservation Department started a special "Kakerori Project" to poison the rats and protect the nests. With hard work by locals and some additional financial support from overseas conservationists, the number of birds has now passed the safer 100 level.

Native land birds are starved out by the mischievous Indian mynah bird, introduced at the turn of the century to eat agricultural pests. It does eat them, and everything else: seeds, nuts, other insects, and even domestic garbage.

The noisy black bird, complete with white wing "targets," is called the *manu kavamani* ("government bird") as a constant reminder of whom to blame for its presence. They became such pests that in the 1980's the government offered a 10-cent reward for each dead bird. As air rifles are the only firearms allowed in the islands, the wily *manu kavamani* won that particular battle.

The Cooks are also home to millions of seabirds. Suwarrow, Palmerston and Takutea are important international breeding sites for terns, noddies, boobies, and the unique frigatebirds and tropicbirds.

The Great Frigatebird (*kota'a*) has a wingspan of seven feet, a deeply-forked tail, and a hooked bill. The Red-Tailed Tropicbird (*tavake* or bosun bird) is famed for its long red tail-feathers, which are highly-prized for traditional ceremonial costumes.

Visitors with avian interests should pick up McCormack and Kunzle's booklets and posters about the *kakerori*, the birds of Takutea and Suwarrow, and the Rarotonga cloud forest.

## Lagoon Life

The liveliest spot in the Cooks---aside from the Banana Court on a Friday night---is the lagoon and its underwater reef. Both are home to multitudes of colorful tropical fish, but there would be no reef without those little coral animals and their plant buddies, the algae.

## Corals

A single coral is called a polyp, and a coral branch in the lagoon contains millions of these tiny tube-shaped animals. The main food of a coral polyp is plankton, which it catches with its stinging tentacles. As the plankton is digested, the coral secretes a mineral compound which hardens into a coral skeleton, and thus the reef is born.

A tiny algae lives in each polyp, and also supplies food to its host. The more the algae grows, the faster the coral grows. Since the algae is a plant, it likes shallow sunlit lagoons rather than deep, dark oceans, and thus its coral host thrives in lagoons as well.

The lagoons and shallow offshore waters of Rarotonga and Aitutaki have a good variety of plate, branch, brain and mushroom corals.

Cold, freshwater currents from mountain streams are deadly to lagoon coral. Over the years these have cut large passages in the reef at Avatiu and Avarua Harbors, and smaller ones near Muri Beach and along South Beach.

The deeper the shade of blue, the deeper the water. Pale turquoise water, as in Rarotonga's lagoon, is rarely more than fifteen feet deep, while on Aitutaki the aquamarine sections reach thirty feet. Areas that appear yellowish or brown from a distance are usually less than four feet deep.

### Fish and Shellfish

The lagoon hosts a bewildering variety of colorful species, including angelfish, butterflyfish, damselfish, trumpetfish and parrotfish. At night locals catch *maroro* (flying fish) by torchlight.

Blue starfish, clams and crabs are common, as are six-inch sea slugs, also called *beche de mer*. These are revered in some Asian cultures as aphrodisiacs, but not considered such by locals.

### Marine Life

Tuna frequent offshore waters, but are seriously threatened by driftnet fishing boats of Taiwan, South Korea and Japan. These floating factories use 30-mile-long nets which not only over-harvest tuna, but also kill whales, porpoises, sea turtles and everything else in the neighborhood. It's not surprising they are nicknamed "walls of death." At their current rate of operation, it is estimated Pacific tuna will be gone in a dozen years.

Other offshore fish include marlin, sailfish, wahoo, bonito, mahi mahi and barracuda. Whales pass by in August and September, and sea turtles are found in offshore waters, but sightings of both are less frequent each year.

## CULTURE AND CUSTOMS

The islanders are referred to as Cook Island *Maoris*, which in their own language simply means "indigenous to." They are part of the great Polynesian race, culturally and linguistically similar to the Maoris of New Zealand. Both groups came from eastern Polynesia, and Rarotongans settled New Zealand several hundred years ago. Cook Islanders also have ties to Hawaii, Tahiti, Samoa and Tonga. Almost all have relatives in New Zealand, and, in fact, more Cook Islanders live in New Zealand than in the Cook Islands!

The islands have similar cultures, except for Pukapuka and its "suburb" of Nassau. Pukapuka was settled from Samoa and Tonga, and Nassau was settled from Pukapuka.

### Family Structure

The typical household starts with the basic nuclear family, adds some in-laws, grandparents and cousins, and may take in a "feeding child" from relatives or friends. Everyone may not be living there at the same time, but all are welcome if they need a place to call home.

Everyone you meet seems to be related to everybody else you meet, usually as the generic "cousin." This makes the whole country seem like a small town, which it pretty much is in terms of area and population.

The original tribes provide basic family lineages, although intermarriage has blurred these lines considerably. Many families trace their roots to

Tangiia and Karika of the 13th century. Prepare for a long night if you ask a local to describe the family genealogy.

One difference between Polynesian and modern Western society is the respect given the elderly. Here seniors are considered teachers of skills and knowledge, and are valued members of the family, church, and government.

In sharp contrast to earlier eras, women have a greater role in shaping society. Many *ariki* are women, and their numbers have grown in business, journalism and other professions.

## Land Use and Ownership

All land was originally owned by tribes, and assigned to families for their use. Intermarriage has led to numerous disputes, and a separate Land Court was created. Land cannot be sold, although rights of use can be inherited. Leases over 5 years must be approved by a majority of family members and the Land Court. Foreigners need special government approval to lease land.

## Housing

Tourists are often surprised to see everyone living in modern houses. The days of the grass hut are gone, except on some remote outer islands. Many locals purchase kit homes, which are shipped in from New Zealand.

Coconut trunks could be milled for lumber, but this is rarely done. Two tourist accommodations that do make extensive use of coconut materials are the Atiu Motel, on that island, and the Tiare Holiday Cottages, on Mauke.

Many homes have solar hot water tanks to take advantage of the abundant sunshine. Some have solar electrical panels for refrigeration and lighting, and little Nassau has gone totally solar in household electricity.

## Education

Schooling is free and compulsory for children six to fifteen. English and Rarotongan are used in primary school, but the colleges (high schools) only use English. Several church-sponsored schools operate, and receive some financial support from the government.

Some islanders attend high school and university in New Zealand. The Fiji-based University of the South Pacific has an extension center on Rarotonga, with many classes taught via satellite and videotape.

## Religion

Islanders are active churchgoers, and much social life is centered around the church. The London Missionary Society of earlier days became the Cook Islands Christian Church in 1947, and 65% of locals are members. Another 15% are Catholic, with Seventh Day Adventists, Mormons, Apostolics, Assembly of God and Baha'i making up the balance.

The church is a strong influence in the community. A National Prayer Day (Takamoa Day) was established on the first Sunday in August, and Gospel Day, October 26, is an official holiday commemorating the arrival of the first missionaries.

Church influence is reflected by the official acceptance of Sunday as a day of rest. No domestic flights operate, most sports facilities are closed, and on Saturday evening bars cannot serve alcohol past the stroke of midnight. The liquor ban is relaxed at restaurants, and international flights are also allowed to operate on Sunday.

The Sunday ban led to an unusual incident in 1977. With several other tourists I was inadvertently "stranded" on Aitutaki, 160 miles from Rarotonga. The pilot of the local airline's only plane

*Church services in Avarua---1840's*

became ill as we landed there late on a Saturday afternoon. His condition was not serious, but he would not be able to fly for several days.

The only reserve pilot was on Rarotonga, a 20-hour freighter ride away. By the time he had chartered a ship it was a few minutes past midnight, and no one would load the fuel since it was now Sunday. We were "rescued" a few days later (what a shame!) by the reserve pilot, who, ironically, was seasick most of the voyage.

Today there are several local planes, but that incident may have helped convince the airline that a second plane was an idea whose time had come!

### Dance and Music

Cook Islanders are considered among the finest Polynesian singers and dan-

cers, and awards come often in international contests. The real national sport is dancing, not rugby or cricket. Unlike most Western dancing, Polynesians tell a story with their bodies that matches the words of the song.

If you were expecting the slow and subtle movements of Hawaiian hula dancers you're in for a big surprise. Cook Island dancing is fast, frenzied and erotic in comparison, with more hip swinging, suggestive gestures and amorous advances than ever seen at a Honolulu hotel.

The musicians keep the rhythm on hollowed-out slit drums, called *pate*, and all participants wear colorful costumes made from flowers, shells, bark cloth and feathers.

The sensuality of the dancing was a particular sore point among the missionaries, reflected by the famous quote of William Wyatt Gill:

"I do not believe it possible for any European to move the limbs as a Polynesian loves to do. At a very early age mothers carefully oil the hands, etc., and then knead the tiny limbs, stretching and "cracking" each joint. Respecting the *morality* of their dances, the less said the better; but the "upa-upa" dance, introduced from Tahiti, is obscene indeed."

The sensuous dancing survives, and it's not just in the tourist shows. If you visit the Banana Court on a Friday night—which you must—you'll first see a traditional dance show. This is followed by islanders gyrating to Polynesian rock 'n' roll music, using the same basic movements as in the traditional presentation.

### Traditional Arts and Handicrafts

Woodcarving is very popular, and the phallic male god Tangaroa is a favorite subject. He's one of the few gods represented in human form, as most were viewed as birds, fish and other animals.

Other carvings include bowls, ceremonial stools, food pounders and coconut-grating seats. Carved storyboards from Atiu depict local legends. Canoes are crafted from burned-out tree trunks, using traditional designs and materials. Bindings are from coconut husk fibers, and pearlshell is used as an inlay on canoe paddles.

Palm and pandanus leaves are woven into handicrafts, including the soft and elegant *rito* hats from the Northern Group. Baskets and mats are made from plant fibers, and traditional skirts are crafted from the inner bark of the hibiscus plant.

Pounded bark cloth, called *tapa*, was once the dominant material for clothing. It is now rarely used in the Cooks, although it is still popular in Samoa,

Tonga and Fiji. One recent occasion for making *tapa* was the investiture of a chief (*ariki*) of a village on Rarotonga.

One unique handmade item is the colorful patchwork quilt called a *tivaevae*. The early missionaries introduced fabric cloth, which became the preferred material for clothing, and *tapa* lost its prominence. The skill used in *tapa* patterns found its way into these elaborately handstitched quilts, with colorful floral patches sown into beautifully-designed local motifs.

Each quilt takes months, and sometimes years, to complete, and they're often group projects. Tivaevae are used at weddings, christenings, funerals and family ceremonies, and also serve as wall hangings. Most are for home use, but some are available at shops, at prices reflecting the time and work involved in their production.

The Museum in Avarua exhibits traditional handicraft items, tools and canoes, and is a must-see for anyone wanting to learn more about crafts and traditional culture.

### Customs

Families often bury their dead in elaborate graves in front yards, many with intricately-carved headstones. These are continually decorated with flowers and ornaments as a sign of respect by the family.

One custom which might be more appropriately put under language is the locals' practice of responding to a question by raising his or her eyebrows quickly, with a slight upward movement of the head. To most Westerners this might mean the person was confused or surprised by the question. Here it's just another way of saying "yes". The first few times it confused me, but I soon found myself adopting the habit.

Another custom that speaks a language of its own is the wearing of a flower behind the ear. My single friends told me that behind the right ear means you're single, and behind the left ear means you're taken. A married friend told me the opposite, maybe because I caught him at the Banana Court with a flower behind his right ear!

Time is an imprecise concept in traditional Cook Islands culture, and this approach survives in the modern era. "Maori Time" or "Local Time" means that eventually things will get done, or eventually the person you arranged to meet will show up. Mostly everyone operates on Maori Time, but there are a few important exceptions.

"British Time" means the event will more or less occur at the time stated. This is used for official ceremonies, and announcements often state that "British Time" applies to the function. Church services usually start promptly, and it is considered rude to arrive late. The airlines also operate on so-called British Time, so be on time for all flights.

It's been said the concept of Maori Time is simply a reflection of the islanders' outlook on life. One popular story tells of a European shopowner who asked a young man resting on the beach if he wanted a job to earn some money.

"After you've worked at the shop for many years you can save up some money, and when you get old you can retire to a life of leisure---eating, sleeping and fishing as you like."

The young man slowly rose, and yawned as he rubbed the sleep from his eyes. He picked up his fishing rod and basket of fresh-picked fruit, and placed them in his outrigger canoe. As he gently paddled into the fish-filled lagoon, he turned, smiled, and asked: "Why wait?"

The common canine has had a controversial role in local history. Along with pigs and chickens, dogs were a traditional source of meat, though they were also kept as pets. Aitutaki and Mauke, however, both banned dogs. Some say locals thought canines spread diseases such as leprosy, while others think mutts were banished because they bit kids and ate too much food.

Rarotonga has had a dog problem, but weekly sweeps of unregistered curs have been effective. Rumor has it that some of these have ended up in the *umu*, in their once-traditional role.

A first hair-cutting ceremony is held for a boy when he reaches anywhere from five to eight years of age. Ribbons are used to tie the hair into locks, one for each guest. After some prayers and speeches, each guest kisses the boy, presents a gift, and then cuts off a lock of hair. A huge feast follows, and the boy is officially on his way to manhood.

## Sexual Myths And Attitudes

Ever since Fletcher Christian and his *Bounty* mutineers visited the South Pacific, the myth of indiscriminate

Polynesian sexuality has been part of the popular culture. While Polynesians may be more open about sex, and more open in expressing interest in the opposite sex, they are just as choosy in their selections as anyone else.

It's difficult to generalize about sexual attitudes in the Cooks. On the one hand, topless bathing is frowned upon. On the other, the phallic male god *Tangaroa* appears on coins, carvings and even government publications. Most locals have a keen sense of humor, and few are shy about using it when the topic of discussion is sex.

They are also less judgmental about the conduct of others. Children born out of wedlock are accepted as much as any other child, and the unwed mother is not shamed, as in some Western cultures. Local police don't harass amorous couples found in semi-public places, they simply smile and suggest a better spot for such liaisons.

Openness about sex has helped the islands to avoid---as of this writing---the spread of AIDS. Posters in public places warn of the dangers of unsafe sex, and public health floats in parades may be adorned with condoms, which are also available at the local pharmacy.

## LITERATURE

A complete reading list is included at the end of this guide, but several accounts of life in the islands are particularly fascinating:

**Maretu** (1802-1880) was born on Rarotonga, and was a young adult when the first missionaries arrived. He had engaged in acts of cannibalism in his early years, but was one of the first to convert in the 1820's. He later become a missionary, serving on Manihiki, Mangaia, and other islands. In 1871 he wrote his autobiography, which was translated in 1983 by Marjorie Crocombe, then with the University of the South Pacific. Titled *Cannibals and Converts*, it's an amazing eyewitness account of an entire culture that was radically changed in less than a generation.

Missionary **William Gill** wrote *Gems From The Coral Island* about his years on Rarotonga from 1839 to 1852. He was the force behind the building of the CICC Church at Arorangi, a favorite of visitors on Sundays.

**William Wyatt Gill**---no relation---spent 25 years as a missionary on Mangaia, beginning in 1852, and also spent time on other islands in the group. His *From Darkness to Light in Polynesia* and writings reprinted in *Cook Islands Custom* are excellent accounts of traditional culture, including marriage rites, religious ceremonies and cannibalism.

**Robert Dean Frisbie** (1896-1948) is an American who decided to live in the South Seas. He ended up on tiny Pukapuka in the Northern Cooks, the only foreigner on the island. He learned the language and culture, married a local girl, and wrote about all of it in his captivating classic *The Book of Pukapuka*. His *Island of Desire* includes more on Pukapuka, but it's also famous for the chapters about Suwarrow. It includes the famous story of how he saved his children by tying them to windswept *tamanu* (mahogany) trees during the great hurricane of 1942, which reduced the atoll to a few sandbanks with its 40-foot waves. Frisbie's daughter "Johnny," who still lives in the Cooks, continued the family's true-life adventures in *Miss Ulysses from Pukapuka*, and *The Frisbies of the South Seas*.

Suwarrow cannot be mentioned without thinking of the modern Robinson Crusoe, **Tom Neale** (1902-1977). This ruggedly individualistic New Zealander wanted to live alone on a tropical island, and he picked Suwarrow after reading Frisbie's accounts. He lived there most of 1952-1977, and described his early years in *An Island To Oneself*, written in 1966. He was in the Rarotonga Hospital when I met him in 1977. "Make sure they take care of my stuff when I'm gone" he said. The government has done just that, and today Suwarrow is a National Park, with Tom's things protected for posterity. (More on Tom's story is in the Suwarrow chapter; photo at Plate 39.)

More pertinent to Rarotonga are books by the late **Ron Syme**. His *Isles of the Frigate Bird* and *The Lagoon is Lonely Now* describe life in the islands from the 1950's to the 1970's. He includes anecdotes about Atiu, Mangaia, and other outer islands.

**Dr. Tom Davis**, former Prime Minister, recounts his medical career before entering local politics in *Doctor to the Islands*. Also look for his autobiographical *Island Boy*, and his novel *Vaka*, based upon early Polynesian sea voyages.

If you're a history or culture buff, a must is **Dick Scott**'s authoritative and entertaining *Years of the Pooh Bah*. He gives an in-depth picture of the colonial era, and how the local culture somehow survived the machinations of its New Zealand administrators.

## LANGUAGE

All the islands, except for Samoan-influenced Pukapuka and Nassau, have a similar language, with some variations in dialect. The early missionaries first translated the dialect of Rarotonga into English, thus Rarotongan became known as Cook Islands Maori.

Conversations between locals are often in their own language, but almost everyone speaks English. Signs, menus and the newspaper are in English. Learning Rarotongan is not necessary, but using common greetings and words will add spice to any vacation.

### Alphabet

Rarotongan has only 13 letters, so it should be only half as difficult to learn as English! The same vowels of *a, e, i, o*, and *u* are used, as are the consonants *k, m, n, p, r, t*, and *v*. The only difficulty is the unusual combination consonant *ng*, pronounced as in "rang".

Vowels may be pronounced as short or long, but for most purposes learning the short sound will get you by:

> *a* ---as in aloud
> *e* ---as in set
> *i* ---as in pit
> *o* ---as in for
> *u* ---as in put

Written Rarotongan also uses the apostrophe ( '). This denotes a "glottal stop," a short hesitation of breath between two vowels. It has essentially replaced the *H* and *L*, and other letters not in the language. (As there is no *l*, a lei becomes an *'ei*.) To give you an idea of how it works, say the English phrase "Uh-Oh." The short hesitation between the two words is the glottal stop.

The glottal stop has achieved some measure of notoriety in the example of *ika*, the word for fish. If you put a glottal stop in front of it you get *'ika*, which means the female genitalia. So, be careful with those glottal stops!

### Pronunciation

Everything is pronounced just as it looks, and each vowel is a separate syllable. Almost every word ends in a vowel. Unlike English, two vowels together do not make a new sound. The word for small child, *tamaiti*, has four syllables, not three. Despite this rule, don't believe any local who smiles and says cows on Rarotonga say "mo-o" instead of "moo"!

## Some Useful Words

*Kia Orana*---Hello (May you live)
*'Aere Ra*---Goodbye
*Meitaki*---Thank you/Good
*Meitaki ma'ata*---Thank you very much
*'ae*---yes
*kare*---no
*tane*---man
*vaine*---woman
*manea*---pretty/handsome
*'ura*---to dance
*akaipo*---to make love
*mataora*---happy
*umu*---earth oven
*kai*---food
*umukai*---feast
*teia ra*---today
*apopo*---tomorrow
*ra*---sun
*marama*---moon
*moana*---ocean
*maunga*---mountain
*Papa'a*---European/Foreigner (literally "four layers," from the clothes worn by early missionaries)

If you visit the outer islands, a sure way to evoke a smile is to use that island's version of "Thank you very much." On Aitutaki use *Meitaki atupaka*; on Atiu, Mauke and Mitiaro use *Meitaki ranuinui*; and on Mangaia use *Meitaki ngao*.

As in most languages, many words are simply combinations of two smaller words (*umukai*, above). Others are local transliterations of the English word, such as *motoka* for motor car.

Names may reflect the person's birth order, as in *Toru* (three) or *Teina* (younger sibling of same sex), or the child's or a relative's habits, as in *Moeroa* (sleep long). My friend *Nooroa Kairoa* laughed aloud when he translated his name: "Sit long, Eat long"!

Some names serve both genders, such as *Kura*, *Vaine*, and *Tere*. This might seem a Polynesian curiosity, but consider our own Robin or Leslie.

Foreign names are often localized by using the closest available letters, then adding a vowel at the end. Robert thus becomes *Ropati*. Some names are shortened and then translated, as in Dashwood becoming *Rakau* ("Wood").

For more on the language, pick up the slim but informative book *Say It In Rarotongan*, by Mana Strickland. If you just want to try the basics, both *Kia orana!* and *Meitaki ma'ata!* will usually bring a broad smile in response.

## Other Expressions

Visitors from the States may wonder where the bonfire will be if a local asks to borrow a "torch" (flashlight). If you're invited to "tea" (dinner), remember to use your "serviette" (napkin).

The street level of a building is the "ground floor"---you'll have to walk up a flight of stairs to get to the "first floor".

Motorbikes are called "bikes", while bicycles are called "push bikes." The former use "petrol", not gas. All those "panelbeater" signs are for autobody shops. If it's chilly out, don't put on a sweater---put on a "jumper"!

If the newspaper says the "Mamas and the Papas" were at the fundraising dance, don't think Michelle Phillips and her rock group are on the island. The phrase simply refers to anyone from middle-age onward, and it's a term of respect for the older generation.

Plate 1. Dancers at Constitution Celebrations, Rarotonga
2. Kids begin dancing early in the Cooks.  3. Beauty and the Beach, Rarotonga

4. The Needle is a prominent landmark of Rarotonga's inland mountains.
5. Beautiful Muri Beach and its motus (islets) are popular spots on Rarotonga.

6. Rarotonga from the air, with views of South Beach and the Muri Beach islets
7. Lagoon, West Coast of Rarotonga

8. The Needle, up close and personal, on Rarotonga's Cross-Island Track
9. Kids on Mauke have few worries  10. Wigmore's Falls, inland South Coast

## PLANNING YOUR TRIP

### GETTING THERE

The Cooks are served by **Polynesian Airlines** and **Air New Zealand**. ANZ has more flights, but Polynesian usually has lower fares. Always allow plenty of time to connect to your overseas flight ---the next one may not be for a week!

### FROM US/CANADA

The quickest way to get to Raro is on Polynesian (800-592-7100), which has a weekly *non-stop* from Los Angeles, 10 hrs door-to-door. The return is via Western Samoa and Hawaii (14 hrs total). Roundtrip fares start at US$789 from Los Angeles or San Francisco, and reduced-fare add-ons are available from other cities. One free stopover is permitted on the return.

Poly also has great package deals, which include air, hotel and transfers. These start at US$839 (pp/dbl) for one week, US$1128 for two weeks, and are sold though travel agents.

Air New Zealand (800-262-1234, be prepared to wait!) also flies from LA, via Hawaii or Tahiti. Seasonal fares are: low (Apr-Aug) $878; shoulder (Mar, Sep-Nov) $978; high (Dec-Feb) $1178.

From Hawaii, Polynesian flies via Western Samoa. Roundtrip fares range from US$538 to US$698, depending on travel dates. ANZ's seasonal fares, for non-stops, are US$648 to US$948.

From Canada, Air New Zealand offers connecting fares from Vancouver, starting at Can$1168.

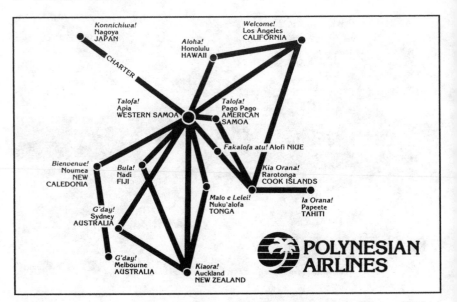

Konnichiwa!
Nagoya
JAPAN

Aloha!
Honolulu
HAWAII

Welcome!
Los Angeles
CALIFORNIA

CHARTER

Talofa!
Apia
WESTERN SAMOA

Talofa!
Pago Pago
AMERICAN
SAMOA

Fakalofa atu! Alofi NIUE

Bienvenue!
Noumea
NEW
CALEDONIA

Bula!
Nadi
FIJI

Kia Orana!
Rarotonga
COOK ISLANDS

G'day!
Sydney
AUSTRALIA

Malo e Lelei!
Nuku'alofa
TONGA

Ia Orana!
Papeete
TAHITI

G'day!
Melbourne
AUSTRALIA

Kiaora!
Auckland
NEW ZEALAND

POLYNESIAN
AIRLINES

**Polynesian Airlines' 30-Day Polypass**
For US$1299 from LA (US$999 from Hawaii) you can island-hop to the Cooks, Samoa, Tonga, Tahiti, Fiji, New Caledonia, New Zealand and Australia. (Not valid December or January.)

**Educational Programs**
The Pacific Islands Institute (808-262-8942) has 14-day Elderhostel programs from US$2400, including room, meals, classes, and airfare from Hawaii.

**Mileage Programs**
Delta and USAir offer mileage credit for Air New Zealand flights. You earn about 10,000 miles for LA-Raro-LA.

**FROM NEW ZEALAND/AUSTRALIA**
Polynesian's 30-day Polypass (US$999) allows travel to the Cooks, Samoa, Fiji, Tonga, Tahiti and New Caledonia. ANZ has non-stop flights from Auckland, with connections from Australia.

**FROM EUROPE/ASIA**
From London or Frankfurt take ANZ to Los Angeles, then connect to Raro. From Tokyo, take ANZ to Raro via Fiji.

**TRAVEL BY SEA**
Most international freighters don't take passengers due to insurance problems. Some yachts do stop in Raro, but rarely during the Nov-Apr hurricane season. If you're adventurous, check out yacht clubs. Look for laundry hung out to dry on the deck, a sure sign of travelers.

## GETTING AROUND
**BY AIR**
Air Rarotonga (22-888) has an excellent safety record and meets all international standards. Flights of under an hour serve Aitutaki, Atiu, Mauke, Mitiaro and Mangaia several times each week, while Manihiki, Penrhyn and Pukapuka have weekly flights (4 hrs each way).

Flights on these 19-seaters are quite memorable, with great aerial views. Locals are decked out in flowers and shell necklaces, and the plane's arrival is often a major social event! Islanders heading home can also offer more tips on what to see and do.

Alas, there's no in-flight movie. When I asked what film we'd see on our flight to Atiu, the pilot pointed to the clouds ahead and laughed: "*Rain Man!*"

Most flights are smooth, and I've never been on a flight where a passenger became ill. On those few occasions when weather conditions make flying unsafe, flights simply don't operate.

Roundtrip fares are NZ$284 to Aitutaki, Mauke or Mitiaro; NZ$254 to Atiu or Mangaia; NZ$1000 to Manihiki; and NZ$1100 to Penrhyn or Pukapuka.

### Discounted Air/Land Packages
These are great deals, and should be used whenever possible. Two-night Aitutaki packages start at NZ$300. A 7-nighter to Atiu, Mauke and Mitiaro is about NZ$650, including some meals.

If you want to go where few have gone before---and can afford to do so ---a new 4-day/3-night package from Raro visits Penrhyn, Manihiki and Pukapuka. This once-a-month all-inclusive tour is about NZ$2500.

Packages can be booked from overseas, or you can decide what outer islands to visit after arrival. Island Hopper and other Raro travel agents may have specials if flights are not crowded. Always book early for the popular Friday flights to Aitutaki.

### BY SEA
**Freighters:** Though it sounds romantic, the reality of freighter travel may not match the dream. The so-called cabins are tiny boxes with bunk beds and little ventilation, and the smell of diesel fumes and old cigarette butts permeates the air. Meals are usually canned and greasy, and you might not even want to eat, depending on the conditions at sea.

On a trip some years ago I slept with a T-shirt over my face to absorb the fumes and smells, and ate only bread

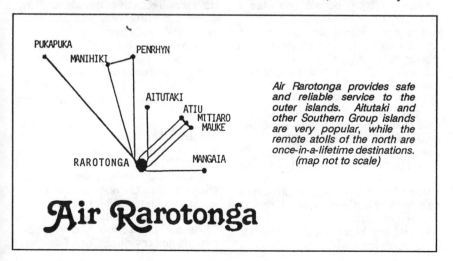

*Air Rarotonga provides safe and reliable service to the outer islands. Aitutaki and other Southern Group islands are very popular, while the remote atolls of the north are once-in-a-lifetime destinations. (map not to scale)*

**𝒜ir ℛarotonga**

and jam to avoid stomach problems. Though there's nothing quite like an evening of gazing at the Southern Cross followed by waking to a tropical island on the horizon, try an overnight in the Southern Group before you take a three-week trip up north!

Freighter schedules are erratic, especially to the Northern Group. Ships serving the Cooks include the *Martha-lina* and the *Avatapu*. The latter's captain is Nancy Griffiths from the US, one of the few female freighter skippers in the Pacific. If a freighter voyage is in your karma, try the **Waterfront Commission** (21-921/fax 21-191), **Triad Maritime** (20-374) or the *Avatapu* (22-369). The *CI News* has shipping notices.

**Yachts:** Those departing Avatiu Harbor pass by the Northern Group if they're heading to Hawaii or Samoa. Renew your visa well in advance if you plan to head north for a while.

## LOCAL TRANSPORTATION

Travel on Rarotonga is pretty easy, since it's only 20 miles around. Rental cars, motorbikes and bicycles are available, as are taxis and a bus. Aitutaki has similar rentals. Other islands may have a rental motorbike or bicycle, or you can usually walk to most places.

Airport transfers are NZ$8 if you're not on a package. Aitutaki has an airport van, and on other islands you'll be met if expected. If not, you can usually hitch into town with a fellow passenger.

## WHEN TO GO

Anytime is a good time to visit the Cooks. The weather is always warm and tropical, and seasonal variations are minor. July to October is peak visitor season, and hotels all fill up during the July/August Constitution Celebrations. Christmas flights are filled by both tourists and traveling Cook Islanders.

## CLIMATE

The weather is similar to that of Hawaii, since Rarotonga is as far south of the equator---1350 miles---as Hawaii is north. Being below the equator, the seasons are the opposite of North America.

From June to September the days are usually warm and sunny. Nights are cool and refreshing, and you may find a sweater or jacket helpful.

From December to March it's a little hotter and more humid, but rarely uncomfortable. It rains a bit more, but often in short bursts, so most days have lots of sunshine. Hurricanes visit every decade or so, but this is not something one can plan around.

### Rarotonga Weather Chart:

|     | Low °F / °C | High °F / °C | Rain in / mm |
| --- | --- | --- | --- |
| Jan | 73 / 23 | 84 / 29 | 10 / 254 |
| Feb | 73 / 23 | 84 / 29 | 9 / 229 |
| Mar | 73 / 23 | 84 / 29 | 11 / 279 |
| Apr | 72 / 22 | 82 / 28 | 7 / 178 |
| May | 68 / 20 | 81 / 27 | 7 / 178 |
| Jun | 66 / 19 | 79 / 26 | 4 / 102 |
| Jul | 66 / 19 | 77 / 25 | 4 / 102 |
| Aug | 65 / 18 | 77 / 25 | 5 / 127 |
| Sep | 66 / 19 | 77 / 25 | 4 / 102 |
| Oct | 68 / 20 | 79 / 26 | 5 / 127 |
| Nov | 70 / 21 | 81 / 27 | 6 / 152 |
| Dec | 72 / 22 | 82 / 28 | 9 / 229 |

Local temperatures are measured in Celsius. The lowest temperature *ever* recorded on Rarotonga was 9°C (48°F), so you can leave the down jacket and wool socks at home!

## FESTIVALS AND CELEBRATIONS

The Constitution Celebrations and the Round-Rarotonga-Road-Race are popular with tourists. The following are more-or-less regular events, but Cook Islanders are always celebrating

something! After arrival, check the *CI News* for events during your visit.

**Cultural Festival Week:** mid-February; Crafts exhibits, Tivaevae Quilt Contest.

**Dancer of the Year Festival:** end of April; National contests, also *Papa'a* Night for tourists and expatriates.

**Constitution Celebrations:** late July/ early August; commemorates independence on August 4, 1965; parades, contests, shows; This is the Cook Islands' version of Mardi Gras!

**Round Rarotonga Road Race:** October (formerly November); international athletes compete in this 20-mile run, shorter fun runs, and lively celebrations.

**Miss Cook Islands Pageant:** late October; visitors welcome at all events.

**Gospel Day:** October 26; commemorates arrival of missionaries in 1821. Religious plays (*nuku*) performed.

**String Band Competition:** Oct / Nov; the best "ukurere" players in the Pacific.

**All Soul's Day (Turama):** November 1; decorations and evening ceremonies at Catholic Cemetery, near the airport.

**Tiare (Flower) Festival:** November; Raro is decked out in flowers; highlights are float parade, Miss Tiare Pageant.

**International Food Festival:** November; Best Restaurant, Best Cocktail, Great Cook Islands Chicken Curry Cookout Contests. Visitors help choose winners.

**New Year's Eve:** special Island Night shows and celebrations.

*The Float Parade is a highlight of the July/August Constitution Celebrations.*

**Legal Holidays:** New Year's Day; ANZAC (Memorial) Day (Apr 25); Good Friday; Easter Monday; Queen's Birthday (June); Constitution Day (Aug 4); Gospel Day (Oct 26); Christmas Day; and Boxing Day (Dec 26).

## TRAVEL PRACTICALITIES

**Entrance Formalities:** On arrival show a current passport and an onward or return air ticket. A visa isn't required for stays up to 31 days. Visas for each additional 30 days are NZ$30, secured from the Immigration Office near the airport. Three extensions are allowed.

Visitors may bring in, duty-free, personal effects and sports gear, 2 litres of wine or spirits, 200 cigarettes or 50 cigars, 2 cameras, 10 rolls of film, and other goods up to NZ$250 in value.

There are no foreign embassies, but a New Zealand Representative is in residence. The closest US consul is in Suva, Fiji, but foreign relations are handled by the Embassy in Wellington, New Zealand. The consular official at the Ministry of Foreign Affairs (tel 20-507) may offer assistance to visitors.

### Time

The Cooks are in the same time zone as Hawaii, which is two hours earlier than California (three hours during US Daylight Savings Time). They lie east of the International Dateline, on the same side as the US and Canada. New Zealand time is two hours earlier, but it's the following day, since NZ is west of the Dateline.

The Cooks used to observe Daylight Savings Time, but it was abolished in

1989, as it served no purpose. Flexible "Maori Time" usually prevails over clock time, except for airline flights.

US visitors should note that numerical dates on hotel vouchers and domestic air tickets list the day first and the month second, as opposed to common US practice. June 15, 1995 would thus be 15/6/95, instead of 6/15/95.

## Electrical Power

Current is 230 volts, 50 cycles. North Americans will need adaptor plugs for dual-voltage appliances and electric shavers, plus converters for other 110-volt items. Buy adaptor plugs listed for New Zealand. Wall outlets have their own on-off switches, so check these if your bedside lamp won't go on.

Rarotonga was notorious for blackouts, but service was recently upgraded. Still, don't be surprised if one hits during your visit. Emergency services and many hotels have backup generators.

When the Rarotongan Resort opened in 1977, we writers were impressed by the numerous candles in each room. Thinking it part of a plan to enhance the hotel's romantic image, we congratulated the manager on such thoughtfulness.

He explained, with some embarrassment, that they were there for safety, since the power often went out in the evening. He added with a smile, however, that they could also be used for romance!

Aitutaki has 24-hr power, but on other islands the generator starts at 6am and shuts off at midnight. Many locals leave their bedroom light switches turned on at midnight, and use the light to wake them up in the morning.

On one occasion a lady on Mangaia went into labor at 3am, and the town generator was turned on to supply power to the hospital. Everyone's bedroom lights went on, and locals got up and began making breakfast---until they saw it was still pitch black outside!

## Telephone/Fax

The phone system is quite modern, with fiber-optic lines on much of Rarotonga. Most outer islands have direct-dial for domestic and international service.

International calls and faxes can be made 24 hrs from the Telecom Centre in town. A 3-minute call to the US/Canada is NZ$17.50; to New Zealand, NZ$6.93;; and to Australia, NZ$9.90. Many hotels have International Direct Dialing. To call the US or Canada, first dial 001, then the area code and number. Dial 0064 for New Zealand, and 0061 for Australia. Many visitors use faxes instead of the slow mail service.

Local calls are NZ10c; use the red pay phones in hotels, bars and restaurants. For directory assistance, dial 010 for local numbers, 017 for international. Dial 015 for operator-assisted calls.

The Cooks' country code is 682. All local numbers have five digits. Calls to the Cooks from North America average US$4/minute. For person-to-person, add a US$8 surcharge per call. Overseas circuits are voice-activated, so take turns talking. If you overlap voices, you may cancel out the entire conversation!

## Mail

Mail *to* the US takes a week or two. Mail *from* the US may take two months, as the US Postal Service may route it to Cocos Island, Costa Rica; Cocos Island, Australia; or, somehow, Papua New Guinea. Friends have forwarding stamps from these places, and more.

Letters are NZ$1.05 to North America, postcards are NZ85c. The Post Office is open 8-4, weekdays. Most hotels sell stamps, which is handy on weekends.

Have mail sent to your hotel, or c/o General Delivery, as there's no American Express office. "SOUTH PACIFIC" should be on all mail, in large type.

There's no home mail delivery in the Cooks. In fact, there are no street addresses! Everyone gets mail at a post office box.

### Film and Photography
Film and other supplies are available on Rarotonga, as is one-hour processing. Prices are 10-20% higher than in the US. Few items are available on the outer islands.

## MONEY AND FINANCES
The New Zealand dollar is the unit of currency, but most transactions use Cook Islands notes and coins. These equal their New Zealand counterparts when used in the Cooks, but they are not exchangeable outside the country.

Colorful $1, $3, $5, $10, $20 and $50 notes are joined by the usual 5c, 10c, 20c and 50c coins. Your pockets will soon bulge with the unique octagonal $5 coin, the triangular $2 coin, and the famous *Tangaroa* dollar, with the phallic god on one side and Queen Elizabeth II on the other. It was rumored she was not pleased with this, but Tangaroa probably wasn't thrilled either.

Collectors should note there are two versions of the Tangaroa dollar. The scarce original, minted from 1973 to about 1985, is much larger than the new one, and worth several times its face value. The new dollar is the size of a US quarter, and worth only its face value.

### Exchange Rate
Visitors from the US have fared well in recent years, with the NZ dollar worth only US44-73c. The rate changes daily, but it's been around US60c:

| | | |
|---|---|---|
| US $1 = NZ$1.67 | NZ$1 = US 60c |
| Can $1 = NZ$1.33 | NZ$1 = Can 75c |
| Aus $1 = NZ$1.18 | NZ$1 = Aus 85c |

Don't buy NZ dollars overseas unless your bank is your favorite charity: you'll lose about 7%. The airport bank in Raro is usually open for international flights, so there's no need to change currency in advance. Bring traveler's checks, as the exchange rate is 5% higher than currency. Also take a few US$1, $5 and $10 notes, which can be used in a pinch.

### Banks
In Avarua, both Westpac Bank and ANZ Bank handle foreign exchange (Mon-Fri, 9-3). Hotels may exchange currency, but the rate is *much* lower. On the same day I received NZ$1.67 for US$1, the hotels were giving NZ$1.50. Outer island Post Offices may change currency, but at a very low rate.

### Credit Cards
Hotels, restaurants and most shops accept Visa, Mastercard, and Bankcard. Some accept American Express and Diner's Club. Exchange rates are similar to traveler's checks.

### Typical Costs
The Cooks are pretty middle-of-the-road compared to most tourist destinations. The rock-bottom bargains of Mexico are rare, but so are the outrageous prices of Tahiti and much of Europe. You can find a comfortable room with kitchenette for NZ$60 and up. Breakfast or lunch is about NZ$10, dinner is NZ$12 and up. Cars average NZ$55/day, motorbikes NZ$20/day.

*Rick Welland's* Ina and the Shark *drawing is featured on this unique banknote.*

You'll get good value in all price ranges. Those wishing to avoid the tourist traps of the world will find the Cooks a safe haven.

## HEALTH

The Cooks pose no special health problems for the visitor. Sunburn is the most common health hazard, as the sun is usually directly overhead and very strong. Use SPF 15 suntan lotion, especially the first few days. If you do get a burn, the pharmacy has the usual offerings, or try the local Mauke Miracle oil.

The water is generally safe, but I boil drinking water. If your hotel has solar hot water panels, the hot water may be cleaner than the cold---use the bathroom sink to test this out.

Mosquitoes are common inland, but shore breezes keep them away from most hotels. None carry malaria, but they have occasionally spread dengue fever. Mosquito repellent is recommended for inland hikes.

There are no poisonous snakes or lethal insects. Reddish-brown 6" centipedes have a nasty bite, but are not common enough to worry about. Avoid red (biting) ants that hang out near outdoor rubbish cans. Common brown ants (non-biting) love unclean kitchens.

Look at, but don't touch, the underwater coral in the lagoon. The tiny tentacles contain a mild toxin to ward off predators. Coral cuts can become infected if not thoroughly cleansed.

The lagoon is generally safe, but avoid the few reef passages. Wear footwear if reef walking, and go at low tide.

Rarotonga has a hospital, outpatient and dental clinics, and pharmacy. Other islands have a hospital or clinic, staffed by a doctor or nurse. Serious problems are treated in New Zealand or Hawaii.

## TRAVELING WITH CHILDREN

Kids of all ages love the Cooks. Teenagers enjoy watersports and disco night at the cinema. Island Night shows often feature children, and kids will have loads of fun if they join in. Most hotels can arrange sitters, and some hotels especially welcome kids, with discounts for connecting rooms. See "Where To Stay" in the Rarotonga chapter.

## HANDICAPPED TRAVELERS
The Rarotongan Resort offers rooms suitable for the handicapped. The Tourist Authority can also be of assistance.

## LOCAL CONDUCT AND CUSTOM
Cook Islanders are friendly, generous and tolerant, but even they can be offended by rude or insensitive behavior contrary to the norms of their culture.

### Tipping and Bargaining
The first rule is simple: NO TIPPING. This is against Polynesian custom. You may not appreciate the sheer beauty of this until you return home and take a cab or eat out at a restaurant.

The second rule is also simple: NO HAGGLING. The price marked is deemed fair by the shop owner. If you think it's too high, shop elsewhere.

### Appropriate Dress
Dress is casual, but Cook Islanders are *highly* offended by nude or topless sunbathing or swimming. Keep brief attire confined to the beach. Put on a shirt or *pareu* if you go to town or shops.

Wear your best clothes to church, and avoid shorts and T-shirts. Women should not show bare shoulders, or wear short skirts.

On weekends, men must wear long pants at the Banana Court and Reefcomber. Sleeveless T-shirts and flip-flops are also prohibited at the latter. Restaurant dress is informal. Pure swimwear at dinner might cause offense, but shorts and T-shirts are OK.

### Taking Photographs
Always ask before taking photographs of individuals, especially on the outer islands. Locals aren't afraid you'll steal their souls, but---like us---they might consider it an invasion of privacy.

### Crime
There's relatively little crime, and the Cooks are probably safer than most tourist destinations. Nonetheless, use the same caution and common sense that apply to any small town setting. Petty theft is on the rise, so don't leave cameras or purses unattended at beaches or nightspots. Lock motorbike frames, especially on weekends.

### Sunday
This is a day of rest, and most businesses are closed. Drive slowly in villages. The Rarotonga chapter lists restaurants and shops which are open.

### Relax!
Last, but not least, remember that locals have a very easy-going approach to life. It offends them if visitors *demand* service, rather than simply request it. Rarotonga is a pretty laid-back place, and most people like it that way. It's only a suggestion, but try to relax, and remember that patience is a virtue, especially in the Cook Islands.

## WHAT TO TAKE
Experienced travelers always "travel light." This is easy to do, as the weather is warm and dress is casual.

Take lightweight cottons or blends, rather than synthetics. Everyone wears shorts and T-shirts in the daytime. In the evening women wear sundresses or a *pareu*, the wrap-around sarong worn as a dress, top, or skirt. Men wear a knit or island-style shirt, and slacks or jeans.

Bring sandals, sneakers or walking shoes, and reef shoes or old sneakers for reef walking. Socks minimize mosquito bites on inland hikes. Don't forget your swimsuit, sunglasses, and maybe a hat for the midday sun.

It can get cool in the evening, especially from June to August. Take a light jacket, sweater or flannel shirt. Keep it in your carry-on bag, as airplane cabins are usually just a notch above freezing. A rainshell or poncho is handy for the occasional downpour, but I've never found an umbrella necessary.

Suntan lotion and insect repellent are highly recommended. Bring medications, and copies of your prescriptions.

I bring a travel alarm clock for early morning flights, and find a pocket flashlight always useful. Voltage converters and/or adaptor plugs may be needed for hairdryers, etc. Snorkeling gear can be rented on Rarotonga and Aitutaki, but if you have a perfect-fit mask it might be worth taking. If you'll be staying at hostels or outer island guesthouses, bring soap and a towel, and maybe flip-flops for the shower.

Don't forget the big three: **passport; airline ticket; traveler's checks**. Take some US currency and a credit card. Don't forget your driver's license, as you'll need it to get a Cook Islands license for rentals. The International Driver's License is not accepted.

Camera, film, radio/tape/CD player, a paperback for the beach, and your copy of *Cook Islands Companion* are other suggested items.

Use a carry-on bag for camera, toiletries, swimsuit and valuables. If somehow your checked baggage is misplaced (rare on these airlines) you won't be totally inconvenienced. This smaller bag is also handy for the beach, or for carrying items on a motorbike.

**What NOT To Take**
Suits and fancy dresses aren't necessary, but can be comfortably worn at restaurants. Agricultural products, pets, firearms and illegal drugs are prohibited.

**FURTHER INFORMATION:** Contact the **Cook Islands Tourist Authority:**

**Main Office:** PO Box 14, Rarotonga, Cook Islands, SOUTH PACIFIC; Tel (682) 29-435/Fax (682) 21-435;

**USA/Canada:** 6033 W. Century Blvd., Ste. 690, Los Angeles, California, 90045; Tel (800) 624-6250/Fax (310) 216-2868.

**New Zealand:** 330 Parnell Road, PO Box 37-391, Auckland; Tel (09) 379-4140/Fax (09) 309-1876;

**Australia:** 1/177 Pacific Hwy., North Sydney, NSW, 2060; (02) Tel 955-0446/Fax (02) 955-0447.

**Hong Kong:** Pacific Leisure, 40 Des Voeux Rd., Box 2582; Tel (5)247076.

**US Consulate:** Robert Worthington is the Honorary Consul in Honolulu. He can be reached at (808) 847-6377.

**Regional Information:** If you plan to island-hop around the South Pacific, David Stanley's *South Pacific Handbook* is a must (Moon Pubs., Box 3040, Chico, CA 95927). Good regional magazines include *Pacific Magazine* (Box 25488, Honolulu, HI, 96825), *Pacific Islands Monthly* (Box 1167, Suva, Fiji) and *Islands Business* (Box 12718, Suva, Fiji).

**And Finally:** If all else fails, call us at Pacific Publishing (510-525-1441). If we don't get back to you in a day or two, we're probably in Rarotonga!

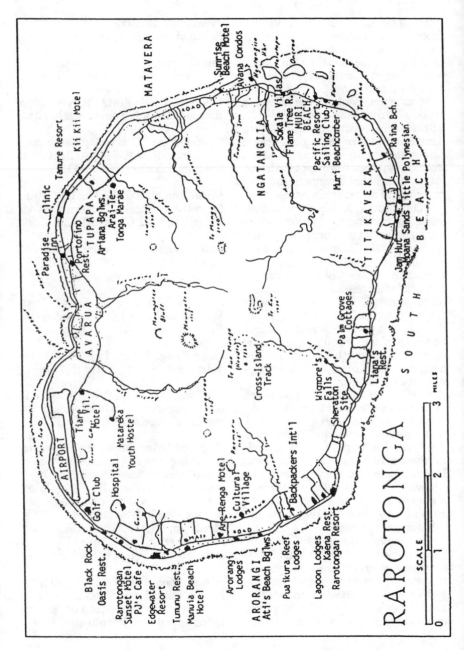

# RAROTONGA

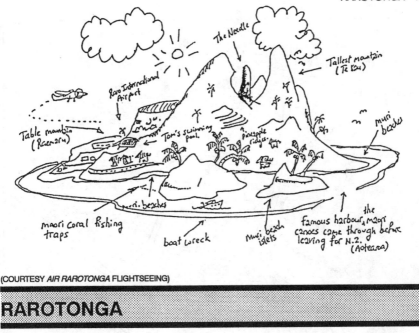

The labels on the illustration read:

The Needle

Tallest mountain (Te Kou)

Raro International Airport

Table mountain (Raemaru)

Tom's swimming pool

pineapple ridge — runs

muri beaches

maori beaches

maori coral fishing traps

boat wreck

Muri beach islets

the famous harbour, maori canoes came through before leaving for N.Z. (Aotearoa)

(COURTESY *AIR RAROTONGA* FLIGHTSEEING)

# RAROTONGA

Population:   10,918
Area:        26 sq.mi.

Rarotonga is a spectacularly beautiful island, with a turquoise lagoon and white sand beaches surrounding a lush mountainous interior. It's the largest island in the country, and half the nation's population lives on "Raro", as everyone calls it. It's the administrative and commercial center of the islands, and the site of the modern international airport.

The tourist facilities are excellent, but they don't overwhelm the local culture, as in some vacation areas. Recreational choices are numerous, and as it's only 20 miles around the island, you're never very far from pristine beaches and other island attractions.

The name itself comes from early Polynesian explorers, who found it by sailing *raro* (down) and *tonga* (to the south) of Raiatea, in French Polynesia. An earlier name was *Tumu-te-Varo-varo*, Source of Booming Sounds, from the large waves breaking on the reef. You'll occasionally see this tongue-twister in print, as it's now the name of a top island dance group.

Raro is a place of fun and relaxation, and the enchantment that comes when the beauty of an island is matched by the friendliness of its people.

## Orientation
The island's center is a series of rugged mountain ridges and peaks, including the unique outcrop known as **The Needle (Te Rua Manga)** (Plates 4, 8).

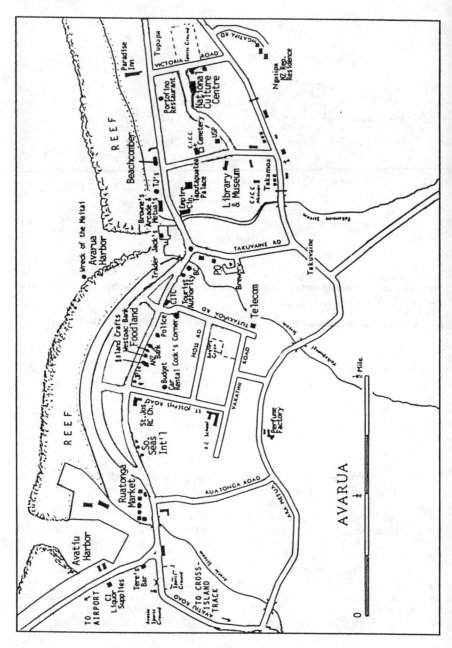

The highest mountain is **Te Manga**, at 2140ft (653m) above sea level. Two dozen valleys fan out to the coast, with crystal-clear streams draining the misty high country. Orange, papaya and banana groves are sprinkled throughout the valleys, and thrive on the rich volcanic soil.

A wide band of fertile soil surrounds the mountainous interior, allowing cultivation of fruits and vegetables. This is ringed by a belt of low, swampy soil, perfect for taro, the popular starchy root crop. Villages in pre-missionary times were located on the inland edge of this swampy area, and were joined by the historic coral road, the *ara metua*. Parts of this ancient road are still in use today.

Between the swamp and coast is a narrow sandy plain, where a newer palm-fringed road circles the island. All villages and most tourist facilities front this road, only yards from the beach.

A reef surrounds Rarotonga, enclosing a beautiful lagoon on the west, south, and southeast (Plate 6). Several passages open to the ocean, including two on the north that have been widened into harbors.

Though roughly circular in shape, Raro has four distinct coasts. The north is the most populous, and includes **Avarua**, the commercial and administrative center. It's a pleasant seaside town, with two small harbors, dozens of shops, two banks, several restaurants, and many historical sites. Half of Rarotonga's population lives in this area.

The lagoon here is rocky, and not good for swimming. Avarua is for shopping, sightseeing, dancing and dining. It's 8 blocks long and 2 blocks wide, a 15-minute walk from end-to-end. The airport is 2 miles west, and serves both domestic and international flights.

On the west coast is **Arorangi**, six miles from Avarua. It has the most tourist facilities, with two large resorts and several smaller lodgings. The beautiful beaches offer good swimming.

The south coast is essentially one long, pristine beach, which I shall now dub "**South Beach**", as it deserves its own identity. The deep, coral-filled lagoon near **Titikaveka** is perfect for snorkeling and swimming. Inland is popular **Wigmore's Falls** (Plate 10).

The east coast includes picturesque **Muri Beach** (Plate 5), the best spot for windsurfing and sailing. The wide lagoon has a sandy bottom, and four palm-clad islets (*motus*) laze in the sun. North, past **Ngatangiia**, the beaches are pretty, but not good for swimming as the reef fronts the shore. This area, near **Matavera**, is peaceful and quiet, and is rich in historical sites.

**On Arrival**
Customs and Immigration officials are friendly and efficient. Look for the representative from the **Tourist Authority**, who will help you find your hotel van. If you don't have a pre-paid voucher, it's NZ$8 to most hotels.

If you arrived without hotel reservations, turn right as you exit and stop at the new **Accommodations Bureau**, which can help you find a room. There's no charge for the service. You can also check luggage, at a flat fee of NZ$10 per bag for as long as it's stored.

Westpac's **airport bank** is usually open for international flights. Change some currency and put a NZ$20 bill in your passport for the departure tax you'll pay when you leave (NZ$10 for children).

On arrival at your hotel, remember that there is **no tipping**. A smile and a *Meitaki ma'ata!* will do just fine.

If you arrive after an all-night flight, try to sleep for a few hours, then stay up until evening. This may help reduce jet lag. Regardless of when you arrive, walk down to the beach, sift some sand through your toes, and think about what everyone back home is doing at that moment!

## WHERE TO STAY

Tourists are required to stay in licensed accommodations. It's best to reserve *before* you arrive, as you may not be allowed in if all the hotels are full. Although this rarely happens, you should at least reserve for the first night or two. You can always move if you're not satisfied, and you need not inform the Immigration Office of any changes.

Camping is definitely prohibited. Choose instead from one of the hostels listed below. If you do try to camp, you may find yourself on the next flight out.

Buildings can't be taller than a coconut tree, so most hotels are one or two stories. Many rooms have kitchenettes, handy for snacks or for saving on food costs. Air-conditioning is not common, and most visitors find it unnecessary. Most rooms have ceiling fans, which provide a gentle breeze on the few nights the trade winds are sleeping. All lodgings charge 10% government tax.

All rates are quoted in NZ dollars, per night. For quick conversion use: **NZ$100 = US$60/Can$75/Aus$85.**

### LARGE RESORTS

Two large resorts on the west coast account for almost half the island's 800 rooms. At press time the new Sheraton Resort was still under construction on South Beach, but the completion date was uncertain. Tourist Authority offices can update you on its status.

**The Rarotongan Resort** (Box 103/tel 25-800/fax 25-799) sits 8 miles from town, on a beautiful white sand beach with good lagoon swimming. The beachside bar and restaurant are adjacent to the large pool, and tennis courts and gift shops are close by. Island Nights, dance lessons, *pareu*-tying classes and other activities are offered. Snorkeling gear and outrigger canoes are available, as are vehicle rentals.

The 151 rooms sit in lush tropical gardens, in one and two-story blocks. All have balconies, phone, fridge, minibar, and coffee/tea facilities, but no kitchenettes. Some are air-conditioned, others have ceiling fans. Many rooms were upgraded in recent renovations, which will eventually cover all units.

Garden rooms are NZ$160 (all rates are single or double). Renovated beachfront units are NZ$240, older ones are NZ$190. The larger Paradise units are NZ$290 for renovated, NZ$210 for others. Four beachfront suites, all renovated, are NZ$430.

**The Edgewater Resort** (Box 121/tel 25-435/fax 25-475), 4 miles from town, is the island's largest hotel, and popular with those traveling on packages.

The nice beach offers fair swimming; the lagoon is deeper 100 yds to the south. A fine restaurant, cozy bar, tennis courts, pool, watersports shop, gift shop, vehicle rentals, and squash courts round out the facilities. Sunday barbecues and bridge tournaments are popular. Don't miss the Thursday crab races!

The 182 rooms are in two and three-story blocks, on a relatively small parcel. They're clean and comfortable, with private patios, air conditioning, in-house movies, and tea/coffee facilities.

Rates are the same for single, double or triple, and range from NZ$165-220, depending on proximity to the beach. Connecting rooms for kids under 12 are only NZ$75. Two owner's suites go for NZ$300. Nine deluxe beachfront VIP units have kingsize beds, spa baths and air-conditioning, for NZ$350.

**SMALLER HOTELS AND MOTELS** Two dozen smaller lodgings dot the island, including upscale lodges, backpackers' hostels, and everything in between. "Motels" are much more comfortable than their American cousins.

**West Coast**
Fine white sand beaches are the main attraction, with fair-to-good swimming. The lagoon is dotted with coral, but can be shallow in spots. The sunsets are marvelous, and restaurants are close by.

The upscale **Rarotongan Sunset Motel** (Box 377/tel 28-028/fax 28-026) is just north of the Edgewater. There's a sandy beach, good swimming, large pool, and the cozy Birdcage Bar. Nigel and Irene Purdie offer 20 spacious studios, each with sliding glass doors, kitchenettes, dining area, tiled bathroom, ceiling fans, TV and phones.

Nine beachfront units are NZ$185 single or double, and 11 garden units are NZ$150. Units 1, 4, 5 and 9 are beachfront end units, which I highly recommend. Book early, as this popular place always fills up.

The **Manuia Beach Hotel** (Box 700/tel 22-461/fax 22-464) fronts a nice beach, with fair swimming. The six beachside and 14 garden rooms are closely set in ten duplexes, with pool and jacuzzi near the beachfront restaurant and bar. Beachside dining is a tradition, as are tropical drinks at sunset. Their Bounty Restaurant features a la carte dining.

Rooms have a queen and single bed, fridge, mini-bar, and coffee/tea facilities. Service is excellent, and includes nightly "pillow gifts." Rates are NZ$375 garden and NZ$465 beachside, including tropical breakfast for two. Watersports equipment is complimentary, as are both golf and tennis at local clubs. Children under 12 are not allowed.

**Puaikura Reef Lodges** (Box 397/tel 23-537/fax 21-537) has 12 motel-style rooms across the road from the beach. Eight 1-br units and 4 studios all have kitchens, and offer good value at NZ$106, single or double. Paul and Susan Wilson look after their guests, who are personally met at the airport.

**Lagoon Lodges** (Box 45/tel 22-020/fax 22-021), near the Rarotongan Resort, is more like a cozy village than a motel. The 14 spacious units are spread over 4 manicured acres, across the road from a nice beach. A large pool, barbecue, tennis court, children's play area and guest laundry are on-site. Cassey and Des Eggelton take obvious pride in their well-maintained establishment.

All are quite comfortable, have upscale furnishings, and are among the best units on Raro. Studios are NZ$130, 1-br's are NZ$145. Huge 2-br lodges are only NZ$160. The exquisite 3-br VIP lodge, with its own pool, is NZ$350.

**Ati's Beach Bungalows** (Box 693/tel 21-546/fax 26-174) include 4 deluxe beachfront units at NZ$105 (sgl/dbl), and 5 garden units for NZ$70. The deluxe 2-br, 2-bath beachfront family unit sleeps 6, for only NZ$235. Ati and Jim are warm and congenial hosts.

A new offering is **Oasis Village** (Box 2093/tel 28-213/fax 28-214), four self-contained cottages near the beach at Black Rock. Rates are NZ$150.

Budget travelers enjoy the Estall's **Are-Renga Motel** (Box 223/tel 20-050). The 16 units are basic, but large and comfortable. Some have a kitchen and bath, others share both. Hot water is solar-powered, so use the electric back-up switch if it's raining. Rates are NZ$25/40, sgl/dbl. Their aptly named **Airport Lodge**, near the Meteorological Station, has 6 units at similar rates, plus shared rooms at NZ$15/per person.

The nearby **Arorangi Lodges** (Box 584/tel 21-687/fax 26-174) is basic and inexpensive. The eight rooms have kitchenettes, and rates of NZ$30/sgl, NZ$40/dbl, and NZ$15/pp share basis.

On the side road near the Kavera Market is **Backpackers International** (Box 878/tel & fax 21-847), a good place to meet other travelers. Bill Bates offers 2 singles, 6 twins and one double, with communal lounge, kitchen and dining area. Toilets and showers are in a separate block. Rates are NZ$25/sgl, NZ$15/pp share basis. His family also runs the budget **Rutaki Lodge**, near the Rarotongan Resort, with similar rates for the 3 triples, 3 doubles and 1 single.

## South Beach

For peace and quiet, try one of the small upscale lodgings along South Beach, near Titikaveka. The beaches are uncrowded, and snorkeling and swimming are excellent.

The quietest of the quiet is definitely **Palm Grove Cottages** (Box 23/tel 20-002/fax 21-998). Grant and Marie Priest's spacious and comfortable units are "popular with older couples, and others seeking peace and quiet." Five are right on South Beach, and eight are across the road, near the pool and barbecue. These pleasant studios have nice kitchens, verandas, and lots of glass. Rates are NZ$185, sgl/dbl for beachfront, NZ$140 gardenside.

The **Moana Sands Resort** (Box 1007/tel 26-189/fax 22-464) has 12 beachfront

The "Honeymoon Cottage" on the beach at the Little Polynesian Motel

rooms in a two-story block. Each has a queen-size bed, upscale furnishings, tropical cane decor, fridge and cooking facilities. Rates start at NZ$150.

A guest restaurant and bar are on-site, and room service is available at breakfast and dinner. "Kids are very welcome here, and they'll also enjoy the game room and TV" says Manager Jolene Bosanquet. Snorkeling, canoeing and sailing gear is complimentary.

Also on this prime section of South Beach is the cozy **Little Polynesian Motel** (Box 366/tel 24-280/fax 21-585). "Little Poly" has nine studio units, all with lots of glass so you can see the lagoon right from your bed! There's a pool and barbecue, and free use of watersports equipment.

Eight units in duplexes are NZ$147, while Unit #9 (NZ$177) is the famous "honeymoon cottage," set off by itself on the beach. All have kitchenettes, though it's smaller in #9 due to the kingsize bed! Jeannine and Junior host several weddings a year, with special rates available.

**Raina Beach Apartments** (Box 1047/tel 20-197/fax 23-602) are two lower and two upper 1-br units, in a modern building across the road from South Beach. All have kitchens and lounges, and are NZ$145; children under 5 not allowed. The rooftop deck has a 360° view.

### Muri Beach Area
Tropical islets dot the lagoon, and this is an excellent spot for swimming, windsurfing, sailing, and watersports.

My favorite upscale lodging is the **Pacific Resort** (Box 790/tel 20-427/fax 21-427), a 46-room beachfront property with lush gardens, picturesque stream,

and freshwater pool. Snorkeling and watersports gear are complimentary.

Units are large, with kitchenette, lounge, bedroom, bath and veranda. The 2-br garden suites are NZ$250 (sgl or dbl), and 1-br garden units NZ$240-260. Closer to, but not on the beach, are the 1-br Units 5-10, at NZ$275.

The 1-br "honeymoon suites"---Units 11, 12, 13 and 14---sit right on the beach. Rates are NZ$325. These are among the choicest rooms on Raro, and are booked many months in advance.

The Resort also manages seven adjacent deluxe VIP homes, called the **Pacific Villas**. These absolutely exquisite 2-br houses include three beachfront villas at NZ$515, and four garden villas at NZ$475.

A short walk to the south, the pleasant **Muri Beachcomber** (Box 379/tel 21-022/fax 21-323) has ten beachside units in duplexes, plus two garden units, all at only NZ$135/160, sgl/dbl. (No kids under 12 in beachside.) Immaculate kitchens and baths, upscale furnishings, and well-tended grounds all reflect the personal attention of Helen & Peter Kemp, and Bill & Lynley Tillick. Pool, barbecue and laundry are on-site. Most units are booked 4-6 months in advance.

The same group manages the nearby 4-br beachfront **Lodge**, which sleeps 7 or 8. Families find it a bargain at NZ$300/dbl, NZ$50 each extra guest.

The seven luxurious **Sokala Villas** (Box 82/tel 29-200/fax 21-222) are set in coconut palms and ironwoods fronting the lagoon. Five of these spacious 1-br masterpieces have their own pool, built right into the deck! All have queen-size beds, kitchenettes, slate floors, pine interiors, log exteriors, and gorgeous views of the islets and lagoon.

Four one-story cottages are right on the beach, and three two-story villas are in the lush garden. Rates range from NZ$160-NZ$315, with pool units at the higher end. The excellent Flame Tree Restaurant is next door.

The two self-contained **Aroko Bungalows** (Box 850/tel 21-625 or 29-312) sit right on the lagoon. At only NZ$50, these are usually booked up.

I was extremely impressed by the six new **Avana Marina Condominiums** (Box 869/tel 20-836/fax 22-991). One 3-br and five 2-br townhouses sit on a small beach at the end of Muri lagoon. These deluxe 2-story units are nicely furnished and maintained. Each has queen-size beds, lounge, veranda, kitchen with dishwasher and microwave, TV, phone, and nearby laundry and barbecue. Watersports equipment and rowboats are complimentary, as are arrival breakfasts and other amenities. It's a comfortable place to stay, and kids are welcome. All units are NZ$350/night.

**Northeast and North Coast**
Above Muri the reef fronts the beach, and swimming is not good. There are, however, some **bathtub beaches**---small reef holes---good for cooling off.

The **Sunrise Beach Motel** (Depot 8/tel 20-417/fax 21-323) has 6 nice beachfront cottages, with kitchenettes and great views, for only NZ$85, sgl or dbl. Two budget units sleep 3 each, at NZ$25/pp share basis. Cool off in their tiny pool, a "bathtub beach" 100 yds south, or at Muri Beach, a ten-minute walk.

**Ariana Bungalows** (Box 925/tel 20-521/fax 26-174) is one of the few inland lodgings. Nine cottages sit in tropical gardens near the large pool, barbecue area, self-serve laundry and TV/video/billiard lounge. Rates are NZ$44-60. Bob Healy meets many flights, and also offers budget travelers shared hostel rooms at NZ$16 per person, and 11 beds in "Bob's Dorm" at NZ$14/pp. All units have kitchens and hot showers.

The long-established **Kii Kii Motel** ("key-key"), (Box 68/tel 21-937/fax 22-937) is a pleasant 24-room American-style motel. Beach swimming is not good, but the pool is inviting. Manager Pauline Napa gets rave reviews from our readers, and lots of repeat business. Budget rooms start at NZ$54/67, sgl/dbl. Two newer end units--- #21 up, #17 down---have ocean views and private verandas, for NZ$92/114.

Close by is the **Tamure Resort** (Box 483/tel 22-415/fax 24-415), a small, budget-style resort with a beach but no lagoon swimming. The 35 rooms have fridges, and coffee/tea facilities, but no kitchenettes. There's a good restaurant and friendly bar, and barbecue area near the pool. The Tamure has excellent Island Night shows each week.

Rates are NZ$110, sgl/dbl. The quietest rooms are #18-25, while #21 and #22 also have nice ocean views.

The **Paradise Inn** (Box 674/tel 20-544/fax 22-544) is the only motel in Avarua. Karen Leisen and staff provide a comfortable home-away-from-home at moderate rates. The building was once the largest dance hall in the South Pacific, and much of it was preserved during the 1985 remodeling.

Most of the 16 rooms are split-level affairs, with lounge, kitchenette and shower/WC on the main floor. A spiral staircase leads to the loft bedroom.

*These two "Honeymoon Cottages" at Pacific Resort sit right on Muri Beach.*

Rates are NZ$60/66 sgl/dbl. Children under 12 are not allowed.

Swimming is not an attraction, but the seaside deck offers great views and magnificent tropical sunsets (Plate 19). A self-service bar, lounge, and upstairs TV/VCR area adjoin the deck. The Paradise is a recommended choice for those on a moderate budget.

Two popular hostels are a mile from town, on the airport back road. Their hosts often meet incoming flights.

**Tiare Village/Dive Hostel** (Box 719/tel 23-466/fax 20-969) has three A-frame cottages which sleep four, and four rooms in the main house which share a kitchen and lounge. Rates are NZ$16/ share basis in this pleasant and friendly lodging. Room 4 in the house has a double bed and private bath, and is often saved for couples.

Hugh Baker's **Matareka Heights Youth Hostel** (Box 587/tel 23-670/fax 23-672) is on the hill behind Tiare Village. The upper house has a shared lounge and kitchen, and 3 triples, each with its own bath. The lower house has shared kitchen, lounge and bath, and 3 dbl/twin rooms. All are NZ$25/40, sgl/dbl, with weekly discounts. The views are great, and if you don't have a motorbike you'll be in good shape by the time you leave!

**Houses For Rent**
For stays of a month or more, consider renting a house. Rates vary from NZ$900-2000/month, based on size and proximity to the beach. Try CI Commercial Realty (Box 869/tel 23-840/fax 23-843), or Villa Services (tel 25-264/fax 25-265). We at Pacific Publishing also hear of house rentals from friends in Raro. You can reach us in California at (510) 525-1441/fax (510) 525-1275.

# RARO PRACTICALITIES

**Information:** The *Cook Islands News* (Mon-Sat) lists current activities. The **Cook Islands Tourist Authority** has lots of pamphlets at its office in central Avarua. Freebies at hotels and the CITA include the informative *What's On in the Cook Islands, Jason's Passport Map* and the *Cook Islands Sun* tourist newspaper.

## TV and Radio
CITV's one channel broadcasts 5pm-11pm. *Seinfeld* and *Melrose Place* are favorites, as are local and international news shows. AM (630) and FM (103.3) radio stations offer music and news.

## Bookstores
The main shop is the **Bounty Bookshop** (near ANZ Bank) with maps, cards, magazines, NZ newspapers, paperbacks, and South Pacific books. The affiliated **Post Shop** in the Taio Centre (Arorangi), **Pen Mart** in the Tangaroa Shopping Centre (airport back road), and **Pacific Supplies** (near South Seas International) carry similar items.

The **CITC Main Store** has a good selection of books. Also try **Island Crafts, University of the South Pacific (USP)**, and the **Library and Museum**.

## Libraries and Museum
The lending library is the **Cook Islands Library and Museum** (opposite USP), open Mon-Thurs, 12-4:30; Friday, 9-4:30; and Saturday, 9-11am. Their large Pacific collection is open to the public. Temporary cards are NZ$10/month, plus a refundable NZ$25 deposit.

Sharing the same building and schedule is the Museum, with displays of canoes, statues, artifacts, tools, and weapons. Original maps and period photos highlight the informative exhibits. No entrance fee is charged, but donations are gladly accepted.

The **Cook Islands National Library**, in the National Culture Center, is a reference library. It's open 9-4 on Tuesday, Thursday and Friday, and 9-8 on Monday and Wednesday.

## Banks
**Westpac** (22-014) and **ANZ Bank** (21-750) are open Mon-Fri from 9-3. Exchange rates are comparable. For cash on nights or weekends, check to see if an international flight is arriving---Westpac's **airport bank** may be open.

## Post Offices
The main Post Office is near the traffic circle, and open Mon-Fri, 8-4. Branches are in Arorangi and Titikaveka. Stamps can be purchased at most hotel front desks or gift shops, even on Sundays.

## Telephone/Fax
**Telecom** (29-680), is on Tutakimoa Rd., past Cook's Corner Arcade, and open 24 hours for international phone, fax, telegram and telex. See the "Planning Your Trip" chapter for more details.

## Local Travel Agents/Airlines
For outer island packages, try **Island Hopper Vacations** (22-026) near Foodland. Also check with **Hugh Henry and Associates** (25-320), **Matina Travel** (21-780), and **Stars Travel** (23-669).

All the airline reservation offices are now located at the main terminal:

| | |
|---|---|
| **Air Rarotonga:** | 22-888 |
| **Polynesian Airlines:** | 20-845 |
| **Air New Zealand:** | 26-300 |

## Photographic Supplies
Try the **Rarotonga Pharmacy, South Seas International** or **Cliff's** (near the

# What's On In The
# COOK ISLANDS

**FREE VISITORS' GUIDE**

market). The pharmacy and Cliff's offer one-hour print processing, and Cliff's may do slide processing.

**Beauty Salon/Barber**
In addition to hotel salons, Avarua has **The Salon** (22-210), and **Top Shape Hairdressers** (21-274) at the Health Club. In Arorangi, try **Paradise Hair and Beauty** (22-774).

**Health Club/Massage**
If you need that aerobics class to stay in shape, or a massage to unwind from windsurfing, **Top Shape Health and Fitness Center** (21-254) is the place to go. It's located in town on the main road, east of the traffic circle.

**Service Clubs**
Members are welcome at the **Rotary Club** (27-450, meets on Wednesdays), **Lions Club** (20-428) and **Chamber of Commerce** (20-295). The **Returned Services Association (RSA)** (26-026) is across from the airport terminal.

**Medical/Police/Fire**
The **Tupapa Outpatient Clinic** (20-065) is a mile east of town and open daily. Serious problems and emergencies are treated at the **Hospital**, up the hill near the golf course. The well-stocked **Rarotonga Pharmacy** (29-292) is next to the main CITC store. The **Police Department** is on the main road in central Avarua.

| Ambulance/Hospital: | 998 |
| Police: | 999 |
| Fire: | 996 |

**Laundry**
Many lodgings have self-service washers and dryers. **Snowbird Laundry** (20-952) has branches near the Empire Theatre and another in Arorangi. They'll pick up, wash, dry, fold, and deliver, for about NZ$10 per load.

**Public Restrooms**
The most-centrally located are: at Cook's Corner; next to the Banana Court/Tourist Authority; next to Avarua Harbor; and near the Ruatonga open-air market.

Visitors can use facilities in restaurants, hotels or bars without any problem. The WC at Trader Jack's merits a special award for upkeep.

# GETTING AROUND

Rarotonga is only 20 miles (32 km) around, so nothing is very far away. Buses and taxis operate, but most visitors rent motorbikes or cars---especially on weekends, when bus service is limited. Sample distances are:

| Heading West From Avarua (counterclockwise) | Miles | Km |
|---|---|---|
| Airport Terminal | 1.4 | 2.2 |
| Golf Club | 3.2 | 5.1 |
| Edgewater Resort | 4.2 | 6.8 |
| Rarotongan Resort | 8.0 | 12.8 |
| Liana's Restaurant | 9.5 | 15.2 |
| Palm Grove Cottages | 10.0 | 16.0 |

| Heading East (clockwise) | | |
|---|---|---|
| Tamure Resort | 1.4 | 2.3 |
| Muri Beach area | 6.0 | 9.6 |
| Little Polynesian Motel | 7.6 | 12.2 |
| Palm Grove Cottages | 10.0 | 16.0 |

Drive on the left, as in New Zealand, Australia and Great Britain. Speed limits are 40km/h (25mph) in town and 50km/h (30mph) in rural areas. Gasoline ("petrol") is about NZ$1/liter, or US$2.40 per US gallon. Avarua petrol stations are near CITC, Budget Rent-A-Car and Portofino. Hogan's in Arorangi, and Countryside near the Sheraton site, are open late and on Sundays.

You'll need a Cook Islands Driver's License to rent a vehicle, and it's also a unique souvenir. The International Driver's License is not recognized. Show your home driver's license at the Police Department in Avarua, have your photo taken, and pay NZ$10.

Motorbike renters must take a driving test to the traffic circle and back, unless your home license covers motorbikes. (Theoretically, you can't drive a motorbike until you've passed the test, but you have to drive your motorbike to the Police Station to *take* the test. So much for logic in paradise!)

The main road is level and paved ("sealed"), with no traffic lights or stop signs. The traffic circle in town is a challenge if you're not used to driving on the "wrong" side of the road. Go slowly and you'll soon get used to it.

Look out for kids, pigs, horses, and especially dogs, which can appear anytime and anywhere. The "seawall curve" west of the airport can be dangerous when wet, and on busy weekend nights.

To avoid dents, don't park cars under coconut trees. Don't leave car windows open when you park, as this is an ancient signal to the Polynesian Rain God to start a tropical downpour. "Rush hour" on Rarotonga is from 4:00-4:05pm, but don't expect to hear helicopter traffic reports on the radio!

## Car Rentals

The newer cars are NZ$50-60/day, but you might find some older models for NZ$40/day. Versatile "Jeep-style" convertibles are NZ$55-85/day. Rarotonga Rentals has replica MG convertibles for NZ$70/day. Weekly discounts, which apply to all rentals, save about 20%. Unlimited mileage and basic insurance are included. Minimum driver age is 21.

For newer models, I found **Budget Rent-A-Car** (20-895/fax 20-888) to be reliable and efficient, with free delivery to hotels and the airport. The office is in town behind Ronnie's, and branches are at the Edgewater (21-026) and the Rarotongan Resort (20-838). Other reputable companies include **Tipani Rentals** (22-328/fax 26-458), **Rarotonga Rentals** (22-326/fax 22-060), **Avis Car Rental** (22-833/fax 21-702), **TPA Rental Cars** (20-611) and **Rental Cars C.I.** (24-442/fax 24-446).

## Motorbike Rentals

These are popular with both locals and tourists. They seat two, and the automatic clutch makes shifting easy---but use care if you're not used to them.

Drive slowly in gravel, as you can easily slide out sideways. Don't tailgate, since dirt can get thrown into your eyes. Wearing sunglasses at dusk keeps bugs out of your eyes. The larger bikes (100cc) vibrate less than the smaller ones (50cc), but the latter are easier to kickstart (no electric starters). Keep clothes and legs away from the exhaust pipe. Helmets are not usually available.

Rates are NZ$15-25/day, with weekly discounts available. Check the tires and brakes on older bikes. Newer bikes have a frame lock, which should be used.

**Polynesian Bike Hire** (20-895) is part of Budget, and rent clean and reliable bikes. Also check with **Tipani Rentals** (22-327), **TPA Rentals** (20-611), **Vaima Rentals** (22-222), and **Odds and Ends** (27-595). Many lodgings also rent bikes.

## Bicycle Rentals

Bicycles ("pushbikes") are NZ$5-10/day. The main road is flat, as are most inland roads. **Hogan's** (22-632) has mountain bikes and tandems. Try **Polynesian Bike Hire** and **Tipani Rentals**, listed above. Some lodgings also rent pushbikes.

## Buses

There are no buses on Sunday, and limited service on Saturday. The **Cook's Corner Bus** (25-512) departs every half-hour from that arcade, alternating directions (only clockwise on Saturday). Some routes serve the airport back road. Hours are weekdays from 7am-4:30pm, and Saturdays from 8am-noon. Fares are NZ$3/OW, NZ$4/RT, NZ$5 for a day pass, and NZ$15 for a 10-ride ticket, which can be shared.

Their separate **Night Service,** for NZ$4/RT, runs Mon-Thurs from 6-10pm; Friday night from 6pm-1:30am; and Saturday from 6pm to midnight.

To catch a bus when outside of town, just go to the main road and flag one down. The driver will be glad to stop.

## Taxis

**B.K. Taxis** (20-019) is reliable, as is **Ngatangiia Taxi** (22-238), even though I still can't pronounce it! Others include **Kapi Taxis** (23-510), **Kaikaveka Taxis** (20-213) and **Silver Cabs** (27-021).

Rates are regulated: NZ$1.50 drop charge, plus NZ$1.50/km. Nights and weekends are higher. Always ask for an estimate in advance. Taxis often wait at the shelter opposite Mama's Cafe. The Rotary Club donated it as an *Are Tapaeanga*, "a place to stop and rest," but it's also a taxi stand and notice-board, to the mild chagrin of its donors.

## Restaurant Transport

Some offer reduced-rate transport for Island Night diners, with further discounts for parties of 4 or more.

## Hitchhiking

While this is officially frowned upon, most locals will pick up a stranded tourist, especially in rural areas. On one occasion the bus was down so I hitched in from the Rarotongan Resort. A family gave me a ride, a dozen oranges, and invited me to dinner! One rainy New Year's Eve a driver went 3 miles past her home to drop me at my hotel. I wouldn't hitch as a primary means of travel, but it's probably OK in a pinch.

## Maps

If you plan to do much inland hiking, or visit an outer island, get a topographic map (NZ$8) from Bounty Bookshop.

## FOOD AND DRINK

Polynesian fare centers around pork, chicken, fish and shellfish, with lots of fruits and vegetables on the side. A decade ago it was difficult to find Polynesian-style food on restaurant menus, except at special Island Night dinners. Local restaurants have responded to visitors' suggestions, and most include local dishes in their nightly offerings.

Delicacies include *ika mata*---marinated fish in coconut sauce---and *eke* (octopus) dishes. Fresh tuna, mahi mahi and parrotfish are favorites, along with the occasional barracuda or shark.

*Taro* is a popular starchy tuber served at most traditional meals. The main variety is wet taro, grown in the swamps, while the rarer dry version, called *tarotarua*, grows on higher inland plots. Wet taro cooks up grey, dry taro stays white. Both taste pretty bland. One expatriate described taro as "tas-

ting like soap." It's more palatable if you add sauces to liven up the taste.

Taro has a leafy top called *rukau*, which has a deliciously sweet spinach taste when cooked. *Rukau* is considered a male aphrodisiac---"I feed it to my husband to put lead in his pencil!" joked one lady---but nothing has been published in this fascinating area of science.

Breadfruit (*kuru*) is also a popular starch, but these wrinkled, grapefruit-sized carbohydrate bombs grow on trees. Captain Bligh of the *Bounty* was bringing breadfruit trees from Tahiti to Caribbean slave plantations when he was rudely interrupted by Fletcher Christian and his mutineers. Cooked breadfruit has a nut-like flavor, and fried *kuru* chips, served at takeaways, are a delicious snack.

Local sweet-potato (*kumara*) is tasty, as is *poke* ("po-keh"), a starchy dessert pudding of baked arrowroot (tapioca) and bananas, papayas or other fruits.

Papayas, called pawpaws in local English and *nita* in Rarotongan, grow year-round and are popular at breakfast. Bananas come in many varieties, and some stay green even when ripe. To check ripeness, examine the long edges of the fruit. If they're sharp, wait a day or two. If they're rounded, they're probably ripe. Plantains resemble bananas, but aren't sweet, even when ripe. Ask if you're not sure what you're buying.

Delicious mangoes drop from the trees from October to March. Sweet pineapples are grown inland in the south coast area. Oranges, once abundant, are now available in lesser quantities, but are still sweet and juicy. Like bananas, some orange varieties are green when ripe. The yellow starfruit tastes like a tart melon. Watermelon is a very popular snack, and avocadoes grow wild on Rarotonga.

Coconuts are a versatile food. Drinking nuts, or *nu*, are young nuts right off the tree. Machetes are handy for opening this ecologically-sound container. The hard meat is eaten as is, or grated and squeezed to make coconut cream and sauces. After the mature coconut sprouts a leaf or two, the inside becomes a sweet, spongy food called *uto*, which can be baked, or eaten as is. Look for sprouted nuts along the beach.

*Kava*, the mildly narcotic drink made from the root of the pepper tree, was banned by the missionaries, and is not used in the Cooks today. It's still popular in Samoa and Fiji. It tastes like woodsy dishwater, and its effects are greatly exaggerated---you're not missing much.

After *kava* was outlawed, locals used hollowed-out tree stumps to brew "bush beer" from oranges. This is still popular on Atiu, as part of a ritual called the *tumunu*. Visitors there can participate in the ceremony, but bush beer is hard to find on Rarotonga. Atiu also produces fine coffee, which is available on Rarotonga.

Mangaians used to grow pineapples, can the juice for export, and make a pineapple liquor called *Mangaia Ara*. Shipping and production problems led to financial losses, and Mangaians closed down the cannery and distillery. Bottles of *Mangaia Ara* are still around, but you'll have to look hard to find this exotic drink.

Locally-produced fruit juices are quite good, including orange, guava, passionfruit, mango, and other tropical flavors. Look for the pure "juice," not the watered-down "fruit drink."

**International Influences**
The New Zealand influence is felt in restaurants, cafes and takeaways. Popular light meals include fish and chips, sausages, egg dishes, burgers and mince and meat pies.

New Zealand-style offerings are complemented by great seafood, and Italian, German, Southeast Asian and Indian cuisines. Chinese food is becoming popular, although Chinese immigration was prohibited for many years by the colonial government. This is the main reason Chinese restaurants don't dominate the culinary field, as they do on Tahiti and some other islands.

Beverage choices include fruit juices, fresh ground coffee, tea, soft drinks, beer, Australian and New Zealand wine, and most types of liquor. New Zealand's Steinlager is the beer of choice, with locally-brewed Cook's Lager gaining in popularity. The brewery also makes a decent mineral water, bottled under the *Avaiki* label.

## WHERE TO EAT

There's a good range of choices, from upscale dinner spots to takeaways at the harbor. Many nightspots also serve meals, and resort restaurants are popular with both tourists and locals.

### UPSCALE RESTAURANTS

Several restaurants have an upscale dinner menu, although they may also be open for other meals. Reservations are recommended, especially on weekends. Note that some are closed on Sunday.

**Portofino** (26-480), near the Paradise Inn, is my favorite. Bill Carruthers specializes in Italian, seafood, and other European dishes. It's a large place, but the atmosphere is cozy. The seafood marinara is highly recommended (NZ$22), and other excellent entrees are NZ$15-28. The daily specials are usually good choices, and their pizza is always good (takeaways available). Portofino is open only for dinner, Monday through Saturday.

A close second is the excellent **Tumunu Bar and Restaurant** (20-501), near the Edgewater. Eric and Julie Bateman open their comfortable island-style establishment for dinner daily, and it's one of my Sunday favorites. The meals are delicious, and the portions are huge. Two of you will go home absolutely stuffed if you order the "Fisherman's Platter For One"! Dinners are NZ$15-29. There's also a darts night dinner, usually on Tuesdays.

Muri Beach is home to the award-winning **Flame Tree Restaurant** (25-123). Sue Carruthers has Indonesian, Indian, Japanese, Chinese, Thai and

Vietnamese cuisine most nights, and often adds Middle Eastern and West African specialties. Steak, seafood, and local dishes such as *rukau* round out the diverse menu. Prices range from NZ$15-29, but look for their advertised fixed-price specials for about NZ$23.

Also at Muri Beach, above the Sailing Club, is **Sails Seafood Restaurant** (27-350), with a "million dollar view" they properly brag about. If you want atmosphere, a twilight dinner is a must. The fish and continental cuisine are satisfying, and another plus is that it's open daily for lunch and dinner.

First famous as a seaside bar, **Trader Jack's** (26-464) is now a fine restaurant as well. Dinners include fresh seafood, chicken, and grilled steaks, at NZ$12-27. This is another place where you won't go home hungry. Open everyday for dinner, for lunch Mon-Fri, and brunch on Saturday.

Near the Rarotongan Resort is the **Kaena Restaurant** (25-433), which offers a variety of seafood specialties, steak, and local dishes. Entrees are NZ$17-22, and they offer a wide assortment of beer, wine and cocktails. Open daily for dinner.

In the quiet South Beach area is **Liana's Restaurant** (formerly Vaima) (26-123), 2 km from the Rarotongan Resort. The new menu features Chinese cuisine, with some European and local dishes as well. Dine in the bamboo main room, or on the thatched veranda. Entrees start at NZ$15. Open 7 days for dinner, with a light counter lunch available Monday-Friday.

The popular **PJ's Cafe/Turtle's Restaurant** was a recent victim of arson (as were the Outrigger and the Tangaroa), but Peter John McKinley may be back in operation as you read this. The restaurant was famous for its excellent

food, and the bar offered great tropical drinks in a casual and friendly atmosphere. Give them a call (20-367) to see if the party has begun again!

**Resort restaurants** are also good choices, which is unusual for a vacation destination. The **Whitesands** at the Rarotongan has theme buffets, including an excellent "fish market" night. (Don't forget to use the discount coupon in the *CI News*.) The **Reef Restaurant** at the Edgewater, Manuia Beach's **Bounty Room**, and the **Tamure** also have a good selection of steak, seafood, and local delicacies. A new favorite of mine is **Sandals** at Pacific Resort, where both the food and service receive high marks.

## MODERATE CHOICES

Several restaurants offer lighter lunch and dinner choices for moderate budgets. These are mostly in town, or on the west coast. Some are open Sunday.

In Avarua are several good choices, including **Ronnie's** (20-823), formerly the Hibiscus. Ronnie has expanded the lunch and dinner menus to include some excellent Mexican food (try the beef tacos). For those who think taro is bland, his fried taro may be a nice surprise. Eat in the dining room, on the outdoor patio, or the upper deck (my choice), which offers pleasant breezes and a sidewalk-cafe ambience. Open six days a week.

East of the traffic circle are several good spots. **Metua's Restaurant and Bar** (20-850) is open daily, and is a popular bar in the evenings. It's right on the seafront, inside the small Browne's Arcade shopping area. They have great omelettes for breakfast, and inexpensive lunch and dinner.

The nearby **Staircase Restaurant** (22-254) is seaside above the Top Shape

Health Club. Try the tasty barbecue and salad bar, chicken satay, sashimi, and great desserts. The fantastic sunsets add to the comfortable setting. Dinner only, Mon-Fri. Inexpensive.

If you're in the mood for curry, the place is go is **Priscilla's**, near the Portofino. The menu includes a full range of Indian cuisine, at moderate prices.

In front of the Edgewater is the **Spaghetti House** (25-441), offering pasta, pizza and other basic dinners at reasonable prices. Open seven days for dinner, with takeaways available.

The **Oasis Steakhouse** (28-224), near Black Rock, offers fish, pork, pasta and a salad bar in addition to its obvious focus. Main courses start at about NZ$15. Open for dinner 6 days, lunch Monday to Friday.

If you're heading around the island, try the cozy **Jam Hut** (22-872) in Titikaveka, in the South Beach area. Skip and Pepe offer huge sandwiches and tasty grills for lunch, plus a moderately-priced dinner menu. It's a relaxed and informal setting. Open daily for lunch and dinner, with great coffee and tropical ice cream dishes.

## BUDGET CAFES AND TAKEAWAYS

There are several good budget choices, both in town and around the island.

The food and service are great at the little **Blue Note Cafe**, which is part of the veranda of the Banana Court Bar. Sip on cappucino and munch on nachos as you watch the world go by!

The popular **Cook's Corner Cafe** (22-345) is in the patio fronting the arcade and bus stop. Basic grills, fish and chips, burgers, and egg dishes are served at breakfast and lunch, with takeaways available. Also at Cook's Corner is **Simone's Bistro**, open for lunch and dinner 6 nights a week.

In the center of town is **Mama's Cafe**---the locals' favorite for lunch---with sandwiches, grills, and the best ice cream on Rarotonga. Open weekdays 8-4:30, and Saturdays 8am-12:30pm.

Also popular with locals is the small but friendly **Bunny's Diner** (22-718), in the center of Arorangi. Fish and chips and homemade pies are the specialties, with a nice lunch for only NZ$8-10.

The beachfront **Boardwalk Cafe** at the Sailing Club is open for lunch Mon-Fri. The food is good, the service is spotty, and the boom box may be loud.

Near Liana's in the South Beach area is the American-style **Just Burgers**, open Mon-Fri from lunch time until 9 or 10pm, and Sundays after church. They also have good fries, and Heinz ketchup, which is rare on Raro!

Near the Edgewater is **AJ's Takeaways** (20-742), not to be confused with PJ's Cafe or TJ's Dance Hall. It only offers fish, chips and chicken, but it's open Sunday so it deserves a mention.

Popular takeaways are at the Ruatonga Market and Avatiu Harbor. Head there for a quick lunch, or a late-night snack on weekends. My favorite is the pineapple burger at **Palace Takeaways**. It definitely hits the spot---I'm not sure which one---after a night on the town.

Facing it is **Southern Fried Chicken**. The chicken is good, but the chop suey had some ingredients in it I'd rather not discuss. Instead, try chinese food at **Moana Takeaways**, at the market.

On the airport back road try the **Pandanus Coffee Lounge** in the Tangaroa Shopping Center, open daily.

In the South Beach area is the small and aptly named **Halfway Cafe**, as far from town as you can get! Open daily for sandwiches and light refreshments.

The **Hong Kong Restaurant** near the market may not yet be open, but this wouldn't surprise me. I've been hungering for egg rolls since the "Opening Soon" sign went up---in 1992!

## FOOD SHOPPING

For fruits and vegetables, head to the open-air **Te Punanga Nui**, also called the **Ruatonga Market**, next to Avatiu Harbor. Sweet papayas and bananas are always available, and pineapples and mangoes in season. Look for Mano's pickup truck and buy a little round watermelon. Leave it in the fridge overnight. Cut it in half and scoop it out with a spoon for breakfast!

The main grocery store is the well-stocked **Foodland**, near Westpac Bank. In addition to the usual offerings, they have a great deli and meat counter, and roasted chickens to go. They carry fresh NZ milk and yogurt, and NZ strawberries and kiwifruit in season. They also have the best prices on Atiu coffee.

The smaller **Wigmore's Superstore**, in the South Beach area, has fresh produce at good prices, plus meat, fish, bread and basic groceries. Almost across the road is the **Hydroponics Greenhouse**, with tasty lettuce and other vegetables.

Other shops include **Home Market** near the Paradise Inn (excellent pork); **Matavera Village Traders** on the east coast; **Goodluck Trading** at Muri Beach; and **Kavera Central** and **AJ's Mini-Mart** on the west coast. Look for the fresh produce stand along the main road, near Kavera Central. Many locals shop at the wholesale **PNT Store** in Arorangi, near the Snowbird Laundry.

You'll often see fresh-caught fish for sale, strung up in trees along the road between the harbor and the airport.

Good bakeries include the **Turama-tuitui Bakery** on the airport back road, near Tereora College. Fresh bread and

*Bananas can usually be bought in smaller bunches.*

coconut rolls make it worth the trip. In the South Beach area is the large **Turoa Bakery**, which makes excellent French bread and absolutely delicious banana muffins and cheese buns. It's open weekdays, closed Saturday, but open again on Sunday.

Beer and wine can be purchased in most food shops, but for liquor the best bet is the government-run **Cook Islands Liquor Supplies** (28-380), across from Avatiu Harbor. It's open Mon-Fri, 9am-4:30pm, and Saturday, 8am-noon. At other times try village shops, which carry basic liquor items.

## NIGHTLIFE

**Island Nights:** These special dinners, with accompanying dance shows, are a must for any visitor.

First comes the *umukai*, a traditional Polynesian feast. The *umu* is an earth oven, a large hole filled with burning timbers, then stones from mountain streams. Shredded banana trunks are added, and the steam soon begins to rise. The *kai* (food)---pork, chicken and fish---is wrapped in banana or hibiscus leaves and placed inside, then everything is covered with more leaves and earth. After a couple of hours it's cooked to perfection, with all the natural juices retained. *Umukai* foods also include *eke* (octopus), taro, *rukau* (taro tops), *ika mata* (marinated raw fish), *poke* (pudding), and fruit dishes.

The meal is followed by the entertainment (*kariori*), an exciting hour of swivel-hipped dancing, island legends, traditional songs, and plays. Audience participation is a highlight of most shows.

There's an Island Night on Rarotonga most every night, except Sunday. Most are at the resorts, including the Rarotongan, Edgewater and Pacific Resort. The Friday night show at the Tamure gets rave reviews, and the children's shows are a good option if you've already seen the professionals.

The dinner and show are NZ$22-35, and well worth it. Roundtrip transport is often available at reduced rates. You can also see the show only, for a cover charge of NZ$3-6.

11. Smiles come easy to Rarotongans.   12. Smiles also come easy to Pukapukans.
13. Schoolgirls sew fragrant flower 'eis (leis).

14. Bicycles are a good means of transport on Rarotonga.
15. Friendly Mormon missionaries always travel in pairs.

16. The legendary Banana Court Bar and Dance Hall is usually quiet during the day.
17. Avatiu Harbor: yachts, freighters, and a captured Taiwanese fishing boat

18. Mellowing out to "Miss Piggy Sings Her Favorite Love Songs in Rarotongan"
19. Sunset from the deck at the Paradise Inn

The Banana Court doesn't serve an *umukai* meal, but it does have excellent dance shows, usually from Wednesday to Friday evenings. Other nightspots also have island-style shows. Check the *CI News* for current offerings.

Look for shows by **Te Ivi Maori Cultural Group**, which has appeared in North America and Europe, and the exciting dance group te

*dance·drink·make friends*

**Tumuvarovaro** (Rarotonga's former name). Both the **Orama Dance Group** and **Matavera Youth** offer excellent entertainment.

## NIGHTSPOTS

Rarotonga has more than two dozen licensed bars and restaurants, with many offering live music. Local dance bands get your feet moving, and combos provide easy-listening island music. The *CI News* has daily ads and a Saturday entertainment section, and the Tourist Authority also has current listings.

Most nightspots are open until midnight Monday-Thursday, 2am on Friday night, and midnight on Saturday. All bars are closed Sunday, though some licensed restaurants are open.

For a guided trip to the nightspots, try a **Pub Crawl**. The Edgewater Resort (25-345) has a good one, and Hugh Henry and Associates (25-320) and Eric at the Tumunu (20-501) occasionally organize a group. All visit three or four places, and include pickup, return, and cover charges. Prices vary from NZ$30-48, depending on what's included.

**In Town**

The most famous watering hole and dance hall on the island---and perhaps in all of the South Pacific---is the legendary **Banana Court**, known simply as the **BC**. Located in the heart of town, it's open daily, except Sunday. There's live music Wednesday to Saturday, with a NZ$3 cover charge. The moderate dress code requires men to wear long pants on weekend nights.

A Friday night visit to the BC is almost mandatory. Locals and tourists both pack the place, and it can take quite a while to reach the main bar, which is past the sunken dance floor. Head for the patio at the right rear if you need some fresh air, or to the tamer **Vaka Lounge**, at the front. In gauging the crowd, one local noted:

"If it only takes 5 minutes to get to the bar, there's enough tourists...if it takes 30 minutes, there's too many!"

When you're not imbibing you'll be dancing to the uptempo Polynesian rock 'n' roll. Note that in Polynesia both the men and women do the asking when it comes to dancing, so don't be shy.

Despite its downscale appearance, the BC is pretty safe. Anyone caught fighting is out for 30 days. The second offense is 90 days, third costs a year. This can really put a dent in your social life on a small island, so few locals cause any trouble.

The Vaka Lounge is open for cocktails at Happy Hour, and has a live rhythm and blues band Tuesday nights.

Another good choice is **Trader Jack's**, on the waterfront near the traffic circle. It's the choice of many local business people, and packed by both tourists and locals on Friday night. There's usually live music on Thursday and Friday. Stop in before heading to the main dance spots, or for a cocktail on a Saturday afternoon.

A block east is the long-established **Metua's**. The open-air restaurant becomes a bar in the evenings, and usually has a dance band on Wednesdays and weekends. It's a lot tamer than the BC, and a good place to meet locals, or have a drink under the stars.

The nearby **Staircase Restaurant** becomes a dance bar on Saturday evenings, with "Pina Colada" and similar theme nights.

**TJ's** is close by, with karaoke some weeknights. You'll easily find it on weekends---listen for the loud disco music. It's mostly a younger crowd, 18-25, but all are welcome.

Back on the other side of town is the popular combination of **Ronnie's** in the front and the **Reefcomber** in the back. Ronnie has a great stereo system that fills his outdoor patio with good music and tons of people. Like the BC, it may take a while to get to the bar.

The Reefcomber has been called "a cleaner and mellower version of the BC", which is pretty accurate. It's in the former First Club disco, but that's the only similarity. The upscale cabaret has live music Wednesday to Saturday, with excellent island dance bands. It attracts an older crowd than Ronnie's, and proper dress is required (no shorts, flip flops, or sleeveless T's).

Opposite Avatiu Harbor is **Tere's Bar**, a local institution. It's the choice of yachties, and popular Thursday to Saturday, with live music on the open-air patio. Or, stop in for an afternoon drink after a tough day of shopping.

At Cook's Corner, the tiny **Hideaway Bar** features live music on weekends, karaoke on some other nights. Often a local string band entertains on their *ukureres* (no "*l*" in Rarotongan).

### Around the Island

The **Tamure** usually has a dance band on weekends, and they often host visiting groups from overseas. The **Reef Bar** at the Edgewater and the **Nu Bar** at the Rarotongan have combos for dancing or listening. If **PJ's** is back in business, look for some good live music.

Quieter choices include the bars at the **RSA/Citizen's Club** across from the airport, the **Golf Club**, near Black Rock, or the **Game Fishing Club**, near the Tamure. The RSA does have a combo Wednesday to Saturday, but the main attractions at these clubs are the friendly locals, the inexpensive drinks, and the tall tales about whatever happens to be the topic of conversation.

The younger crowd can try the **Big Orange** disco, in Arorangi. The **Empire Theatre** in town becomes an under-21 disco after the Friday night movies, so teenagers have something to do besides get into trouble. This idea could be tried in more "developed" countries.

### Cinema and Other Diversions

The Empire Theatre airs current movies on two screens, at 7:30pm and 9:30pm. The audience is more participatory than in most theaters, and loud conversations are not uncommon. The seats are a bit past their prime, but most of us are also, so settle back and enjoy the experience. All in all it's usually a fun evening, even if you've seen the film!

Videos are available around the island, and may be a good choice on a rainy evening. **Nikao Video** (near the airport) has the latest releases.

*Avatiu Harbor---home to freighters, yachts, and the Cook Islands Navy.*

## AVARUA SIGHTS

The seaside village of **Avarua** (Two Sea Channels) dates from 1825, when the missionaries brought locals together on the coast to receive religious training. Until then all villages were inland, near the taro swamps and plantations.

Today it's a tree-lined commercial center, eight blocks long and two blocks wide, with government offices, banks, shops, restaurants and nightspots. Many historical sites are in the area.

We'll head east through town, starting in the western "suburb" of Avatiu ("a-va-tchoo"). **Avatiu Harbor** (Plate 17) hosts freighters, yachts and some fishing boats. It's moderately protected, but there's no breakwater to deflect sporadic northerlies. The **Waterfront Commission** monitors freighter traffic.

The patrol boat *Te Kukupa* (The Dove), a gift from Australia, comprises the entire Cook Islands Navy. Its primary tasks are monitoring the Cooks' large Exclusive Economic Zone (EEZ) for unlicensed fishing boats, and search-and-rescue missions. It's open on some holidays---check with the Tourist Authority for upcoming tours.

The new open-air **Te Punanga Nui** (Great Market)---also called the **Rarotonga Market**, adjoins the harbor. Look for great deals on fruits and vegetables.

**St. Joseph's Catholic Church**, which opened on Christmas Day, 1896, was recently re-built. Along with the British protectorate in 1888 came religious freedom, and Catholics and Seventh Day Adventists soon arrived in the islands. Their churches thus date from the 1890's, rather than the 1840's and 1850's of the CICC branches.

In the town center, shops line the inland side of the divided road. Parking is under large casuarina (ironwood) trees, which prevent erosion and don't drop nuts on cars and pedestrians.

**Westpac Bank** and **Foodland** mark the town center. **ANZ Bank** and **Bounty Bookshop** are tucked into the modern CIDB Building. The air-conditioned banks are nice respites on hot days.

Stop at the **Police Station** for your new Cook Islands' Driver's License (NZ$10). The motorcades out front are daily driving tests for motorbike renters.

**Tutakimoa Road** heads inland to the **Cook's Corner Shopping Arcade** and **Telecom**. The **Lawn Bowling Club** and **Te Atukura**, the government reception center, are off side roads. Inland, on the *ara metua*, is the **Perfume Factory**.

The century-old **CITC Department Store** and the modern **Pharmacy** were severely damaged in 1987 by Hurricane Sally, which tossed car-sized boulders through their front windows.

At the friendly **Tourist Authority** you find loads of helpful information, which you can review over a cool one at the infamous **Banana Court Bar**.

The "BC" is also an historical landmark. Born as a sanatorium in 1905, it later housed the legislature. Eventually it became the *Otera Rarotonga*, Raro's first hotel. After private motels were built the hotel section was closed, but the bar and sunken dance floor remained open. The present name was adopted in the 1970's, reflecting the original banana grove on the site.

The **Vaikapuangi Stream** flows into tiny **Avarua Harbor**, home to small fishing boats. The cute foot bridge is officially called the **Bridge of Love**.

A large government complex---Post Office, Courthouse, Ministers' Offices, Survey Department and Telephone Exchange---once fronted the **traffic circle**. On Mother's Day, 1992, it was all destroyed in an arson fire. A new center is planned, but for now everything has been squeezed into nearby buildings.

The **Post Office** (open Mon-Fri, 8-4) is now on the west side of **Takuvaine Road**. For collectors' stamps and coins, stop at the adjacent **Philatelic Bureau**.

Past the PO is the **Rarotonga Brewery**. It takes 28 days to brew Cook's Lager, using Australian malt barley. Tours are Tues/Thurs at 10am.

Back at the main road, the **Makea Bridge**---named for the local *ariki*---spans **Takuvaine Stream**, and leads past the **Empire Theatre**. Close by is Queen Makea Takau's **Para O Tane** palace, and the **Taputapuatea Marae**. The Makea chiefs presided over Avarua, and it was Makea Takau who accepted British protection in 1888 as a French warship approached.

The palace was ravaged by hurricanes in the 1940's, and the massive walls collapsed into piles of coral boulders. Architecture students from the University of Auckland, with help from the Makea's descendants and their friends, finished the restoration in 1993.

**Takamoa Road** offers several historical sites. The limestone **Cook Islands Christian Church**, built in 1853 under the guidance of missionary Aaron Buzacott, still has Sunday services at 10am.

In the **CICC Cemetery** is the grave of **Albert Henry**, perhaps the Cooks' most famous son. Look for the impressive life-size bust of the Premier, usually adorned with flowers and shell *'eis*.

In contrast to Henry's elaborate grave is that of **Robert Dean Frisbie**, the famed American writer who lived on

Today Takamoa trains CICC ministers, and remains one of the oldest educational centers in the South Pacific.

Notice the dwarf coconut trees, an experiment that's been repeated around the island. They're safer for nut gatherers, as well as afternoon nappers.

On the main road, facing the CICC, sits the limestone ruin of the old **Sunday School**, built in 1842. In 1992 it was meticulously restored by Joan Rolls and David Gragg as their new **Beachcomber** shop and gallery.

The hull of the yacht **Yankee** once sat nearby, and was a popular tourist attraction. Often featured in *National Geographic*, it ran aground here in 1964. A recent hurricane crumpled it into an unrecognizable ball of rust, and it was buried for safety reasons. The museum has artifacts of the famous vessel.

The largest wreck on Raro is the **Maitai**, a 3,393-ton vessel owned by the Union Steam Ship Company. It ran aground on Christmas Eve, 1916, with a load of Model-T's bound for New Zealand. Only its rusting boiler remains, easily visible off Avarua Harbor.

Past **Portofino** is the **Paradise Inn**, restored from the old **Maruaiai Dance Hall**, largest in the South Pacific. Down **Victoria Road** is the impressive new **National Culture Center**, venue for major island events. The **National Library**, at the front of the complex, is a reference and research center.

Facing it is the **Tupapa Sports Ground**, the site of wild rugby games on Saturday afternoons, May through August. Further on are the **outer island hostels**, which serve as temporary quarters for outer islanders visiting Raro.

Up the hill is **Ngatipa**, residence of the New Zealand Representative. The original house was built in 1891 on land given to Queen Victoria by the Makea.

Pukapuka. His plainly marked grave lies in the southwest corner of the cemetery.

The nearby **Library and Museum** is a must. The Raro Practicalities section has details on hours and library cards.

Facing the library is the Cook Islands center of the Fiji-based **University of the South Pacific (USP)**, which uses satellite, video, and live instruction. USP also publishes and sells books about the South Pacific.

Takamoa Road appropriately ends at **Takamoa Theological College and Mission House**, founded in 1839 to train Polynesian missionaries for overseas work. In 1947 the local branch of the London Missionary Society became the Cook Islands Christian Church.

*The Avarua CICC, built in 1853, is still a center of community activities.*

Rebuilt in 1968, it's not open to the public except on certain holidays. Queen Elizabeth II stayed there during her 1974 visit to Rarotonga.

Our town tour ends here. The Around The Island Tour is the last section of this Rarotonga chapter.

## TOURS AND ATTRACTIONS

**Guided Tours**: A Circle-Island Tour is an excellent way to learn about local culture and history, and to see places to return to later. One of the most informative is given by the guides from **Hugh Henry and Associates** (25-320), who know Raro as well as anyone.

Their 4-hr tour departs each weekday morning. The comfortable coach covers both the main and back roads, stopping at agricultural plantations and cultural, religious and historical sites. The Perfume Factory and Rarotonga Brewery are included on most tours, which are NZ$24 per person.

They also offer a "picnic tour" every Wednesday, and can arrange cross-island hikes and guided reef walks.

**Tipani Tours** (25-266) is one of the oldest tour companies, and Hinano MacQuarie and her staff also know the island well. They offer tours, reef walks, cross-island hikes, and, for groups, a traditional feast at a private home.

**Ariki Tours** (28-647) offers private Circle-Island tours for 2-4 passengers, at NZ$53 per person, and can provide other personalized services.

**Cook Islands Tours & Travel** (27-270) also has island tours, plus a Nite on the Town Tour, which includes dinner. Call for current offerings.

# Pa's Mountain Trek

If you're into exploring the inland mountains and valleys, there's only one person to see: Papa Teuruaa, otherwise known as **Pa, Son of Polynesia**. Despite the name, Pa is a youngish man with blond dreadlocks, and he's one of the nicest guys you'll meet. His little company, called **Pa's Mountain Trek** (21-079/20-457 eves) offers two hikes, depending on your energy level.

The Cross-Island-Hike takes about 5 hrs, and is recommended if you're in reasonably good shape. Trek up lush valleys to the famous rock, The Needle, then slither down the back side of the mountain to fabulous Wigmore's Falls for a refreshing dip in the cold pool.

His easygoing four-hour Nature Walk roams through tropical jungles and plantations. All tours are NZ$30 (NZ$15 for kids), transport included.

## Cultural Village Tours

On the historic *ara metua* in Arorangi is the top entertainment value on Rarotonga, and a must for visitors. The **Cook Islands Cultural Village** (21-314) is a journey into local history and culture. Visit early on your trip, if possible, as it will help you understand much of what you'll see around the island.

The program begins in their mini-museum, then proceeds to theme huts where visitors observe handicrafts, medicine preparation, coconut husking, and other cultural demonstrations.

An island lunch is served on bio-degradable coconut leaves, and the spectacular dance show includes audience participation. The whole package is only NZ$28, plus NZ$2 if you need transport. The village is open weekdays from 9:45am-1:30pm, but arrive before 10am to enjoy it all. They also offer circle-island tours in the afternoon for NZ$20, or NZ$42 for both options.

**Highland Paradise** (20-610) is a botanical garden and historical village atop a 600' hill, overlooking the west coast. Examine edible and medicinal plants, plus the Guillotine Stone, Wedding Pillar, and other ruins. Light refreshments are included in the two-hour tour, which begins at 10am. Cost is NZ$25, plus $5 if transport is required. Open weekdays, 9:30-4pm.

## Piri Puruto Show

Raro's unique showman is **Piri Puruto, Master of Disaster** and **Coconut King of the Cook Islands** (20-309). After climbing a 50-ft coconut tree in 16 seconds, he shimmies down to demonstrate the coconut's many uses.

Piri's most striking presentation, however, is starting a fire by rubbing two sticks of wood together, which has to be seen to be believed. This alone is worth NZ$12. Call for daily schedules.

**Brewery Tours**

Rarotonga Breweries (21-083) offers free tours Tues/Thurs, 10am, with a complimentary glass of Cooks Lager. Don't forget to pick up T-shirts for connoisseurs back home.

**Flightseeing**

Air Rarotonga (22-888) offers a breathtaking 20-minute scenic flight over The Needle, Muri Beach and inland valleys. The views are absolutely spectacular. Flights are NZ$49, and operate Monday through Saturday, as arranged. Bring your camera and lots of film!

Even more breathtaking is **Skydive Tandem** (29-888). Drop 8000' strapped to (clutching?) the instructor, and hopefully keep your eyes open on the way down. This is definitely not for the faint-hearted! Daily dives, with instruction, take about an hour, for NZ$200.

**Outer Island Day Trips**

Air Rarotonga (22-888) offers day trips to the lagoon island of Aitutaki, 160 miles north. If you can't spend a few days there, this is a great alternative.

After a morning pickup from your hotel and a 45-minute flight, you'll take a pleasant circle-island tour. Then it's time to change into your swimsuit and take a cruise on one of the most beautiful lagoons in the South Pacific. After a barbecue lunch on a palm-fringed *motu* (islet), snorkel for a few hours ---gear is included---and return to Raro in time for dinner. These all-inclusive trips start at NZ$289.

A new two-island day trip visits Atiu and Mauke. Highlights include the *kopeka* cave, coffee plantation, tropical gardens, and cultural and historical sites. This is a good way to get a taste of the more traditional islands. These interesting tours start at NZ$299.

# WATERSPORTS

**Beaches and Swimming**: Rarotonga is surrounded by beautiful white sand beaches, all open to the public. The lagoon is usually warm, clear and calm, but avoid the few reef passages due to their strong undertows. Ocean swimming is rare, since the surf breaks heavily on the outer reef.

The best spots for swimming and watersports are at Muri Beach, South Beach, the Rarotongan Resort, and at deeper areas along the west coast. The lagoon gets pretty shallow in many spots, especially at low tide. The deepest sections are along the reef between Muri Beach and South Beach.

The north and northeast coasts are not good for swimming, but **bathtub beaches** (reef holes), sprinkled along the coast, can be refreshing.

**Beachcombing**

This is very rewarding, especially in less-crowded areas such as South Beach. Besides shells, look for green, glass-like sea urchin spines, about 3" long, which are used in wind chimes.

**Reefwalking**

The outer reef has many small pools, home to crabs, sea slugs and other little characters. Larger fish are often trapped in them when the tide goes out, so this is the locals' favorite time for spear fishing. Good spots to reach the reef are near the Rarotongan Resort, along west coast beaches, and opposite the SDA Center on South Beach.

Wear old sneakers or other footwear, as the coral is very sharp. Low tide is usually the easiest and safest time to venture out, but always keep an eye out for sporadic large waves. As the old warning says, "never turn your back on

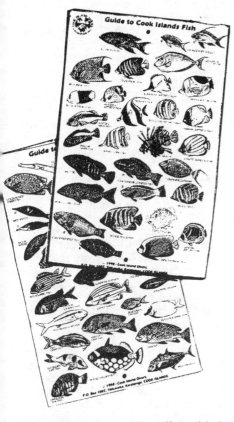

the sea." Tour companies offer guided reef walks, a good choice if you're not familiar with this type of terrain.

### Snorkeling

The lagoon is crystal clear, 4-20 feet deep, and home to dozens of varieties of colorful tropical fish.

Snorkeling is good in the *deep* water off Muri Beach, but not near the beach itself. Try the area past **Taakoka** islet. Along South Beach, try the deep water opposite Akapuao Stream (near T.M. Motors), which has lots of coral heads

and fish. Also try deeper spots off the west coast, from Black Rock to the Rarotongan Resort.

Most beachfront hotels have free or low-cost gear for guests. At Muri Beach both **Pacific Resort** (20-427) and **Aquasports** (27-350, at the Sailing Club) rent gear. Plan on NZ$10/day, NZ$25/week for mask and snorkel, extra for fins and reef shoes. Top grade silicone gear is NZ$35/week. Edgewater's **Sports Center** (25-435) has rentals. In town, the **Dive Shop** (26-675) sells quality gear, while **Toytown** (26-660) has the basics.

Tropical fish come in all shapes, sizes, and colors. A must for snorkelers and divers is the "Guide to Cook Islands Fish" (NZ$10) showing 50 local species. The full-color, two-sided card is laminated so you can take it underwater. Look for it at watersports shops.

The shape of the fish defines its relationship with the coral reef below it. Those with slender, disc-shaped bodies, such as the **angelfish** and **butterflyfish**, maneuver well between the coral outcrops, darting in and out to find a meal, or to avoid being caught by a larger fish. These species often return to the same spot each day to look for food. You may recognize some familiar finny friends if you snorkel in the same area for several days.

The long and thin fishes, like the **trumpetfish, pipefish** and **needlefish**, often float motionless above the coral, waiting for smaller fish to leave the protective coral folds. Their bodies permit quick acceleration for catching these smaller morsels. **Eels** wedge themselves into crevices in the reef, grabbing whatever goes by, including fingers of too-curious snorkelers!

As indicated in our Health section, avoid touching live coral. Be especially careful around the brightly-colored phosphorescent "fire" corals, which pack a nasty toxin in their tiny tentacles.

### Lagoon Cruises

At Muri Beach, both Captain Junior at **Aquasports** (27-350) and Captain Tama at **Pacific Resort** (20-427) offer pleasant glass-bottom boat lagoon cruises, with lunch at an islet. There's plenty of time for snorkeling or exploring the islet. Both run from 11am-3:30pm weekdays, and Tama also goes on weekends. This delightful way to spend a day is only NZ$30 for adults, NZ$15-20 for kids.

Traditional **vakas** (large, oceangoing canoes) were built on each island for the 1992 Pacific Festival of the Arts. The *Maire Nui* from Mauke and the *Ngapuariki Rua* from Aitutaki were recently docked on Rarotonga, and there was some talk of offering day cruises on these unique vessels. Check with the Tourist Authority (29-435) for updates on this intriguing idea.

### Sailing and Windsurfing

At Pacific Resort, Keith Abrams' **Cook Islands Windsurfing and Sailing School** (20-427) rents windsurfers for NZ$20/hr (weekly discounts), and sailing catamarans, dinghies, and kayaks. Keith is also an excellent instructor, with sailing or windsurfing lessons at NZ$40 for a 90-minute lesson.

**Aquasports** (27-350) has similar rentals, and windsurfing lessons at NZ$40/hr. The **Rarotongan Resort** (25-800) also has windsurfers for rent.

The Sailing Club has races on Saturday afternoon, with 13' Sunbursts the choice of most members. Visiting enthusiasts are encouraged to stop by.

### Scuba Diving

The ocean waters around Rarotonga are excellent for diving, with visibility of 100-200ft. The outer coral shelf has numerous canyons, tunnels and caves, in depths of 10-100ft. These are home to **plate, shelf, mushroom, branch** and **brain corals**. The shelf drop-off starts at 80-100ft, and quickly reaches depths of 12,000ft.

Greg Wilson's **Cook Island Divers** (22-483/fax 22-484) has NAUI Qualified Diving Instructors, and offers daily ocean dives at 8:00am and 1:00pm. One-tank dives are NZ$60, and a four-day beginner's course is NZ$425. Greg has gotten high marks from dive groups visiting from the States. **Dive Rarotonga** (21-873) also offers daily dives, and PADI training. Look for them at their A-frame in Arorangi.

**Marineland Pacific Divers** at Pacific Resort (22-450/20-427) offers ocean dives, plus beginner half-day lessons in the shallow (10ft max depth) lagoon at Muri. **Aquasports** (27-350) also offers introductory dives in the lagoon. Rates are NZ$60 for 3 hours.

### Fishing

The waters off Rarotonga are excellent for deep-sea fishing, and the fish are not far offshore. **Bonito, barracuda, mahi mahi, sailfish, wahoo, yellowfin tuna** and other world-class gamefish are typical catches. The local record for **marlin** is 616 lbs (280 kg).

Several fishing boats operate from town. The 34' *M.V. Seafari* of **Seafari Charters** (20-328) is skippered by Canadians Elgin and Sharon Tetachuk. Wayne Barclay and Jenny Sorensen of **Pacific Marine Charters** (21-237) also take their 26' *Te Manu Ka Rere* out on most days. Don Beer's **Beco Charters** (21-525) and Brent Fisher's **Fishing Tours** (23-356) offer trips as well. All boats have full gear and safety equipment, and handle 4-6 lines.

Departures are usually at 9am, with five-hour trips at NZ$90-100/person (non-fishing at NZ$50/person). By local custom, the catch stays with the boat. Some boats are also available for private charters and scenic cruises.

Lagoon fishing is popular with locals, especially **night fishing** by torchlight for *maroro* (flying fish). If you're too shy to join in on your own, tour companies can provide a guide.

One seasonal diversion is **whale watching**. Humpback and pilot whales migrate south in August-September, passing close to the north shore. You can view them from the boats listed above, or from the Avarua shoreline.

## Surfing

Although the waves crash onto the reef with deadly force, the small core of surfers keeps growing. Surfing spots are near the wreck of the *Maitai* at Avarua Harbor; off Norrie Park in Matavera; and outside the Ngatangiia passage.

## SPORTS AND RECREATION

**Golf and Mini-Golf:** The nine-hole course at the **Rarotonga Golf Club** (27-360) is one of the most unusual in the world. It's set amidst the guy wires and antennae of the nearby radio transmitter, and you have the option of a replay if you hit any of these only-in-the-Cook Islands obstacles. The virtually flat course becomes a par-70, 18-hole layout by criss-crossing tees and greens for the second nine. Green fees are only NZ$5 for 9 or 18 holes. Clubs (NZ$10) and handcarts (NZ$1) can be rented.

The course is open 8am-sunset, 6 days a week (no Sunday golf in Polynesia). Weekly competitions are open to visitors with a current handicap. The clubhouse has a licensed bar and pool table, and non-golfers are welcome. If you want to meet some local characters, this is as good a place as any!

If your backswing is not so hot, try the 18-hole **Mini-Golf** course, north of the Edgewater. It's NZ$8/game, and open Monday-Saturday, 9am-7pm.

## Tennis and Squash

The Edgewater (25-435) and the Rarotongan (25-800) have good quality **tennis courts**, some lit at night. Rates are NZ$15/hr (racquets NZ$5/hr), with guests having priority. Excellent instruction is available from Malcom Kajer at the Edgewater. Local schools have courts, but some have seen better days.

The Edgewater has **squash courts**, open 9:30am-8pm (ex. Sun), for NZ$10/hr (racquets NZ$3/hr). The **Catholic Mission Squash Center** (21-056) at St. Joseph's rents courts at NZ$5/hr.

## Lawn Bowls

The **Lawn Bowling Club** (22-077) has visitor roll-ups at noon Saturday (wear whites or creams), and some weekdays.

The international-standard green and licensed bar open at 4pm weekdays, 12noon Saturday. Green fees are $2, bowls hire is NZ$1. The Club is on Moss Road, behind Cook's Corner.

### Horseback Riding

A unique way to see the island is on horseback. **Aroa Pony Trek** (20-048/21-415) offers a two-hour ride Monday-Saturday, at 10am and 3pm, for NZ$28 (kids half-price). Trips visit plantations and Wigmore's Falls. Some readers have expressed general concern for the condition of animals on Rarotonga, so let us know how these are doing.

### Jogging and Running

Join the **Rarotonga Hash House Harriers Hussies and Hoffspring** (David Lobb, 22-000, days) for their 5:30pm Monday fun run. Monday's *News* lists the starting point. International athletes visit in October for the **Round-Rarotonga-Road-Race**, and shorter fun runs.

### Other Sports and Recreation

Some resorts have beach **volleyball**, and grass courts are scattered around the island. Look for friendly games at 4pm weekdays. North Americans can get a taste of home at after-school **softball** games at Tereora College.

For aerobics or weightlifting, try the **Top Shape Health Club** (21-254) near the Beachcomber. It's open 6am-9pm, Mon-Sat, and visitor memberships are available.

If you like less strenuous diversions, **darts** and **pool** may be for you. The Tumunu Bar, Golf Club, Game Fishing Club and RSA all offer one or both.

### Spectator Sports

Rugby, rugby league, soccer, cricket, basketball, boxing, women's netball, and track events are popular. Most are on Saturdays, and visitors are welcome.

**Horse races** on Muri Beach were a Christmas tradition, but these are now rare. Most horses just headed into the lagoon to escape the summer heat! Any races would be listed in the *CI News*.

## SHOPPING

There's a good selection of pearls, clothing, handicrafts, artwork, coconut products and some duty-free items, all at reasonably good prices.

In Avarua, shops line the main road from Avatiu Harbor to the Portofino Restaurant. The **Cook Islands Trading Corporation** (CITC) is the island's largest department store, and **JPI** and **Vanwil's** are smaller versions. **South Seas International** is a wonderful island-style general store, which has just about everything you can't find anywhere else. Three tiny malls---**Cook's Corner**, **Browne's Arcade** and **Mana Court**---each have a half-dozen shops.

Outside of town, the **Tangaroa Shopping Centre** (airport back road) and the **Taio Centre** (main road, Arorangi) each have a half-dozen shops.

**Shopping hours** are 8am-4pm weekdays, and 8am-noon on Saturday. Some resort shops are open Sunday, and the airport shops are open for international flights. Bargaining, as previously mentioned, is considered rude.

### Pearls and Jewelry

The pearl industry is growing rapidly, and recent auctions of Manihiki black pearls fetched more than US$2 million. These beautiful cultured pearls are sold loose, in strands, or in pendants and other handcrafted jewelry. One exquisite strand of perfectly-round black pearls recently sold for NZ$53,000, but most items are from NZ$100-2,000. Natural white pearls from Penrhyn are also available at reasonable prices.

Black pearls come in several varieties, with quality---and price---based upon size, color, luster, shape and purity. The most valuable are the perfectly-round, while the pear-shaped "semi-baroque" are popular in pendants. The barrel-like "circles" and oddly-shaped "baroque" pearls are used in creative designs. The Manihiki chapter has more on pearl cultivation.

Joan Rolls at the **Beachcomber** is a well-known expert on pearls. Her shop near the Portofino has an excellent selection of pearl jewelry and other handcrafted items. The Beachcomber's **Pearl Hut** outlet in front of the Banana Court offers "pick-your-own-pearl" pendants for about NZ$100. The **Pearl Shop** at Cook's Corner also has a large selection of pearls, as does **June's Pearls**, next to South Seas International.

**Handicrafts**
The most popular souvenirs are wooden carvings of the phallic *Tangaroa*. Woven mats and soft *rito* hats from the Northern Group are good choices, as are beautifully-carved slit drums (*pate*). Carved bowls, pandanus bags from Mitiaro, hand-made local pottery, and wooden storyboards from Atiu are all available at reasonable prices.

Look for these items at the **Women's Handcraft Centre** at Ruatonga Market, **Island Crafts** near Westpac, **Pacific Gifts & Souvenirs** at Cook's Corner, the **Treasure Chest** at Mana Court, and at the pearl shops listed above. Also try **Shells and Crafts** at Muri Beach, the **Manavaroa Shop** in Arorangi, and **Erita's Crafts** near the Sheraton site.

On the airport back road is the **Akatikitiki (Visual) Arts Center**, where talented Mike Tavioni and his students create and sell their traditional carvings. In Arorangi, stop at Kay and Ian George's **Akaoa Art Studio** for bone carvings, drawings, tropical wall-hangings, and hand-painted clothing.

If you're lucky you might be able to find---and afford---one of those colorful hand-made quilts called *tivaevae*. These may take months to produce, and can cost over NZ$1000. Try the Beachcomber or Island Crafts, or take a day-trip to Atiu and check out the Atiu Fibre Arts Studio.

**Tropical Clothing**
The basic item for women is the all-purpose wrap-around *pareu*, two yards of brightly-colored cloth. These go for NZ$15 and up, and are available in many shops around the island. Dresses, skirts and blouses of the same material are also popular. Men usually pick up a few island-style aloha shirts, available at the same shops for NZ$25-40.

**Joyce Peyroux Garments** is the Cook's largest clothing manufacturer. Their town outlet is near the ANZ Bank, while the factory store is in Arorangi. **TAV Ltd.** offers their tropical sundresses at half the price you'd pay in Hawaii. Their main shop is at Cook's Corner, near the **Kirsty & Kendrick** outlet, another local wholesaler.

There are a dozen other clothing shops you can check out if you have the time and energy. Traveling east from the airport, try any or all of the following: **Manu Manea** and **Mango Trading**, west of Avatiu Harbor; **Odds and Ends** and **June's**, just past the harbor; **JPI**, **Linmars** and Mana Court's **Troppo Raro**, all downtown; and the **T-Shirt Factory**, **June's Boutique**, **ABC Trading** and **Tuki's Pareu**, all between the traffic circle and the Portofino.

In Arorangi try the shops at the Taio Centre, and **Dynasty Fashions**, both on the main road. The Tangaroa Shopping Centre also has clothing shops. For kids' pareus and tropical outfits, the place to shop is **Vonnia's Nouvelle**, near the Empire Cinema in town.

T-shirts are very popular souvenirs. In addition to the places above, stop by the **T-Shirt Man** at the Ruatonga market, or the **T-Shirt Factory** outlet at the Tangaroa Shopping Centre.

### Local Perfumes, Soaps, and Oils

Rarotonga is blessed with exotically-fragrant flowers, and all are used in locally-produced soaps, shampoos, oils, and perfumes. The most fragrant scents are *tipani* (frangipani), *pitate* (jasmine), *tiare* (gardenia) and plumeria.

**Perfumes of Rarotonga** makes soaps and oils in addition to tropical perfumes. The factory shop is on the main road in Matavera, but Travis Moore also has a little sales hut in front of the Banana Court. Look for coconut oil blended with medicinal herbs in **Mauke Miracle Oil** and **Mauke Maire Oil**. And don't forget their famous **Mokonut** soap, featuring *Moko* (gecko) taking a shower. I always pick up a few of each, both as gifts and for home use.

The **Perfume Factory**, on the back road in Avarua, also has locally-produced fragrances. John Abbott makes tropical soaps on the premises, and visitors are welcome to observe the process. The retail outlet is at the front of the building.

### Stamps and Coins

Cook Islands' stamps and coins are prized for both their beauty and scarcity. The best place to find them is at the **Philatelic Bureau**, near the main Post Office.

*Mokonut Soap: Don't leave Raro without it.*

Stamps come in colorful tropical designs highlighting fish, coral, birds, flowers, and historical scenes. These sets are beautiful gifts, even for non-collectors.

As previously indicated, the most famous Cook Island coin is the original one-dollar *Tangaroa*, minted in the 1970's and 1980's. It's the size of a US silver dollar, with the phallic male god on one side and Queen Elizabeth II on the obverse. These older *Tangaroa* dollars are becoming scarce, but the Philatelic Bureau may have some sets.

The newer one-dollar *Tangaroa* coin has the same famous pairing, but it's only the size of a US quarter. It is, however, uniquely twelve-sided, and is the

perfect gift for the friend who has everything. The triangular two-dollar coin and the gold-colored five-dollar coin are also numismatic oddities.

Cook Islands bank notes are not exchangeable outside the country, but they are avidly sought by collectors throughout the world. The older bills include the famous *Ina and the Shark* design by local artist Rick Welland, with the unique three-dollar bill being one of the world's most unusual notes. The newer notes have colorful cultural and historical scenes representing all the islands in the country.

## Other Choices

Tasty tropical jams and preserves are inexpensive gifts, and if you find a bottle of the pineapple liquor *Mangaia Ara* ---no longer produced---you'll have a real collector's item. Another good choice is a half-kilo bag of sun-dried **Atiu coffee**, about NZ$14. The food markets have the best prices.

If you haven't had a chance to photograph Rarotonga or Aitutaki from the air, consider the aerial photographs available from the **Kenwall Gallery**, near the airport. Colorful posters de-

picting Life on the Reef and Seafood of the Cook Islands are other popular souvenirs.

You can save quite a bit on some **duty-free** items like perfume, liquor and cigarettes. These can be purchased at any time, and delivered directly to your flight. Check out both CITC and South Seas International. Radios, CD players and cameras are also duty-free, but prices may still be higher than at discount outlets back home.

A good souvenir is a tape of drum dances by local groups. A friend looked in one store, but they sent him to another, saying "they have better tapes." That shop recommended JPI, again saying their competitor had better tapes. ("This does not happen very often back home!" he said to himself.)

At JPI the saleslady unwrapped a possible selection, and played it on the store's PA system. When the local shoppers heard the frenzied beat of the slit-drum music they stopped in their tracks and began dancing in the aisles. Needless to say, he bought the tape.

## Local Artists

Look for colorful tropical oil paintings by **Jillian Sobieska** (21-079) at her roadside Galerie near the Tourist Authority. She also does portraits, original cards, and sketches. **Claire Higham** (20-238) offers watercolors of island scenes at her studio near the Edgewater. Longtime resident **Rick Welland** is not currently living in the islands, but his paintings are available at Perfumes of Rarotonga, in Matavera.

The Beachcomber has an exclusive set of numbered lithographs by 93-year-old **Edwin Shorter**, sure to be collector's items. Younger artists include **Ian George**, whose work is on display at his Akaoa Art Studio in Arorangi.

*The beautiful Turangi Valley winds through lush gardens and tropical jungles.*

## AROUND-THE-ISLAND

At some point you should definitely take a leisurely trip around the island. Little houses with manicured lawns and family graves out front share the main road with churches and small shops. On the inland *ara metua*, taro swamps and plantations are bordered by stunning mountain backdrops and quiet streams. Modern Rarotonga is in Avarua, but its Polynesian heart is in the rural areas.

The main road circles Raro, while the *ara metua* is intact in many districts. After trying the main road, return to explore some inland areas.

We'll head clockwise from Tupapa, where our Avarua tour ended. One local calculated that it's 50 meters longer in this direction, since you're on the outside lane. I guess there isn't much to do on a rainy day in Raro!

### NORTHEAST COAST

We come first to the **Kii Kii** (Key-Key) district, near the aptly-named motel. Oral histories recount the legendary battle of early chiefs, when Tangiia broke the sacred necklace---*kii kii*---of Tutapu, The Relentless Pursuer.

The island's most important *marae* (sacred site) is the **Arai-te-Tonga** (Shield of the South), on the *ara metua*. Head inland at the sign, 3.5 km from town. The *marae* adjoins the *koutu*, the Royal Court of the High Chief. Next to the main 7' by 12' platform is the Investiture Pillar, a 7' basaltic rock. Flat rocks nearby were seats for other chiefs. Used for important ceremonies in pre-missionary times, the *marae* is still considered sacred, and should not be walked upon.

## EAST COAST

Matavera means "hot face," from a 13th century incident when Chief Tangiia tried to burn Tutapu (of *kii kii* fame), in a large oven. Archaeologists have not found the oven, but other research indicates the oral histories are fairly accurate accounts of past events.

Today Matavera is a peaceful and quiet village. The **CICC Church** is a good choice for Sunday services, as the few tourists find it easy to meet locals.

Along the road are gravesites from the mid-1800's, and distinctive Norfolk pines, imported from that island by sailors returning to live on Rarotonga.

**Ngatangiia** is named for the family (*nga-ti*) of Chief Tangiia, and has many historical sites. The seven Maori canoes left **Ngatangiia Harbor** for their discovery voyage of New Zealand, circa 1350 AD. The **Seven Stones** at the roadside park mark the departure point, and a *marae* is to the left.

Captain Goodenough anchored here in 1814, seeking sandalwood. He was the first European to land, as the *Bounty* mutineers remained on their ship in 1789. His stay was marked by constant skirmishes, due to his crew's theft of women, food and supplies.

Ngatangiia was home to missionary Charles Pitman, who arrived in 1827 and stayed for 27 years. The impressive **CICC Church** dates from that era.

### Inland East Coast

Matavera and Ngatangiia are in the "Takitumu" district, which stretches west to include the entire south coast. The Chief of Takitumu is the *Pa Ariki*. The original villages were all inland, along the *ara metua*.

Turn right just before the Avana Stream bridge, then bear right onto the *ara metua*. On the left is the small **Kai-**nuku's Marae**, which pre-dates Tangiia. Also on the left, past a large mesa, is the Turangi Valley, which we'll return to. Continue to the remains of **Pa's Palace**, on the left. Nearby is the T-shaped **Pokata Paepae** (meeting place), and the site of an old court house.

Return to the **Turangi Valley** road. This dirt track is 2 km long, and the deep-cut valley is bordered by lush plantations, gardens and taro plots. Ford the stream three times to reach the water intake at the end. The track is easy on foot, passable on a motorbike. If you're looking for a tropical jungle, this is the place to go!

Two modern footnotes are attached to the Turangi Valley. The movies *Angel in Green*, starring Susan Dey (of "L.A. Law"), and *Merry Christmas, Mr. Lawrence*, starring David Bowie, were filmed here. Locals were too well-fed to play prisoners-of-war in the Bowie movie, so New Zealand students on holiday were hired for the parts.

If you enjoyed Turangi, you'll love the **Avana Valley**. Head inland right *after* (south of) the Avana Stream bridge. Avana is wider and longer than Turangi, with taro patches and picturesque spots along the stream. Vehicles can go in 2.5 km, but plan on walking the last 2 km. The dirt track crosses the stream 19 times before it ends at the water intake. Bring mosquito repellent.

The Avana's high volume of cold freshwater---which kills coral---long ago cut through the reef to create Ngatangiia Harbor. Avatiu and Avarua Harbors were similarly created by cool stream waters killing a facing reef.

### Muri Beach

Past Avana is beautiful **Muri**. Stop at the thatched **Vaka Village**, once home to the dozen ocean-going canoes that arrived from New Zealand, Hawaii, and other islands for the 1992 Pacific Festival of the Arts. One or two may still be anchored here.

Four *motus* frame the lagoon: Motutapu, Oneroa, Koromiri, and Taakoka. You can often walk to them at low tide. Look for stone **fish traps**, which confine their prey as the tide goes out the passage. Poisonous *ora* powder, made from kernels of the barringtonia tree, was used to catch lagoon fish.

Across the road is Rarotonga's egg basket, **Scott's Chicken Farm**. Over a million eggs are produced yearly. A dozen at the market cost about NZ$4.

On the left is the Flame Tree Restaurant and Sokala Villas. Continue past Good Luck Trading, and turn left at **Muri Enua Hall**. You'll come to a large sports field, with an *umu* (earth oven) on the left, where local feasts are held.

You're now at Raro's most beautiful spot, **Muri Beach**. The lagoon is calm and clear, perfect for watersports. To really enjoy it, take the main road to the **Pacific Resort** or the **Sailing Club**, and rent snorkeling gear, a sailboat or a windsurfer. Look for Saturday races of the popular 13' Sunbursts.

Beyond Koromiri is the wreck of the Japanese fishing boat **Iwakuni Maru No.1**, which ran aground in 1959. It dropped anchor too far offshore---in 12,000 feet of water! Wind and currents threw the hapless ship onto the reef.

Past Koromiri and Taakoka the lagoon is up to 15ft deep, with good snorkeling. The motus are great for picnics. Rent a canoe for fun, and to keep your lunch dry.

## SOUTH COAST

Like Matavera, this is a quiet and traditional area. Here, however, the lagoon is wide and deep. Still, **South Beach** is less crowded than Muri or the west coast beaches.

Past **St. Paul's Church**, stop near T.M. Motors or the **Akapuao Stream** for a nice beach with good snorkeling.

Quiet **Titikaveka** (Ti-ti-ka'-ve-ka) is perhaps Raro's friendliest village. The ornate **CICC Church** is one of the oldest buildings on Rarotonga, dating from 1841. Near **Titikaveka College** (high school) is *Te Pou Toru*, a small *marae* with investiture pillar and altar.

The **Jam Hut** is a popular stop, or try the **Turoa Bakery** for "cheesies" or banana muffins. Both are open Sunday.

The grassy lagoonside patch I call **Pitcairn Park** is opposite the SDA Center. A plaque commemorates the *Pitcairn*, a Seventh Day Adventist missionary ship that arrived in 1891, after British law opened the island to other religions. The beach here is good for swimming, and for access to the reef.

The **Turoa Stream** is small and shallow, perfect for catching freshwater prawns at night. Locals fashion small snares from coconut fronds and husks, then loop them around the prawn's tail. King prawns reach 8" and are quite tasty. The Tourist Authority can help find a guide for a prawn-hunting trip.

To head up the **Turoa Valley**, turn on the dirt track after the SDA Center. After the taro patch, bear left at the house on the hill. You'll find yourself in one of the largest **orange groves** on the island. The track gets narrow and muddy before it ends at the **Outward Bound** campsite, complete with mini-obstacle course.

**Totokoitu Research Station** is a 50-acre agricultural laboratory. On the right is the unique **coconut house**, with everything but the ironwood veranda posts handcrafted from coconut palms.

*The Taro Patches of Kavera: The Eighth Wonder of the World.*

Look for two unique beachfront **pole houses** near the "Coca Cola shop". Swimming is good in this area, but avoid the reef passages. Soon you'll catch a glimpse of **The Needle (Te Rua Manga)**.

Just before the Sheraton site is the dirt road to **Wigmore's Falls**, the largest cascade on the island. Follow the signs through the construction area. The half-mile track is passable by motorbike, but cars may get stuck if it's been raining.

The twenty-foot falls drop in two or three stages, but the real attraction is the cool and refreshing pool below, a heavenly spot on a hot day.

Locals climb the rocks and dive in, but I don't recommend this for visitors. There's a large rock a few feet below the surface which has caused at least one death. Don't forget to bring insect repellent, as the *namus* (mosquitoes) also love this spot.

Near the Rutaki Store are old stone **fish traps**, which snared their prey as the tide went out the nearby passage.

**Inland South Coast**
Return to St. Paul's Church, head inland to the *ara metua*, then turn left. This area produces just about every crop grown on Raro. Pineapples, papayas, taro, mangoes, oranges, bananas and arrowroot are joined by corn, pole beans, lettuce, tomato and cabbage. Soon the *ara metua* becomes Kauare Road, as it bears left to reach the main road on the west side of Titikaveka.

Another section of the *ara metua* begins right after the **Taipara Stream**. Head inland and make your first left. This area is noteworthy for its highland plots of *tarotarua* (dry taro), and a large pineapple field. You'll eventually reach the main road near Liana's Restaurant.

## WEST COAST

The **Rarotongan Resort**, completed in 1977, was the island's first international resort. Its opening put the Cooks on the international tourism map.

If you long to see acres and acres and acres of taro swamps, turn right at the Kavera market. Before you reach the *ara metua* your dreams will be realized!

The **Puaikura** district occupies most of the west coast, and **Arorangi** is its largest village. The original "Puaikura" village was inland, along the *ara metua*. Both the site and name were changed after the conversion of Chief Tinomana by the famous missionary Papeiha.

As the oft-told story goes, Tinomana met Papeiha and they began talking about their respective gods. Tinomana pointed to the nearby *marae*, and said that his god lived there. He then asked Papeiha to show him where his god lived.

Papeiha looked upward and said "*Arorangi*" ("the face of the heavens"). Tinomana was intrigued by such an idea, and later converted. A new village was built on the coast, and named in honor of that earlier incident.

The limestone **Arorangi CICC Church** dates from 1844, and its Sunday services are popular with visitors. The **preaching stone** in the courtyard commemorates Papeiha first services, and **Papeiha's grave** is nearby.

Next to the church is the **Tinomana Palace**, his second home after the village was moved to the coast. The actual Maori name is *Au Maru* Palace, "the place brought by Christianity." It was in ruins for several decades, but was recently restored as a community project by Puaikura residents.

**Raemaru Park**, past the Palace, hosts many sporting events, especially on Saturdays. Flat-topped **Raemaru** sits behind it, a tropical version of Australia's Ayer's Rock.

Legends say Raemaru was once a high mountain called *Maru*, but warriors from Aitutaki sliced off the top and carried it north, creating that island's Mt. Maungapu. Locals planned to steal it back, as the earlier sunshine kept waking them up. They changed their minds, however, when they found they were catching bigger fish in the early morning. They decided to accept the shortened mountain, but now called it Raemaru, meaning "empty shadow."

Turn right at the Black Rock petrol station and head up the steep road to the **Rarotonga Hospital**. It offers good views towards Avarua, and beyond the chapel are good views of the west coast and those beautiful sunsets.

The hospital opened in 1945, but became famous in the 1970's when controversial cancer specialist Milan Brych ("brick") set up shop with government approval. He supposedly used laetrile from apricot pits, and I did see bags of these lying around during a visit in 1977. Brych charged high fees for his "miracle" cures, and allegedly made another bundle by leasing the then-tiny Edgewater Motel, and re-renting rooms to his patients at high prices.

His cure rate was no better than other practitioners, and many patients died. Some are buried opposite the airport in a small cemetery called the "Brychyard". After Albert Henry was forced from office in 1978 due to the fly-in voter scheme, the new government kicked Brych out of the country.

As it turns out, some who worked for him say he never used the laetrile, he just gave the same chemotherapy drugs available in Australia and New Zealand. The latest rumors have him ending up in the US, supposedly in prison.

*Flat-topped* Raemaru: *The top was sliced off and carried to Aitutaki.*

Return to the main road and head north, stopping at the beach opposite the quarry. The large outcrop is **Black Rock**, the traditional departure point of souls returning to *Avaiki*, the Polynesian spiritland. The traditional name is *Tuoro*, meaning "Welcome".

Papeiha supposedly swam ashore here in 1823, while holding a bible over his head. Since there's no reef passage along this coast, many have doubts about this story.

Black Rock is a popular swimming spot, as is the beach to the north, near the former Nikao Social Center. In 1987, Hurricane Sally picked up the main building and wrapped it around some nearby trees, leaving only its slab foundation.

Across the road is the **Golf Course**, a nine-hole affair with a friendly bar and clubhouse, and visitors always welcome.

**Inland West Coast**

To explore this area, turn onto the hospital road, but turn right (south) before it heads up the hill.

Pass the small **Prison** (jail or "gaol") on the left, and then the must-see **Cultural Village**. The original Puaikura village and the **Tinomana Tribe Settlement** were in the Maungaroa Valley, along **Muriavai Stream**, to the south. The valley road is passable for a kilometer or so. Nearby signs point out the way to the **Highland Paradise** gardens.

Inland Arorangi has well-kept homes, manicured lawns, and lots of fruit groves, and is a nice contrast to the commercialism of the main road.

Turn right at any side road, and pass through the inevitable taro swamp before you reach the main road. The *ara metua* ends at a side road that exits at Rutaki, near the Rarotongan Resort.

## NORTHWEST COAST
North of the Golf Club you can stay on the coastal road, or head inland on the "airport back road."

### Coastal Road
Go slowly as you approach the dangerous seawall curve. In 1973 the runway was extended over the lagoon to handle large jets, and this long curve resulted. Be especially careful at night, and when it's wet or windy.

Past the small **Meteorological Station** is the **Parliament Building**. Sessions are held in February, March, July to September, and sometimes in November. Check at the door to confirm when it's open, and dress properly if attending (no shorts or T-shirts).

The **Rarotonga Airport** was officially opened by Queen Elizabeth II on January 29, 1974. Facing it is the **RSA/Citizens Club**, and tourists are welcome at the cozy bar. In the small **veteran's cemetery** is the grave of **Tom Neale**, the Hermit of Suwarrow.

Along the main road is another cemetery, with graves of a few dozen cancer victims from the 1970's. This is the infamous **Brychyard**. (See discussion under Rarotonga Hospital.)

A more pleasant spot is the disappearing islet of **Motutoa**, opposite the airport. It vanishes after a hurricane, then is reborn by shifting sand and floating coconuts. There's actually a pretty good swimming spot just west of the islet.

The **Catholic Cemetery**, on the sea side of the main road, is decorated with flowers and candles on November 1, All Soul's Day.

The area adjacent to the airport is called **Panama**, named after a canal plan that went very much awry. In the 1940's the colonial government dug canals leading from the freshwater taro swamps to the lagoon. After the swamps were drained, they surmised, the rich volcanic soil could grow more valuable crops.

What actually happened was quite different. At low tide the swamps did empty a little, but at high tide massive saltwater rivers came rushing back the same canals, inundating the low-lying taro patches. Not only did it kill the taro, but now the soil was too salty to grow anything!

The canals were soon filled in with soil from other areas, but not before the locals nicknamed the area Panama, in mock honor of its more successful cousin.

After Panama you'll see Avatiu Harbor, and before you can say *Tumutevarovaro* you're back in Avarua.

### Airport Back Road
This is an alternate route between the west coast and Avarua. From Arorangi, head inland on **Pokoinu Road**, just north of the Golf Course. Bear left as it becomes the Airport Back Road, a section of the *ara metua*.

The **Turamatuitui Bakery** has fresh coconut rolls. **Tereora College** includes the new **Stadium**, built for the 1985 South Pacific Mini-Games. Look for sports events on Saturdays.

The college was operated by missionaries from 1865-1911, and re-opened by the government in 1955. The roadside field may host weekday softball games.

Once opposite the field was the famous twisted coconut tree, but this cracked and blew over in a recent storm.

A new addition in this area is the **Tangaroa Shopping Center**, near the site of the arson-destroyed Tangaroa Restaurant.

Past Tiare Village/Dive Hostel, on the left, is the **Akatikitiki (Visual) Arts Gallery**, where Mike Tavioni creates beautiful wood and coral carvings.

The next intersection is **Avatiu Road**. Avarua is straight ahead, Avatiu Harbor to the left. Let's turn right, to the **Avatiu Valley** and the **Cross-Island Track**.

The wide valley is dotted with plantations. Look for a large **vaka house**, sheltering the 70' *Vaka Uritaua*, one of Rarotonga's two canoes at the 1992 Pacific Arts Festival. The *vaka* was built here, then carried to Avatiu Harbor on the shoulders of eighty men.

The stream bank offers nice picnic spots past the **power station**, a mile inland. Near an upstream bridge is a tiny **swimming hole**, a favorite of local kids. Continue on to the Cross-Island Track, or return to the main road.

### INLAND HIKES
The easiest hikes are up the **Turangi Valley**, **Avana Valley**, **Turoa Stream** and **Avatiu Valley**, all covered above. To explore the higher country, the **Cross-Island Track** is the most popular choice. Great views and a waterfall are your well-deserved rewards.

You can go on your own, with Pa's Nature Treks (21-079), or with another guide. The back half---down the Papua Stream gorge---is not well-marked, and a guide is helpful. Flat-topped **Raemaru** is a popular second choice, and it can also be done on your own, or with a guide. You should be in moderately good shape for these hikes.

Rough trails lead up **Maungatea, Te Kou, Ikurangi** and **Te Manga**, but these are steep and not well marked. You can try them using the pamphlet *A Guide To Walks and Climbs* (available at the CITA), but I'd suggest using Pa or another guide for these tougher hikes.

### Cross-Island Track
Plan on a four-hour trip, although the record in the annual Cross-The-Island-Run is 50 minutes, 39 seconds! Wear hiking shoes or sneakers. Take water, a snack, mosquito repellent, and McCormack and Kunzle's informative booklet, *Rarotonga's Cross-island Walk*.

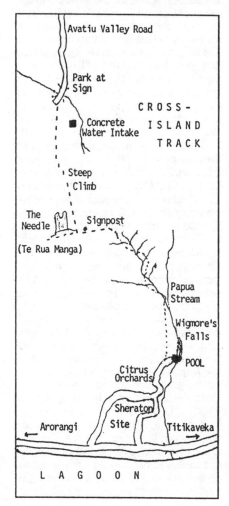

If two of you have motorbikes, leave one near Liana's Restaurant for the trip back. Otherwise you can catch the bus, call a taxi, or hitch a ride home.

Begin at **Avatiu Road**, opposite the freighter harbor. (DON'T take the road in front of the Post Office, as many visitors mistakenly do.) Head inland for 3 km, passing the *ara metua* and the power station. The track begins after the *No Vehicles Beyond This Point* sign.

The easy first kilometer criss-crosses the **Avatiu Stream**, until you reach an old water intake. (Do NOT use the new track dug for the high voltage cable to the Sheraton, which can be dangerous.) Soon you reach a steep, slippery section, where you may spend the next hour grabbing tree roots as you literally pull yourself up the hill. At the top is **Te Rua Manga** (1355ft, 413m), nicknamed **The Needle**, which marks the mid-point of the trip. The rock outcrop is 300ft (91m) above the surrounding ground, and only experienced climbers with gear should attempt an ascent.

Take a break on the flat rocks adjacent to The Needle, and get out your camera. After lunch or a snack, bear left and look for the sign to Wigmore's Waterfalls. You'll be crossing a saddle that separates the north and south drainage systems of the island.

Once you catch the dirt trail down, expect a wet and slow descent of about an hour-and-a-half. The trail crosses the **Papua Stream** and its tributaries ten times, going up and down steep banks on many crossings. The path is often marked by white arrows on trees, but if you lose it, just head downhill along the stream. If it's been raining, you may find it easier to just sit and slide down the muddier parts of the trail. Even so, look back occasionally to admire the idyllic beauty of the stream and forest.

After the trail levels out you go through lots of ferns, then reach a large clearing. **Wigmore's Falls** is on your left. The refreshing pool below is a delightful spot to wash off the mud and relax. Don't dive into the pool, as there's a large submerged rock which has caused at least one fatality.

The dirt road at the pool leads out to the Sheraton site, where you turn left to reach the main road near Liana's Restaurant.

### Raemaru Hike

Flat-topped **Raemaru** (1150ft, 350m) offers excellent views of the west coast, inland peaks, and the Muriavai Valley.

Tracks up the hill seem to constantly change, however, and readers may have to do some moderate trail blazing to reach the top. As on the Cross-Island Track, wear walking shoes, and bring liquids, mosquito repellent, and camera.

Start at the Betela Meeting House, south of the Latter Day Saints (Mormon) Center in Arorangi. Go inland on the side road to the *ara metua*, then turn left. After you pass an old shack on the right, look for a dirt track up the hill.

You'll soon reach terraces from an abandoned pineapple project. If you bear left you can follow the track to the north side of Raemaru, as it switchbacks up to the ridgeline. A narrow trail leads to the summit, unless it's been washed out. If so, look for recent signs of hikers and a new trail to the top.

You can also bear right when you reach the pineapple terraces, and head through the bush skirting the southern slope. This follows a ridge to the base of Raemaru, but then you have to make a rock climb to reach the summit.

The round-trip hike should take about three hours, depending on your skill at scrambling and climbing.

# SUNDAYS ON RAROTONGA

Sunday has been a day of rest in Polynesia since the coming of the missionaries. Most shops, businesses, restaurants, and sports facilities are closed, and inter-island flights do not operate on Sunday.

## CHURCH SERVICES
Many visitors attend morning church services, with most going to branches of the **Cook Islands Christian Church** (CICC). Services start at 10am, and last until 11:30 or noon. The beautiful hymnal singing is known throughout the South Pacific. The women wear their *rito* hats, and everyone is decked out in their finest attire.

There are CICC churches in Avarua, Arorangi, Titikaveka, Ngatangiia and Matavera. Hotels can arrange transport, but most are within walking distance of one of these churches.

## OTHER ACTIVITIES
You can always relax at the beach, but some tours do operate on Sunday. Reservations are recommended for tours, and for dinner.

### Getting Around
For more flexibility, rent a car or motorbike on Saturday, and return it on Monday. Taxis operate on Sundays, but buses do not. Petrol stations that are open include **Hogan's** in Arorangi, and **Countryside** on the south coast.

### Where To Eat
Most resort restaurants are open for all meals. Many offer a **beach barbecue**, as do some of the smaller lodgings. The **Tumunu, Liana's, Sails, Metua's** and the **Spaghetti House** are all open for dinner, and some are open for lunch. You can also try **AJ's Takeaways** in Arorangi, and the **Halfway Cafe, Just Burgers** and **Jam Hut** along South Beach. For basic food items try the **Home Market,** near Paradise Inn, **Hogan's** in Arorangi, and **D & D Dairy** and the **Turoa Bakery** on the south coast. All may be closed 9:30-noon.

### Recreational Activities
The Golf Course is closed, but **tennis courts** are open at the Edgewater and Rarotongan Resorts. Pacific Resort has **lagoon trips** and rentals, and **Aquasports** at the Sailing Club also rents **watersports** equipment. **Scuba boats** often head out, and non-divers are welcome. The **fishing boats** may offer Sunday trips. If you're feeling adventurous, Sunday may be your day to try **Skydive Tandem** (29-888).

**Piri Puruto** usually has a show. Call for time and location (20-309). Call the Rarotongan (25-800) or Edgewater (25-435) about **hikes** and other Sunday offerings, all open to non-guests if there's room. The Edgewater has a Sunday **Bridge Club**, open to visitors.

Sunday is a good day for **exploring** the *motus* of Muri Beach, or having a **picnic**. The Cross-Island Track is usually open, but closes occasionally, as it goes through private land. Call the Tourist Authority weekdays (29-435) to check on current rules. Even if it's closed to the public, tour companies may be permitted to guide small groups.

Finally, Sunday on Rarotonga is still a good day to lie on the beach, take a swim, or do absolutely nothing!

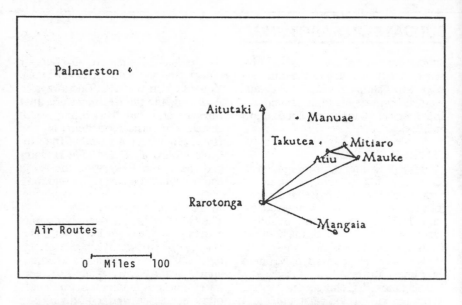

Palmerston

Aitutaki

Manuae

Takutea · Mitiaro
Atiu Mauke

Rarotonga

Mangaia

Air Routes

0   Miles   100

## OUTER ISLANDS OF THE SOUTHERN GROUP

Most visitors spend all their time on Rarotonga, but some are lucky enough to visit the outer islands of the Southern Group. About 15% visit Aitutaki, while only 1% visit the other seven islands.

**Aitutaki** is considered by many the most beautiful island in the Cooks, and perhaps in the South Pacific. It's surrounded by a beautiful turquoise lagoon and palm-studded *motus* (islets). If you like beaches, watersports, and a slow pace of life, you'll love Aitutaki.

**Atiu, Mauke** and **Mitiaro** are called *Nga-Pu-Toru*, "the three roots." With **Mangaia**, these raised coral atolls are famous for their ring of *makatea*---razor-sharp dead coral---often 50' high and a mile wide. There are no lagoons, but try a dip in a "bathtub beach" (reef

pool), sea cave, or inland water cave. These islands attract travelers who appreciate a more traditional culture. Bring a flashlight, walking shoes and "mud clothes" to explore the caves.

While the above islands all have regular air service, three rarely-visited islands can only be reached by sea. **Palmerston** is an atoll 300 miles from Rarotonga, often mistakenly considered part of the Northern Group. Its inhabitants are all descendants of William Marsters and his three native wives. Uninhabited **Manuae** atoll is owned by Aitutaki, and Atiu owns the uninhabited sand cay of **Takutea**.

Consider taking a couple of days to visit an outer island, and return to the South Pacific of thirty years ago.

# AITUTAKI

Population: 2366
Area: 7 sq.mi.

This is the classic Hollywood-movie South Seas island! Palm-clad islets surround a large turquoise lagoon, and white sand beaches dazzle the eye. The pace is slow, with few commercial distractions. Accommodations are comfortable, and watersports are excellent.

I'd recommend a minimum two-night stay, and include Friday night to catch the show at the Rapae Hotel.

## Orientation
The main island sits in the north of a triangular lagoon, which stretches 7 miles on each leg. Small islets (*motus*) dot the east and south.

The fertile soil produces lush tropical gardens and banana, mango and arrowroot plantations. The main village of Arutanga is a sleepy collection of government buildings, shops, and a small wharf. Low hills dominate the interior, with Mt. Maungapu reaching a height of 408ft (124m). The offshore *motus* are uninhabited, except for the small resort near the airstrip.

## Getting There
Air Rarotonga makes the 45-min flight daily (ex. Sun). Roundtrip fares start at NZ$284, with discounted packages and day-trips available.

Keep your camera ready during your flight, as the aerial views of both Rarotonga and Aitutaki are excellent.

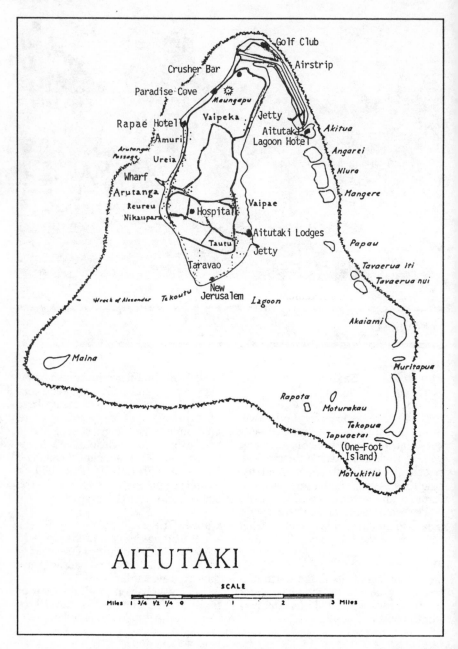

# AITUTAKI

SCALE

Miles 1 3/4 1/2 1/4 0     1        2     3 Miles

## HISTORY

The great Polynesian chieftain **Ru** reached Aitutaki about 900 AD, with his four wives, four brothers, and twenty *tamaine tapairu* (royal virgins). Many years later his grandson, **Taruia**, became the *ariki* (chief) of the island.

**Ruatapu**, another chief from eastern Polynesia, arrived during Taruia's reign. He tricked Taruia into taking a short trip to Rarotonga, then declared himself the *ariki* before Taruia returned. The three chiefly families of Aitutaki are all descended from Ruatapu.

The origin of the name is disputed. Some say it comes from Ru's choice of *Utaki-Enua-O-Ru-Ki-Te-Moana*, meaning "Ru's cargo of people he led to land over the ocean." Others claim it was named after the early warrior *Utataki-Enua*. A traditional name is *Ara'ura* ---"fragrant wreaths for dancing."

### European Contact

The first European discoverer was the infamous **Captain Bligh** in the *Bounty*, who stopped offshore April 11, 1789 after departing Tahiti. A canoe approached, and its paddler was invited on board. He rubbed noses with Bligh, gave him a pearlshell breast ornament tied with human hair, and told him the island was called *Wytootackee*.

This was the Bounty's last stop before Fletcher Christian and his mutineers set Bligh and some men adrift 17 days later. Bligh miraculously survived and returned to England. Captain Edwards' *Pandora* stopped in May, 1791, searching for Christian, as did Bligh on July 25, 1792. Neither found the mutineers, who landed on remote Pitcairn in the eastern Pacific.

**Captain Goodenough** of the *Cumberland* stopped in 1814 after his disastrous visit to Rarotonga. He left the two Rarotongan women he had kidnapped---**Tepaeru** and **Mata**---before he continued on to Australia.

### The Missionary Era Begins

The famous missionary **John Williams** made his first landfall in the Cooks at Aitutaki, on October 26, 1821. He observed that some of the locals

"were tattooed from head to foot; some were painted with pipeclay and ochre, others were smeared all over with charcoal; and all were dancing and shouting in their canoes."

When Williams departed he left the Polynesian missionary **Papeiha** (from Raiatea, near Tahiti), who changed the course of Cook Islands history. Papeiha converted **Chief Tamatoa**, then Tepaeru, one of the Rarotongan women. By the time Williams returned in 1823, many Aitutakians had been converted.

Williams returned to Rarotonga with Papeiha, Tepaeru and Tamatoa. The latter two were instrumental in convincing the locals of Papeiha's sincerity, and most Rarotongans soon converted.

October 26 is Gospel Day, a national holiday commemorating the first missionaries' arrival in the country.

No missionaries came for another 16 years, but naturalist Charles Darwin stopped in 1835, in the *Beagle*.

Aitutaki became a frequent stop for whalers, traders, and escaped convicts from Australia's penal colony. Drinking and violence were common, and it was said custom allowed a man to marry one day and divorce the next. Measles and other introduced diseases decimated the local population, and Christian converts soon became demoralized without a resident missionary.

It was a society of "debauchery and disorder," as one writer put it, when Reverend Henry Royle arrived in 1839.

*Captain William Bligh*

His church was twice burned to the ground, and his family threatened. Despite these hardships he restored some semblance of order, and stayed 37 years, one of the longest periods of European missionary service.

Albert Royle Henry, the country's first Premier, was a grandson of one of Royle's devoted followers, and was named for the early missionary.

## British Annexation
Of all local rivalries, none is greater than that of Rarotonga and Aitutaki.

Rarotonga became a British "protectorate" in 1888. Aitutaki, however, was fully "annexed," as the British coveted its lagoon as a mid-Pacific harbor. When Rarotongans learned Aitutaki was "more British" by the annexation, they were quite jealous, until Raro's own annexation in 1900.

## Dogs and Disease
Early this century many Pacific islands had outbreaks of leprosy, and little treatment was available (until the

1950's). Isolation kept it from spreading, and lepers were quarantined for life on small islets. Rapota was Aitutaki's leper colony until 1926, when all were transferred to a new hospital in Fiji.

Some historians claim locals thought dogs spread leprosy, so the canines were killed during an epidemic. Others think villagers simply tired of dog fights during town meetings, while some say the dogs were eaten during a famine. Whatever its origin, dogs are still prohibited on Aitutaki (and Mauke). Pigs have filled the pet void in some families.

## The War Years
When World War II began many Cook Islanders enlisted in NZ's armed forces, but the biggest effect was on little Aitutaki. About 1000 US servicemen arrived in 1942 to build an airstrip and defend the area if the western Pacific was lost. The airstrip was the largest in the Cooks at the time, and is still in use today.

The island experienced an economic boom unmatched to this day. The military paid wages twice that of the NZ colonial administration, and everything grown or sewn sold at high prices.

Local ladies also enjoyed their companionship. Writer James Norman Hall once said of Aitutaki women:

"I have seen girls from that island who would be called beautiful in any country."

Many servicemen agreed. From 1943 to 1946 three-quarters of the children born had American fathers.

The economic boom ended with the war, but spawned the Cook Islands Progressive Association, which lobbied for higher prices and better shipping. Albert Henry headed the Auckland branch, and the CIPA later became the core of the successful independence movement.

## The Flying Boat Era

After the war, regular air services began from Auckland to Rarotonga. DC-3's stopped at Fiji, Tonga, Samoa, and Aitutaki. When this three-day route was abandoned, Aitutaki was chosen as the Cooks' sole air link to the world.

Tasman Empire Air Lines (TEAL) ---later Air New Zealand---flew huge Solent seaplanes from Auckland to Tahiti, via Fiji, Samoa, and Aitutaki. The route operated from 1951-1960, and was Tahiti's only service until 1961, when its airport was built to serve the filming of *Mutiny on the Bounty*.

The Solents were not your typical little seaplanes. These 34-ton, four-engined "flying boats," as they were called, carried 45 passengers on two decks, and stewardesses cooked meals in flight. The Solents often flew only 1000 feet above the ocean, and it took a minute-and-a-half to become airborne on their lagoon "runways."

They landed near Akaiami islet, and were refueled by hand using dozens of oil drums. Passengers had a couple of hours to swim and stretch their legs. Passengers for Raro were transferred to the main island, to wait days---or weeks---for the inter-island freighter.

On one trip an engine died on take-off, but the Solent landed safely in the lagoon. The 40 passengers were moved to the main island, while the crew flew the disabled plane to Tahiti for repairs. Eight days later it returned for the passengers, many of whom had second thoughts about leaving this tropical paradise.

A Solent is on display at Auckland's Museum of Transport and Technology. There are some remains of Akaiami's jetty and buildings, and it still claims fame as once being the world's only uninhabited international airport!

## Economy

Tourism is steadily increasing, but agriculture is the backbone of the economy. Bananas ruled for years, but shipping problems have taken their toll:

"We get a call saying the ship will arrive in two days, so we pick the bananas and haul them to the packing shed. On arrival day we get another call, saying the ship is still in Samoa. When it finally comes a week later the bananas are all ripe, and would spoil on the way to New Zealand. Well, at least the pigs are happy!"

Many growers replaced bananas with arrowroot, which is dried and made into a flour that lasts months. Some make dried bananas (*piere*), for sale on Rarotonga and overseas export.

Valuable paua (clam) and trochus (turban) shells are used in jewelry. Local trochus are prized as seedlings for other islands, but overharvesting has led to strict quotas. Paua shells are so scarce they're listed as an endangered species, and this has hurt the economy.

## WHERE TO STAY

The only resort is the **Aitutaki Lagoon Resort Hotel** (Box 99 Ait/tel 31-201/fax 31-202), on tiny Akitua *motu*, near the airstrip. A concrete footbridge spans the narrow channel, leading to 25 well-kept bungalows, restaurant, bar, pool, and gift shop. Beachfront units are NZ$310, while garden bungalows are NZ$215. All have fridges and tea/coffee facilities, but no kitchenettes. Guests can snorkel or windsurf off the beach, one of the best on the island.

It was originally named the Akitua Resort, then Aitutaki Resort Hotel, then Aitutaki Lagoon Hotel, before its current incarnation. Locals remain undaunted by marketing strategies and just call it "the resort".

*The "Bridge Over Untroubled Waters" leads to the resort.*

The resort's only drawback is its distance from town, but if you want all the amenities, this is the place to stay.

For a location closer to town, choose the **Rapae Hotel** (Box 4/tel 31-320/fax 31-321), one of my favorites. Duplexes house 12 studios, each with fridge and coffee/tea facilities. The family unit has a kitchenette. All have verandas facing the lawn and beach. The open-sided restaurant/bar has a *kikau* (thatch) roof woven from 4700 palm fronds.

You're a kilometer from town, a pleasant walk or canoe ride. The beach is nice, but the lagoon is shallow. Swimming is better 100 yds north. If you plan to snorkel, head out to the *motus*.

Rates are at NZ$100/sgl, NZ$105/dbl. The family unit sleeps six, and is NZ$130/dbl, then NZ$20/pp.

On the east coast, 2 miles from town, sits the well-appointed **Aitutaki Lodges** (Box 70 Ait/tel 31-334/fax 31-333). Six hillside bungalows offer kitchenettes, queen beds, and verandas with fantastic lagoon views. The beach, however, is muddy, and not great for swimming.

Meals are served in the open-air dining room facing the lagoon, or on your veranda. There's a well-stocked bar, and small shop. Rates are NZ$145, sgl/dbl, with meal, bike rental, and lagoon cruise packages available.

Several basic **guesthouses** are popular with backpackers. All have shared rooms, kitchen and dining area, and cold water shower/toilet block. Most prohibit smoking or alcohol inside. Bring a towel, soap, drain plug, and flip-flops for the shower. All charge about NZ$30-35/pp, with weekly discounts. Most include a light breakfast.

The **Tiare Maori Guesthouse** (Box 16/31-119) is owned by friendly Mama

20. Aerial view of Aitutaki, with One-Foot Island in the left foreground
21. Approaching One-Foot Island on the popular lagoon cruise

22. Coconut husking the native way.   23. Everyone enjoys snorkeling.
24. This inland stream is on Rarotonga's Cross-Island Track.

25. There's no need to bring your own umbrella to Aitutaki.
26. An intrepid CITV reporter searches for stories along the back roads of Aitutaki.

27. *The landing barge at Atiu, with the now-wrecked* Manuvai *in the distance*
28. *Matavai Tumunu, Atiu*

and Papa Tunui. This may be the least restrictive guesthouse. There are 7 rooms, some for couples. Dinner is usually available at a reasonable price.

In front of Mama Tunui's is **Josie's Lodge** (31-111), with six rooms available on a shared basis. Josie may also provide an evening meal for NZ$10-15.

Across the road is **Tom's Beach Cottage** (Box 51/tel 31-051/fax 31-409), which, appropriately, is on the beach. Nine rooms, shared basis, meals as arranged. No smoking, alcohol, tea or coffee is permitted in the house.

**Rino's Cottages** ("Ree-no's") (31-197) are really 4 units in a 2-story duplex, opposite Josie's. The upper two units are quieter. There are no stoves yet, but an electric frypan and kettle are available. Rates are NZ$85, sgl/dbl.

**Paradise Cove** (Box 64/tel 31-218/fax 31-456) is on the coast, a mile north of the Rapae. The main house has 5 bedrooms (NZ$30/40, sgl/dbl), and 6 huts ---with bar fridges---sit on the beach, (NZ$40/60, sgl/dbl). All share kitchen and facilities in the main house.

## WHERE TO EAT
The resort and Rapae offer all meals. Breakfast/lunch is NZ$10-17, dinner NZ$20-35, Sunday barbecues NZ$25. Reserve in advance if possible. Aitutaki Lodges may also take non-guests.

Facing the Rapae is **Ralphie's Bar & Grill** (31-418), which gets lots of repeat business. It's open daily for dinner, Mon-Sat for lunch, all NZ$12-25.

The **Crusher Bar** (31-283), named for the nearby quarry's rock crusher, is 2 miles north of the Rapae, and open daily (ex. Fri) for dinner. Fish, roast pork and salad bar are NZ$12-20.

Most guesthouses have shops nearby, which are usually open 7:30am-7:30pm (ex. Sun). Stop at **Taua's Bakery and Shop** near the Rapae for the best bread on Earth! Closer to town is **Rirei's Food Shop**, with frozen lambchops and great ice cream.

The only shop open Sunday is the tiny **donut shop**, almost opposite Tom's Cottage. There's no sign on it, and the door is only open a few inches on Sunday, but if you really need that can of spaghetti or bag of rice you'll find it!

## GETTING AROUND
On arrival, catch the van to your lodging (NZ$6). For departure, call the airline to reconfirm your pickup time.

There are no buses or taxis. Rent a motorbike or car if your stay is short, or if you're at the resort or Lodges. The roads have lots of potholes, and are very muddy after it rains (Plate 26). Pushbikes are good on the flat coastal road, but inland roads can be steep. The resort has a town shuttle, NZ$10 each way, and Island Night shows offer transport for NZ$6-10/RT.

Werner Tschan's **Swiss Rentals** (31-372 or 31-223/fax 31-329), near the main wharf, has cars for NZ$55 and motorbikes for NZ$20, with discounts available. Also try **Aitutaki Rentals** (31-127) near Paradise Cove, and **Rino's Rentals** (31-197), near his cottages. Pushbikes are NZ$10/day. Some lodgings also rent vehicles. Try to reserve *before* arrival.

## NIGHTLIFE
The premier attraction, and one which I never miss, is the Friday **Island Night** at the **Rapae**. The Polynesian buffet is NZ$27, with tasty delicacies like *ika mata* (raw fish), *eke* (octopus), and *rukau* (taro tops). A whole grilled tuna is often the centerpiece.

Food is only the appetizer, however: the frenetic dance show, with audience participation, is the entree, and Polynesian rock 'n' roll afterwards is the dessert. The bar is well-stocked, and the band plays until 1am. There's no cover charge if you don't partake of the meal.

The **Resort** has an Island Night buffet/show on Saturday, for NZ$30. Again, you can watch for no charge, and the bar is open until midnight.

**Ralphie's** has its own Island Night show on Thursdays, and a band on weekends. There's no cover charge, and it's a good place to meet the locals. I'm constantly amazed at how they can drink so much and still stand up.

A favorite of mine is the **Crusher Bar**. Riki and Lesley have a Saturday Island Night buffet, followed by an excellent dance show. Dinner is NZ$22, and there's no charge for just the show. They have other entertainment nightly.

The local equivalent of the friendly corner bar is the **Aitutaki Game Fishing Club** (31-077), behind the CITC-Donald Store. It's open 6 days from 4pm, and you're welcome even if you're not into fishing. "Shouting" a beer works wonders if you want to meet the locals.

## PRACTICALITIES

The **Air Rarotonga** (31-888) office is on the main road, just north of town.

**Money/Credit Cards:** The PO changes currency, but the rate is poor. Credit cards are accepted at the resort, Rapae, Lodges, Paradise Cove, Tom's, and Bishops Cruises, and some shops.

**Post Office:** Located in Arutanga, it's open 8am-4pm, weekdays. It's also the government liquor store. Liquor sales stop at 2:30pm on Fridays, so afternoon sports matches don't get too rowdy.

**Telephone:** There's a modern phone system. International calls can be made

at the Post Office and some hotels. Most shops let you make local calls for 20c, if they charge you at all.

**Medical/Emergencies:** There's a good hospital on the hill behind Arutanga, with New Zealand-trained doctors and dental staff. Prescriptions are filled here, as there is no private pharmacy.

Hospital/Ambulance: 998
Police: 999

**Laundry:** The hotels have guest laundries, and may allow others if it's not crowded. You'll only be wearing shorts, T-shirts, and swimsuits, so shower in them and clean everything at once!

**Language:** Almost everyone speaks English, although Aitutakian---similar to Rarotongan---is the native language. For "thank you very much" say *meitaki atupaka* instead of Raro's *meitaki maata* and you'll instantly make a new friend!

**Island Tours:** You can visit most places on your own, but a tour adds insight into local culture. **Mike Henry** (31-379) offers a Circle Island Tour for NZ$25.

**Information:** Teina Bishop (31-009) is the friendly Tourist Authority representative on Aitutaki. There's no formal office, but call him for the latest updates. Before you leave Raro, pick up a topographic map at Bounty Bookshop, and pamphlets at the CITA.

**Shopping:** Try the sometimes-open **Handicrafts Center** near the Police Station. **JPI, Maina Traders, Taua's** and **Mango Trading** have *pareus*, handicrafts and souvenirs. Mango has snorkeling gear. The Aitutaki PO prints its own stamps, prized by collectors.

## AROUND ARUTANGA

There are technically 5 villages on the west coast: Amuri, Ureia, Arutanga, Reureu and Nikaupara. It's essentially one town, with Arutanga the downtown section. We'll head south from Amuri.

**Amuri** is home to the Rapae, Ralphie's, Taua's Bakery, Mango Trading and JPI. You never have to leave Amuri to sleep, drink, eat or shop, but head downtown anyway. You pass two **sports grounds**, where Friday afternoons see wild rugby matches. Slip down to the beach here, or pretty much anywhere along the road to town.

**Ureia** is home to Josie's, Maina Trading, and Air Rarotonga.

**Arutanga** is the commercial center, with shops and the **Post Office**. The adjacent **Town Hall** hosts weekend dances. Opposite the **Cook Islands Christian Church (CICC)** is the *kautea ta'unga*, a former meeting place for chiefs and traditional priests. The CICC is perhaps the oldest structure in the Cooks. Built by Reverend Henry Royle in 1839, it was twice burned to the ground by anti-mission locals, and rebuilt for good a year later. The altar is off on one side, rather than on the end. Sunday services are open to all.

There's a **memorial monument** on its north side, honoring missionaries John Williams and Papeiha. It was dedicated on October 26, 1971, the 150th anniversary of their arrival. The limestone **CICC Mission Hall** was also built in the mid-1800's.

The divided road facing the Post Office leads past the **packing shed** to the **wharf**. The former is often empty due to little freighter traffic at the latter.

The Americans planned to extend the jetty towards the **Arutanga Passage**, but when World War II ended the project was abandoned. Freighters must wait offshore and unload their cargo onto small diesel barges, which somehow make it through the passage with their top-heavy loads. If a freighter is unloading, watch for a while to see an interesting aspect of life on an atoll.

Yachts can enter the lagoon through the narrow passage, and usually anchor

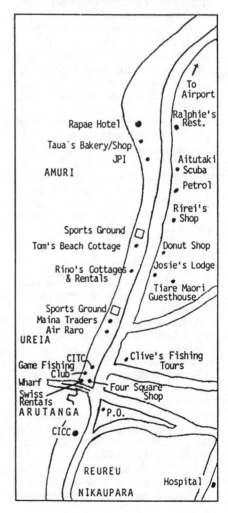

off the jetty. A friendly bribe of a cold beer at the nearby **Aitutaki Game Fishing Club** might convince a skipper to offer a tour of his or her vessel.

The divided road itself is of some historical interest. The south lane is **Sir Albert Henry Drive** and the north is **Lady Elizabeth Drive**, for his wife. Aitutaki was the first outer island with electricity, and this road was the first to have electric lights. It pays to have friends in high places!

A few yards south of the Post Office is **Reureu**, and the road ends at the beach in **Nikaupara**. At low tide you can walk or motorbike around the southern tip of the island.

Return and head inland on the road just north of the Post Office. You pass the **Courthouse**, and the **Police Station** behind it. The friendly Chief Constable is often at the Rapae on Friday nights. Nearby is the small **Handicrafts Center**. If you're lucky enough to find it open, you may be able to get carvings, mats and *rito* hats at half the price of Rarotonga's shops.

## AROUND THE ISLAND

The road is rough past the Handicrafts Center, but you're amply rewarded by the colorful flowers and fruit orchards, where mangoes or papayas may literally drop in front of your eyes. Picking up roadside fruit is usually OK, but ask permission if the owner is nearby.

For great views, go up the hill and turn right to the **Hospital**, built in 1950. Then continue to the next intersection and go left, towards the east coast.

On the rough tracks south of the hospital are several historical sites, including **Te-Poaki-O-Rae** (The Stone of Rae). This unusual *marae* has several small volcanic rocks arranged in rows, all facing a 6' main pillar. Other *maraes*,

including the large **Are-O-Te-Mango** (Temple of the Shark), are also located in this agricultural **Taravao District**, where the houses are few and *namus* (mosquitoes) plentiful. The *maraes* are not well marked and may be hard to find, but there's a better reason to see these attractions in a tour van.

Unlike our guide's leisurely stops at the other jungle sites, he kept the motor running when we reached The Stone of Rae. He recounted its history, but didn't get out to show us around. The eight of us foolishly hopped out for some photos, and within 10 seconds we were attacked by three zillion mosquitoes. We dove head first back into the van, and the guide gunned the engine and headed for the coast. It took ten minutes of vigorous swatting, amidst hysterical laughter, before the few thousand mosquitoes that came along for the ride were deceased or ushered out the window. To accurately reflect its guardians, Te-Poaki-O-Rae should be renamed Te-Poaki-O-Namus.

If you survive the *maraes* of Taravao, continue east to clean and quiet **Tautu**, usually deserted by day while everyone works in the fields. The first dirt track north of the CICC leads to the **Tautu Jetty**, built by the Americans during the war for easier access to the *motus*. Some lagoon cruises depart from here.

From here, or on other tracks leading south from Tautu, you can reach **New Jerusalem**, a religious commune founded in the past decade. Buildings are made of local materials, and members share work, meals and most possessions. There are no formal tours, but you can visit daily, except Sunday.

North of Tautu is a small *marae* near the cutoff to **Aitutaki Lodges**. Stop at the lodges to check out their nice cottages, and the view across the lagoon.

Past the **Vaitau School**, named for the two neighboring districts, is the friendly village of **Vaipae**. Kids play near the **CICC** and large **Vaipaepae-O-Pau** (meeting hall). The latter was built during an intra-island rivalry in the 1970's, started by little Reureu trying to out-build the Arutanga town hall. I think Arutanga finally won, but Vaipae came in a close second.

If you head inland (west) from Vaipae you'll pass **Araura College** (high school), which reflects another name for the island. This road continues on to the west coast, into Arutanga.

If you head north from Vaipae on the coastal road, and bear right at the main fork, you'll come to a pristine area facing a quiet part of the lagoon. This is the **Vaipeka** district, with just a few houses and a small shop. The views are soothing and tranquil. Follow the footpaths through the palms to discover your own private beach.

To try some *uto* (sweet coconut sponge), find a sprouted brown coconut with leaves about 2' long. Inside the nut is the sweet chiffon-like treat. Husk it on a sharpened stick (Plate 22), or use a machete back at your lodging.

The road turns inland (west) and you pass the **quarry** and rock crusher. Next is the **Crusher Bar**, a good spot for a break. Turn right to the airport and the **Golf Club**. It's a typical Cook Islands nine-hole affair, but instead of wire masts you've got an airport runway in the middle of a fairway!

In the 1970's you would play right across the runway, and momentarily stop when the occasional plane landed. Flights now are more numerous, and the runway is out of bounds altogether.

Guests are welcome, and a Saturday round of golf is a great way to meet the locals. Green fees are only NZ$5, and

clubs can be rented. Golfers from Raro come up to play in the Aitutaki Golf Open, held in early December.

The **airport**, built in 1943, has the Cooks' only double-angled runway, allowing landings in most prevailing winds. When the 1983 upgrade made 737 landings possible, there was some thought of allowing international flights. Tourism would increase, but so would customs, immigration and fuel storage costs. Many locals are wary of a possible onslaught of tourists, and the proposal has been tabled.

Head east from the airport to the **Akitua footbridge** and the resort. Hurricane Sally washed out the old bridge in 1987, and for months guests were ferried across on a pontoon barge. The new bridge has reinforced concrete to reduce problems in the future.

The lagoon here is relatively deep, and popular with local kids. The nearby passage is where the legendary Ru entered, with his entourage of wives, brothers and royal virgins.

An old **jetty** is off a track to the west. It was used in the 1950's to ferry fuel drums and supplies to Akaiami, for use by the Solent flying boats.

*In the background is* Maungapu: *Would the Rarotongans try to steal it back?*

Head back past the airstrip to the west coast road, then go south to the beachfront **Paradise Cove** guesthouse. Across the road is the trail up **Mt. Maungapu** (408ft, 124m). It's a half-hour walk through long and prickly grass, but the path is well-marked. Wear long pants and socks to avoid scratches. There are good views, and lots of mosquitoes. Take your camera and insect repellent, but forget the picnic lunch.

Maungapu is another source of rivalry between Aitutaki and Rarotonga. Legends say that in the old days Aitutaki was a flat island. Some warriors canoed down to Rarotonga, sliced off the top of the high-peaked Raemaru (behind Arorangi) and brought it up here in their canoes. That's why Raemaru is now flat-topped, and this hill is called *Maunga Pu*, meaning "Top of the Mountain." Like I said, this was a long

time ago, and canoes were probably a lot stronger than they are today!

For nice sunset views, head up the dirt road near the sports field closest to town. Bear left all the way up the hill, and stop at the crest near the water tanks above Amuri. From here you can continue to Vaipeka, or return to town.

**AROUND THE LAGOON**
**Beaches on the Main Island:** At low tide the lagoon is pretty shallow. On the west, swimming is good 100 yds north of the Rapae. You can swim near Arutanga wharf, but stay well clear of the passage, which has strong currents.

The east coast can be muddy, but spots near Vaipeka are sandy. As mentioned, the Akitua footbridge area is deep and good for swimming.

There are lots of ugly but harmless sea slugs---also called *bêche de mer*---

which are considered an aphrodisiac in the Orient, but not here.

## The Offshore Motus

Swimming and snorkeling are best off the *motus* to the south. The warm, clear water is up to 35 feet deep, and beaches are glistening white sand. If you visit Aitutaki, a *motu* visit is a must.

Fifteen are permanent enough to have names. Another dozen may temporarily exist, depending on recent storms. In 1977 we sighted a tiny *motu* with a lone coconut tree. An Australian on our boat named it after himself. By 1980 "Fitzgerald's Island" was gone, but another islet was forming nearby, literally from the shifting sands of time.

Permanent *motus* are owned by local families, who harvest coconuts for copra. Aside from the resort on Akitua, all *motus* are uninhabited, except for an occasional stray cat or wild pig.

Parts of the lagoon have coral heads just below the surface. Locals know these areas well, but if you rent a boat be very careful, especially when heading into the glare of the sun.

Take insect repellent on your *motu* trip, since sand flies and mosquitoes may be a problem. Don't forget your towel, sunglasses and suntan lotion.

## A Short Tour of The Motus

The first few *motus* south of Akitua are not on most tours. Stop at their secluded beaches if you manage to rent a boat.

Further south is **Akaiami**, the "international airport" in the flying-boat days of the 1950's. There are some remains of the old jetty and outbuildings, and the beach is clean, white, and beautiful.

Before the Solent flights began, all the shallow coral heads had to be blasted out. Engineers dragged a 40-foot sweep bar from a raft, then tied a coconut to whatever it hit. Explosive charges were then dropped at each coconut, and the engineers had six minutes to clear out before the lagoon exploded.

"You may be sure we were well clear of the explosive area by the time the "jelly" went off---although we had quite a few near misses!" recalled one engineer.

Past Akaiami is little **Muritapua**, with good swimming. The long *motu* of **Tekopua** has good swimming but not much coral. It's well wooded, and a nice place for exploring or a picnic.

The most popular *motu* is **Tapuaetai**, "One-Footprint," but known to all as **One Foot Island**. From the air it resembles the left foot, but legends offer other explanations.

A tribe once attacked the main island, and a man and his son escaped by canoe. On this unnamed islet he carried the boy across the beach, and hid him in a tall coconut tree. He then paddled to Rarotonga for help. When the bad guys reached the islet they saw only one set of footprints on and off the island, and didn't realize the boy was there. He remained safely hidden until his father returned with reinforcements to save the day. From then on the islet was called "Tapuaetai".

If I had to pick one place in the entire Cook Islands to spend a day it would definitely be One Foot Island. The water is a dazzling shade of turquoise, the beach is pristinely white, and the lagoon is clean and sandy. It really has to be seen to be believed.

The last southeast *motu* is **Motukitiu**, with good swimming. It's remote and not often visited. Beyond it lies Rarotonga, 160 miles to the south.

Two *motus* to the west---**Moturakau** (Tree Island) and **Rapota**---are volcanic in origin, rather than sand cays. Tourists don't visit often, but locals use them for mini-vacations. Rapota was used as a leper colony until 1926.

In the southwest corner of the lagoon, off by itself, is **Maina** (Little Girl), the closest to the Arutanga wharf. There are lots of coral heads, so boating is tedious but snorkeling is excellent! Some Oregon divers saw more fish while snorkeling here than they had on an earlier ocean dive. One counted 75 species in these rich coral gardens.

From Nov-Feb the waters are the mating grounds of large sea turtles. On the islet is a rare red-tailed tropicbird rookery. Don't forget your camera!

On the reef to the north is the wreck of the *Alexander*, which ran aground in the 1930's with a load of Model-T Fords. In 1954 a beacon was erected on Maina to prevent similar mishaps.

## WATERSPORTS AND CRUISES

Aitutaki is great for snorkeling, fishing and diving. Offerings change frequently, depending on who has a new boat, and who's gone overseas for a while. Tours are always available, but boat rentals may be hard to find. Call Teina Bishop (31-009) to update all listings, or to find people below who have no phone. Also try the Game Fishing Club (31-077). Note that most cruise and fishing boats don't operate on Sunday.

### Lagoon Tours

**Bishops Cruises** (31-009/fax 31-493) has a full-day One-Foot Island trip for NZ$40, which includes transfers, snorkeling gear and barbecue lunch. You head out at 9am in Teina's canopy-covered motor launch, and there's plenty of time for snorkeling and swimming before the 4pm return.

A full-day trip is also offered to Maina and its coral gardens. Snorkeling

gear and lunch are included in the NZ$35 price. The half-day trip, for NZ$20, includes light refreshments.

A sunset cruise to One-Foot, with barbecue, beer and wine, is NZ$55. Teina can also drop you at an islet in the morning and pick you up at sunset ---or perhaps arrange a unique overnight stay on your own tropical island!

**Tere Viking** (31-180) offers tours to One-Foot, Maina, and other *motus* in his motor launch, at similar rates. **Ru's Cruises** does lagoon tours in his 16' skiff. **Paradise Islands Lagoon Tours** (31-368) handles Air Rarotonga daytrippers, but may take others as well.

### Fishing

Gamefish include **marlin, wahoo, tuna, barracuda, snapper** and **trevally**. Australian Ben Grummels, who once ran sailing trips here, holds the world record for the unusual **Hump-headed Maori Wrasse**. He hooked his 13lb, 3oz (6kg) winner in 1989, between Maina and the wreck of the *Alexander*.

**Clive Baxter** (31-025) offers deepsea fishing, while **Ian Guinea** does both lagoon and deepsea fishing. **Don Watt** (31-281) and **Junior Maote** may take visitors along. Visitors are welcome at the June **Queen's Birthday Surfcasting and Game Fishing Tournament**.

### Diving Trips

Ocean visibility is 100' +, with plenty of coral and fish close by. Visiting divers highly recommend Neil Mitchell of **Aitutaki Scuba** (Box 40/31-103/fax 31-310), near the Rapae. He's a licensed NAUI/CMAS/NZUA instructor, and specializes in diving trips. One-tank dives are about NZ$60, and a four-day certification class is only NZ$400. Gear rental is available, and Neil occasionally offers snorkeling tours as well.

# MANUAE

Population:    Uninhabited
Area:         2.4 sq.mi.

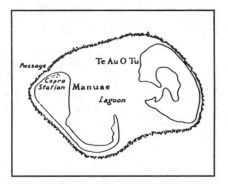

Situated halfway between Aitutaki and Atiu, Manuae's two islets are owned by 11 Aitutaki families, who harvest copra from its 85,000 coconut palms. Thousands of red-tailed tropic-birds also call it home.

Atiuans arrived a few centuries ago. Aitutakian **Chief Ruatapu** later named it *Manu Enua* (Bird Land), which became *Manuae*. His son **Tupui** moved here and shared it with the Atiuans. He modestly named the larger islet *Te Au-O-Tupui* (The Kingdom of Tupui), now known as *Te Au-O-Tu*.

Manuae was the first island in the country sighted by **Captain Cook**, on September 23, 1773. He passed by, but saw no one ashore. He named it Sandwich Island, but later gave that name to Hawaii. He renamed this Harvey Isle, for the Lord of the Admiralty. On maps this became **Hervey's Island**. Missionaries and the British called the entire Southern Group the Hervey Islands, a name which still appears on some maps.

Cook returned April 6, 1777 and noticed the natives had different practices than the Atiuans and Mangaians:

"not one of them had adopted that mode of ornament, so generally prevalent amongst the natives of this ocean, of puncturing, or tattooing their bodies."

In July, 1823, missionary **John Williams** saw 60 inhabitants, but a few years later only a dozen remained. They were soon moved to Aitutaki by that island's chief, who declared Manuae his personal possession.

In 1863 a merchant vessel found **William Marsters** and his wives here, and hired them as Palmerston's caretakers. After Britain took over the islands in 1888, Manuae was used as a penal colony, as Rarotonga had no jail. Prisoners worked for the CITC, which had leased Manuae as a copra plantation. This program ended when the Rarotonga jail was built in 1915.

More recently, scientists visited in 1965 to observe a solar eclipse, commemorated by a postage stamp. A small airstrip was built in 1982, and copra cutters come every few months to harvest the thousands of coconuts.

The CITC lease ends in 1997, and a controversy erupted when some families wanted to lease the whole island to foreign investors for a luxury resort. This was voted down, but there are proposals to allow day trips for tourists. Others suggest making it a National Park, like Suwarrow.

There are no scheduled flights, and ships rarely stop. Yachts need special permission to visit.

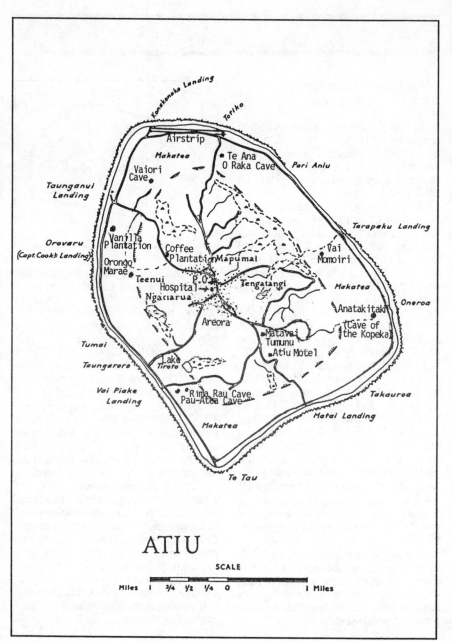

ATIU

SCALE

Miles 1   ¾   ½   ¼   0                1 Miles

# ATIU

Population:   1003
Area:   10.4 sq.mi.

Lying only 135 miles from Rarotonga, Atiu is a good choice for those
who want some adventure without
forsaking all creature comforts. It's for
those who enjoy exploring jungles and
caves, and don't need watersports all
the time. It's a place to get muddy,
drink bush beer with the locals, and
experience communal island life.

Atiu is famous for its rare swiftlet,
the **kopeka**, and its bush beer tradition,
the **tumunu**. Along with Mauke and
Mitiaro, Atiu makes up the island
grouping called **Nga-Pu-Toru**---The
Three Roots. Atiu has clearly been the
dominant root throughout history.

**Orientation**
Atiu was a volcano island which slowly
sank, leaving a coral reef around a low
plateau. 100,000 years ago volcanic
action thrust it up 70', killing the now-
exposed reef. This razor-sharp band of
dead coral is called **makatea**. If you go
to Atiu, Mauke, Mitiaro or Mangaia,
you'll never forget the word.

The coastal strip has nice beaches,
but the reef fronts them and swimming
isn't good. Inland is a band of swamps,
and a lake where tasty eels thrive.
Fertile lower hills once supported a
pineapple industry, but this collapsed
due to marketing problems. The coffee
plantation, however, is doing quite well.

The uppermost hills are less fertile,
and, unlike other islands, are the site of

all the villages. They were originally down near the taro swamps, but were relocated to the plateau by the missionaries. There are technically five villages, but they're so close together they're usually referred to as **Areora**, the largest pre-missionary district.

**Getting There**
Air Rarotonga has flights daily (ex. Sun) for NZ$254/RT. Ships stop in every month or so. The *Edna* hit the reef shortly after service began in 1990.

**HISTORY**
Legends say **Tangaroa**, the divine entity, was the first inhabitant, and his oldest son **Mariri** the first human settler. Mariri named it *Enua Manu*, "land of insects and animals," to indicate no prior human habitation.

Mariri had two younger brothers, including **Atiu-Mua**. He was the most prolific, and his descendants changed the name to honor him.

Three chiefly lines shared power, with **Rongomatane** the most famous of the *arikis*. He is well known to the people of both Mauke and Mitiaro, which he attacked quite often.

Atiuans were the most warlike islanders, and had conquered Mauke and Mitiaro before the missionaries arrived. As writer Charles Nordhoff, of *Mutiny on the Bounty* fame, wrote:

"Time after time, in the old days, they raided Mauke, stealing by night upon the sleeping villages, entering each house to feel the heads of the sleepers. When they felt the large head of a warrior they seized his throat and killed him without noise; the children and women---the small heads and the heads with long hair---were taken back alive to Atiu.

In one legendary battle the Atiuans attacked Mitiaro, and conquered the inland fortress *Te Pare* by using one of their many military strategies. To quickly move through the sharp *makatea* they laid double rows of spears end-to-end on the rough coral rock. They moved so quickly across the terrain that the Mitiaroans were taken by surprise, and most of the population was massacred.

Not content with domination of its small neighbors, Atiuans once attacked Rarotonga, using their *te tara* formation, a version of the flying wedge. They won some battles in the Takitumu district, but never conquered the larger island.

**European Contact**
The first European to sight Atiu was **Captain Cook**, on March 31, 1777. On April 2 he sent three boats ashore, which landed at Orovaru Beach on the west. The locals "saluted us by applying their noses to ours," related a crewman. The natives' long hair was tied in topknots, legs were tattooed from knee to heel, and the chief wore long red feathers, probably from the tropicbird.

There was one apprehensive moment when the crew saw a huge earth oven being dug, and the chief wouldn't allow them to return to the ship. They "could assign no other reason for this, than that they meant to roast and eat us." Their thoughts were eased when a nearby pig was prepared for the oven, and they returned to the ship without incident. The natives later traded for one of the ship's dogs, as there were none on Atiu.

**The Missionary Era**
Rongomatane ruled Atiu in 1823 when two Polynesian teachers were dropped off by a European missionary from Bora Bora. When missionary **John Williams** arrived a few months later, these teachers were devoid of possessions and on the brink of starvation. Rongomatane was going to be a tough nut to crack.

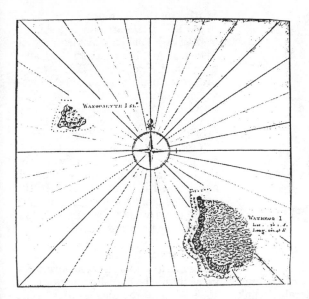

Captain Cook's original map of Atiu, shown as "Wateeoo," and Takutea, shown as "Wanooaette," for Enuaiti (as Atiuans called it then, meaning "small island").

Williams, his young son, and the native missionary **Papeiha** came ashore. Rongomatane was friendly, but a rival chief kidnapped Williams' son, and was preparing him as a dinner entree until Rongomatane came to the rescue.

To test the power of the visitors, Rongomatane challenged them to eat from a sacred grove of sugar cane. If they lived, he would accept the strength of this new religion. If they died, he would know his gods were greater. The missionaries ate the sugar cane and lived, and Rongomatane, as promised, soon converted.

Rongomatane told Williams of Mitiaro and Mauke, where, he explained, he had some influence. They soon visited both islands, and---not surprisingly ---those natives also converted, at the not-so-subtle urging of Rongomatane.

Changes were immediate on Atiu, as the missionaries convinced the na-tives to move all five villages from the taro swamps to a single settlement on the central plateau. Rongomatane regretfully gave up all but one of his twelve wives, and numerous mission-sponsored blue laws, including a curfew, were put into effect.

### The Tumunu Tradition
Before the missionaries' arrival the natives drank *kava*, a mildly narcotic brew made from the root of the pepper tree (*piper methysticum*). The missionaries banned this practice, although it continued in secret for some time.

In the 1850's a method of brewing beer from oranges was introduced from Tahiti, and Atiuans soon mastered the technique. The missionaries quickly banned this "orange-beer," as did later colonial governments.

Having acquired a taste for the drink, locals continued to secretly brew

*Early Missionary John Williams*

it in hollowed-out trunks of coconut palms. *Tumunu* means, literally, "trunk of the coconut tree". Drinking was done in hideouts surrounded by bushes, thus the term "bush beer" became popular for the illegal brew.

Bush beer has survived the years of prohibition, and the *tumunu* tradition has evolved into a significant social and cultural institution.

### The Tahitian Connection
Many islands in the Cooks have historical connections with Tahiti, but Atiu is one of the few that still retains close ties.

Atiuans first went to Tahiti in the 1860's to work on sugar plantations. In 1868 they purchased land from the government, and formed a new community at **Patutoa**, near Papeete. The self-governing village still exists, and disputes are often referred to the Atiu Island Council, 700 miles away! There's a new hostel for visiting Atiuans, and ties remain strong.

### Mutiny on the Ngamaru
In the 1890's, Atiuans bought a ship for trading with Tahiti and visiting Patutoa. They named it the *Ngamaru Ariki*, after their chief. From 1895-1903 Atiuans prospered from this trade, and ballads recount those glory days. The ship's captain, however, was an Atiuan version of Captain Bligh, paying low wages and providing poor working conditions.

One night, when the captain was ashore, the disgruntled crew ran the ship onto the reef near Orovaru Beach and burned it to the ground. In the morning the villagers tried to save it, but by then only twisted iron bars and some tattered riggings remained.

### British Protectorate
Religious freedom and centralized law arrived with the British protectorate in 1888. Most of the missionaries' "Blue Laws" (see p. 16) were abolished, but restrictions were kept concerning alcohol. Manufacturers of "orange-beer or other liquor of an intoxicating nature" were fined ten dollars; mere possession resulted in a fine of seven dollars.

In 1902 the New Zealand administration finally terminated Atiu's control over Mauke and Mitiaro, and Atiu was longer a "colonial" power.

### Atiu Today
Atiu has one of the strongest communal traditions in the Cooks. Agricultural cooperatives cultivate taro and other crops, and volunteers built the around-the-island road and the two successive airstrips.

Atiuans call themselves *Toke-enua no Enuamanu*---worms of the land Enuamanu---expressing their hope to be buried on the island of their birth. At childbirth, custom requires that the placenta---also called *enua*---be buried under a newly planted tree. Their saying "We come from the Enua and go back to the Enua" derives from this practice.

## WHERE TO STAY AND EAT

The only licensed lodging is the **Atiu Motel**, four comfortable A-frame cottages a kilometer south of town. Roger and Kura Malcolm are the busy but friendly owners.

Units are handcrafted from coconut trees cut at Roger's small sawmill across the road. The cottages sit in gardens near the grass tennis court, open-sided dining area/bar and barbecue, and have great views of the island.

All have a double or twin beds, plus a sleeping loft, and nice veranda. The newer family unit has a separate bedroom. Kitchenettes and showers use solar-heated water.

Rates are NZ$80/90, sgl/dbl. Call or fax direct (33-777/fax 33-775), or reserve through Air Raro (22-888).

On Saturdays from January to August the tennis court becomes the **Atiu Lawn Bowling Club**. From September to December it's the **Atiu Tennis Club**. The *Nga-Pu-Toru* Tennis Tournament is held in December, alternating between Atiu and Mauke.

You'll be preparing your own meals, as there are no restaurants. Units are stocked with dry and canned foods and liquor. Tick off items on the list as you use them, and settle up when you leave. Tea, coffee and fruit are on the house.

In town, opposite a bakery, the little **Tivaivai Cafe** has Atiu coffee and light refreshments, and displays of local handicrafts. The **Centre Store** has produce and ice cream, and other food staples. There are two bakeries and three donut shops in the village. Donuts come looped on a string of leaf fiber, perfect for motorbike handlebars.

## GETTING AROUND

Roger or Kura will meet you at the airport; round-trip transfers are NZ$7. They rent motorbikes (no bicycles) for NZ$25, but reserve in advance so they can siphon gas to them before arrival. They also arrange visits to the *kopeka* cave and the *tumunu*. Kore Samuel (33-067) sometimes offers island tours.

The roads are mostly gravel and sand. Be careful on downhills in sandy areas. The coastal road is basically flat, about 23km (14mi) around. You can walk most places, but rent a motorbike if you're only staying a day or two so you can see everything.

## NIGHTLIFE

The motel often has a barbecue and dance band on Saturday night. They arrange an occasional Island Night, with the **Hinano Cultural Theater Group** or the **Puna Korero Dance Troupe**. Atiuan dancers win many national contests.

Look for Friday night dances at the **village hall**, owned by the CICC. They thought of stopping these during the Jan-March hurricane season, thinking they might cause bad luck. If the CICC doesn't allow them, they'll be held at other church halls.

### Attending a Tumunu

As indicated, the **tumunu** tradition began in the 1850's, as bush beer replaced the outlawed *kava*. There are several tumunus around the island, and visitors are welcome.

While the word *tumunu* technically means a tree trunk, it is also used when referring to the hollowed-out trunk where the bush beer is brewed; the thatched hut where one drinks the beer; and the social institution of sharing ideas while drinking the brew. Tumunus are also called "bush beer schools."

The **Matavai Tumunu** (Plate 28) is close to the motel. Hours are Mon/Wed/Fri from 6pm, and Sunday after church. Visitors should contribute a few dollars, or bring a large bag of sugar. While the tumunu is generally for men, women tourists are usually allowed if accompanied by Roger.

A tumunu is nothing like a commercial bar. Drinking is part of an elaborate ritual, which the visitor should respect.

The *tangata kapu* (barman) sits in the center of the thatched hut, next to the tumunu container holding several gallons of bush beer. Everyone else sits on log benches around the barman. A single coconut shell is dipped in and handed to a participant, who drinks it in one gulp. The shell is passed back to the barman, who refills it for the next person. An initial three or four rounds are served, and coconut or fruit may be set out for nibbling.

When the barman raps on the container, everyone becomes silent and drinking stops. A prayer is said, and is sometimes followed by short hymns or a verse from the bible.

Drinking then resumes, and guests are introduced. You'll be asked to say a little about where you're from and what you do, and may be asked your thoughts about Atiu and the islands. The locals then share a little about their lives, and drinking continues for an hour or two, or three or four.

A tumunu visit is a great way to meet the locals. The orange-beer has a sweet taste, and there's no pressure to drink more than one desires.

## PRACTICALITIES

The **Post Office** is in the center of town, and serves as the government liquor store. The motel handles small sums for **currency exchange**, but bring enough with you. There's a small **hospital** with a doctor and a nurse. **Electrical power** is 6am-midnight. **Dress** is very conservative. Men should always wear a shirt (T-shirts are OK). Some locals frown on women wearing shorts in town.

**Church services** at the CICC begin at 9:30am. Catholic Church services start at 9am. The Seventh Day Adventist service is 9am Saturday. Ladies should wear a dress with sleeves, and a hat (available at the motel). Men should wear long pants.

**Language:** Most Atiuans speak English. The local version of "Thank you very much" is *Meitaki ranuinui* (Ra'-nui-nui).

**Shopping:** The Atiu Fibre Arts Studio has hand-made pandanus mats, jewelry and purses, and beautiful *tivaevae* quilts for NZ$700 and up.

Wooden storyboards depicting Atiuan legends are NZ$30 and up. Handcrafted wind chimes, made from sea urchin spines, are sold in town. The unusual *Nga-Pu-Toru* T-shirt is popular. The locally-produced book *Atiu---An Island Community*, recounts island customs and history. Edible souvenirs include fresh-roasted Atiu coffee and local fruit products.

## AROUND THE ISLAND

**Get a Guide:** While you can find beaches and some points of interest on your own, you'll need a guide for the *kopeka* cave and most of the *maraes*. Roger and Kura can arrange guides for caves and *marae* visits.

It's considered proper etiquette to have a guide for caves, since most are privately owned, and families must give permission to visit. Remember, never touch the bones in a burial cave.

**The Main Settlement**
This appears to be one town, but it's technically five separate villages, each at the tip of a pie-shaped slice of the island. The largest district is **Areora**, the southern third of the island. Smaller **Tengatangi** and **Mapumai** are in the east and northeast, respectively.

In the northwest is **Teenui**, with Taunganui landing and Orovaru Beach. The chief of Teenui was the traditional greeter of visitors to Atiu, since everyone, including Captain Cook, arrived at landings in Teenui. Small **Ngatiarua** occupies the rest of the west.

Pineapples once covered the surrounding hills, but irregular shipping and stiff overseas competition put an end to this thriving industry.

As you head to town you may notice the **old airstrip** on your right, which was in the middle of a pineapple field. Using it on a wet day was quite an experience! The new coral airstrip was built in 1983.

As you enter town, you'll notice the **CICC Church** on the left. Built in the 1850's, it's probably the largest church in the country. About 70% of Atiuans are CICC members.

The nearby **Catholic Church** was built in the early 1900's, after Britain opened the Cooks to other religions. About 20% of Atiuans are Catholic.

The 10-bed **Hospital** in Ngatiarua includes a **Dental Clinic**. Dr. Maris Smalley, from Duluth, Minnesota, visited in the 1980's, then raised NZ$37,000 with his Rotary Club to fund it.

Across from the **Post Office**, behind some tennis courts, are stone markers near *Te Apiripiri Marae*, where Papeiha first preached the Gospel in 1823.

You'll surely notice lots of **tennis courts**. In the 1980's the sport became popular, and each village tried to build bigger and better courts than its

*The Crest of Atiu, where the five triangles represent the villages*

neighbors. It seems strange to see so many in one town, but it makes sense when you remember that it's really *five* towns which simply look like one.

The **Atiu Primary School** and **Atiu College** (high school) are in Mapumai. There's a tiny library/museum at the college, which may be open after lunch.

The **Power Station** is in Teenui, and nearby is the **Coffee Plantation**. German-born Juergen Manske-Eimke revived it in the 1970's, and it now produces 5 tons a year. Two-hour tours are NZ$10, and end at the Tivaivai Cafe.

**Lake Tiroto**
The lake is west of the motel, and home to tasty eels, fat tilapia fish, and wild ducks. It's connected to the ocean by underwater caves, and rises and falls with the tides. My guide said there are sometimes sharks in this freshwater lake, but I assume this is very rare.

In the rough *makatea* near the lake is **Rima Rau Burial Cave** and **Pau-Atea Cave**, both accessible with a guide.

You may notice lots of goats and pigs. This is where my guide's piglets came out of the bush and begged for food. Dogs are allowed on Atiu, but pigs are often treated like pets. Atiu actually has more pigs than people.

## West Coast

There are several nice beaches. Now, remember, I didn't say you could *swim* at them, but there's fine white sand, and lots of exotic shells.

Te Tau, Tumai, Taungaroro, and Orovaru are good for picnics and beachcombing. The latter two have nice bathtub beaches (reef holes), very refreshing on a hot day.

Captain Cook's crew landed at Orovaru Beach in 1777, so it's also called Cook's Beach. The large Toka Oonu (Deep Rock) near the beach was the signpost Rongomatane used to direct John Williams to Rarotonga in 1823.

For swimming, try the mini-harbor at Taunganui Landing. The angled breakwater shelters the diesel barge serving the freighters (Plate 27). Piled high with produce outward and supplies inward, this trusty, rusty, barge is pulled up the ramp when done. If you come by ship you'll enjoy trying to hang onto this bouncing metal cork to get ashore. It's fun once. Take the plane back.

Nearby is a beautiful little seaside park, good for a picnic. Outriggers are stored on the ramp, and fishing near the breakwater is good.

On some nights in July and August the waters off Taunganui are thick with flying fish (*maroro*), and thousands are caught as they glide to the coast to spawn. *Maroro* are also caught around the island from June to December.

South of Taunganui is the vanilla plantation, which has had experimental plots since 1983. It's unique in that it uses pockets of soil found in the otherwise infertile *makatea*. Results have been mixed, but hope springs eternal.

Nearby is Orongo Marae, where chiefs were anointed. Earthwatch helped restore the site in 1985, but as it's on private land the "get a guide" rule applies. A burial cave in the *makatea* is nearby, and Vaiori Burial Cave is on a track to the north.

## Other Coastal Areas

On the northern tip is Konakonako, a secondary landing with a concrete ramp and storage building. On the road between the airstrip and town is Te Ana O Raka burial cave. Nearby is the rock quarry and crusher, used for road work.

The coast near Pari Aniu is the most forbidding. Their are high cliffs, and the strong easterlies cause waves to constantly smash the narrow reef below. There are blowholes down there, but be careful when trying to get a good view. Further south is little used Tarapaku Landing, where cargo has to be carried up the steep cliffs by hand on makeshift ladders.

Inland from Tarapaku is a walking track that passes the Vai Momoiri water cave, which is used for bathing and soaking hibiscus bark. The nearby Vai Inano was a man-made bathing pool used by the twelve wives of Rongomatane, but you'll need a guide to find what's left of it. The track leads through a low swampy area past another *marae*, then up a steep hill to the Tengatangi road and town.

The road between Tarapaku and the beach at Oneroa (Long Sand) was cut through very thick *makatea*, and was among the last sections completed. To the south of Oneroa there's an old pig fence and a trail to Takauroa Beach. Some sink holes are in the nearby reef, and snorkelers can try the section between the sink holes and Matai Landing, if the water is calm.

**The Cave of the Kopeka**
Last, but definitely not least, is the famous **Anatakitaki**, also called the Cave of the Kopeka. *Ana-Taki-Taki* is literally translated as "the cave to which one needs a guide." You had better believe it!

The tedious forty-minute hike through the razor-sharp *makatea* is usually led by Tangi Jimmy, and he's kind enough to slow down to a visitor's pace through the rough sections. Cost for the tour is NZ$18, and it's available most days, including Sunday.

You'll need a flashlight for the cave. Roger has extras, but bring a pocket model just in case. Wear your grungiest clothes, and sneakers or walking shoes.

There's a short climb down a hole to the cave entrance, but the main cave is large and not a difficult walk. As you head into the darkness you suddenly hear the rapid "click-click-click" of a tiny black swiftlet. Soon a dozen more fly by, heading to their nests in the high ledges of the pitch-black cave. This is *kopeka* country.

Atiu is the only island in the world where this little bird lives. It's a unique creature in other ways, as it never stops flying once it leaves the cave. It collects small flying insects and nesting material in flight, then returns to the cave to feed its young and rest at night.

Ornithologists theorize that the clicking is used as an echo-location system, as they only click in the cave. Tangi says the birds---which are all over the island during the daytime---usually don't click in the open, but will just before it's about to rain.

**The Legend of Ake**
A legend tells of young Rangi, who married his beloved Ake. They were happy for some years, but Ake soon became depressed as she had not produced a child for Rangi. He thought her depression was due to her working alone at home, so he had a young woman move in with them. Ake grew even more depressed, thinking he preferred the younger woman. Ake and Rangi quarrelled, and Ake ran away.

Rangi and the villagers searched the island for weeks, then months, but there was no trace of Ake.

Years passed, and Rangi still longed for his beloved Ake. He could not work or grow food, so his friends fed and clothed him. He searched for many years, until he was old and grey.

While resting in the bush one day, a small red bird fluttered by in a curious manner. Rangi followed it for an hour into the thick *makatea*, where no one had ever gone.

He came upon a deep hole in the ground, surrounded by sharp *makatea*. There, sitting at the bottom of the hole, was an old woman. It was Ake!

She had run into the jungle after their quarrel, and slipped while wandering in the *makatea*. She fell down the hole and broke her leg, and was unable to climb out, even after her leg healed. She lived for all these years on fruits and berries that dropped into the hole.

Rangi hurried back to the village for help, and Ake was saved. They spent the next few years together, happy once again, and eventually died within a few days of each other.

There are many lessons to be learned from this tale, but for visitors thinking of searching for caves on their own in the thick *makatea*, the most appropriate advice is "get a guide!"

# TAKUTEA

Population:    Uninhabited
Area:        0.5 sq.mi.

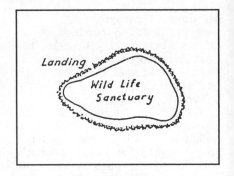

This small coral sand cay lies only 9 miles northwest of Atiu, and is communally owned by the Atiuans as native trust land. The highest point is only 20 feet above sea level, and most of the island is covered in coconut palms.

Takutea has been designated a **Wildlife Sanctuary**, and thousands of red-tailed **tropicbirds** (*tavake*) and red-footed **boobies** nest on the island. It's one of the most important sea bird breeding areas in the entire Pacific.

There is no coastal lagoon, but a **submerged coral shelf** spreads for a half-mile to the southeast, at a depth of 600 feet. Numerous channels in the shelf provide perfect conditions for sea life, and fishing is excellent.

**Mariri**, an early chief of Atiu, often fished offshore, and once caught a rare white *ku*, a cousin of the common red *ku* (squirrelfish). To commemorate this event he named the island *Taku-Ku-Tea*, My White Fish. This was later shortened to its present name.

**Captain Cook** sighted the island on April 4, 1777, after leaving Atiu. Some crew members went ashore to gather coconuts and swamp grass. They saw some huts, but no permanent settlement. Atiuans had told Cook it was called *Enua-Iti* (Small Land), a name still used on occasion.

Takutea was declared a British protectorate in 1889. In 1902 the Land Court awarded it to an Atiuan chief, who then presented it as a gift to the King of England. In 1903 it was considered as a possible penal colony, but Manuae was chosen instead as it had a resident plantation manager. In 1938 the court declared Takutea native land, and voided the gift to Britain. In 1950 the Land Court finally ruled that it should be managed by the Atiuan chiefs as trustees for the people.

Takutea is the only island in the country that has not had a permanent population. Copra cutters visit each year, and **feathers** from the red-tailed tropicbird are collected for traditional costumes. Small numbers of **seabird eggs** can be legally collected for food.

The tiny **landing** on the northwest is dangerous due to offshore currents. A small **freshwater well** in the center of the island is named *Vai-Piro* ("Stink Water") due to its odor and rusty color.

Government permission is usually required for a visit, but if you're on Atiu you could probably go along on a copra or egg-gathering trip.

Air Rarotonga has day-trips to Atiu and Mauke, and a fly-over of Takutea is usually included.

# MAUKE

Population:   639
Area:        7.1 sq.mi.

Mauke, the easternmost island, is part of *Nga-Pu-Toru* (The Three Roots), with Atiu and Mitiaro. Like Mitiaro, it was ruled by Atiu until 1902.

It's even less commercial than Atiu, but does have two pleasant accommodations. There's no lagoon, and hikes, caves, and the friendly Maukeans are the main attractions. The beaches are quite nice, but swimming is not good, as the reef fronts the shore. There are some refreshing water caves, sea caves and bathtub beaches (reef holes).

Mauke doesn't get many tourists, but those that do visit will feel like family members after two or three days.

If you want peace and quiet, this is the place to go. There are few vehicles, no dogs, and minimal distractions. As one local friend succinctly said, "There's plenty to do---mainly nothing!"

**Orientation**
Mauke is a smaller version of Atiu, and was similarly formed by an upthrust of a coral atoll about 100,000 years ago. It's flatter than Atiu, but the ring of fossilized coral---the *makatea*---is a mile wide, twice that of Atiu. Caves, both wet and dry, dot the *makatea*, which is not quite as rugged as that on Atiu.

The central plateau is rich volcanic soil, which supports a wide variety of crops. Like Atiu, large taro swamps lie between the plateau and the *makatea*.

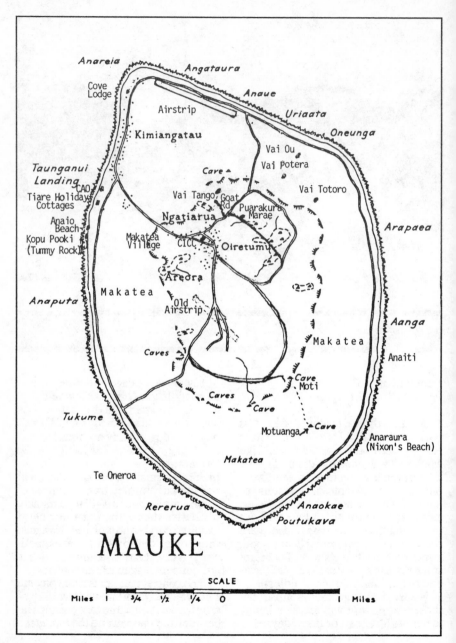

MAUKE

SCALE

Miles 1 ¾ ½ ¼ 0 1 Miles

The settlement pattern is unusual. **Areora, Ngatiarua**, and tiny **Makatea** are clustered in the center, and are collectively called **Oiretumu**. On the northwest coast is **Kimiangatau**, founded by Catholic converts at the turn of the century. Both accommodations are in Kimiangatau, but the central settlement is not far, as it's a pretty small island.

### Getting There
Air Rarotonga has flights Monday-Friday, for NZ$284/RT. Some stop at Atiu or Mitiaro, which can be included in a package at a slight additional cost. For packages, reconfirm your routing *before* you leave Raro, *and* during your trip. Be sure your flights will stop as planned, and not return to Raro.

Always make sure your baggage is not unloaded if you stop at Atiu. Few tourists go to Mauke and Mitiaro, and Atiu's airport crew may assume all tourist-type luggage is destined there.

### HISTORY
Chief **Uke**, descended from gods, arrived after a long voyage from Avaiki, fatherland in the sky. After a peaceful sleep he awoke and named it **Akatoka-manava**, Place Where My Heart Rested. Later generations called it **Ma-Uke**, Land of Uke, but the original name is used in songs and on formal occasions.

Uke's beautiful daughter married a son of Chief Atiu-mua of Atiu, and their descendants settled both islands.

Despite this relationship, Atiuans treated Mauke as a feudal serfdom. Rongomatane and other chiefs raided Mauke, stole the women and food, and killed and ate the men. Our Atiu chapter details a typical raid.

The three Atiuan chiefs each had a district on Mauke, and appointed a Maukean chief to carry out their dictates. Commoners not abiding the local chiefs had to answer to their Atiuan superiors, who were rarely sympathetic.

### European Contact
After Rongomatane was converted by **John Williams**, he took the missionary to Mauke and Mitiaro. Williams was the first European to land here, on June 23, 1823. The conversion of Mauke came quickly, as Rongomatane's strong suggestion to burn their idols was readily accepted by the fearful Maukeans.

The raids stopped after both islands had converted. In 1902 the colonial government granted self-rule to Mauke.

### The Divided Church
The large **Ziona CICC Church** in Areora was built in 1882, but it was not your typical cooperative project.

Having decided a new church was needed, the people of Areora and Ngatiarua decided to build one large church to serve both villages. Each contributed workers and material, and the exterior was soon completed.

Trouble began when they couldn't agree on the interior's design. Tempers flared, and a compromise was finally reached: they built a wall down the middle, and each village finished half the church in its own way. Two entrances were cut, each with its own design, and one large church became two small ones, joined at the hip.

When a new pastor arrived he convinced the villagers to accept another compromise: remove the wall, put the pulpit on the centerline, and he'd keep one foot on each side during the service.

The church remains that way today, with two entrances, two interior halves with different designs, and the pastor still straddles the centerline on Sunday.

**The Divided Island**
The British allowed religious freedom in 1888, and Catholics soon arrived. By 1904 one chief had converted, and disputes arose with London Missionary Society (LMS) members in his district.

Partly due to his new-found power after Atiuan rule ended in 1902, the Catholic chief took the extraordinary step of relocating his followers to a new village. After exploring the island he chose its present site, and named it **Kimiangatau**, "a proper search."

Mauke is one of the few islands with a large Catholic following, about 45%. CICC membership is comparable, while the rest are split between the Seventh Day Adventists and Mormons. This small island of 700 has two CICC churches, two Catholic churches, an SDA church, and a Mormon church.

**Mauke Today**
Mauke has become self-supporting through centralized planning and hard work. Cooperatives export snow peas, mangoes, watermelons, peppers, cabbages and pole beans. Schoolboys have a cooperative which produces taro, arrowroot, sweet potato and bananas.

The rare *maire* vine is extinct on most islands, but it grows well on Mauke. The leaf is used in **Mauke Maire** medicinal oil, and NZ$100,000 is earned from the sale of *maire* garlands in Hawaii, where they are used on special occasions. There are some *maire* vines on the way to Motuanga cave.

**WHERE TO STAY AND EAT**
Both accommodations are near---but not right on---the coast in Kimiangatau. **Tiare Holiday Cottages** (35-102, 35-077, or via Air Raro) sit amid palms on the south. Tautara and Kura Purea are friendly hosts. He's the Government Representative, and may show you around if he has the time.

Three older cottages are handcrafted in part from coconut fronds (*kikau*). You feel very "South Pacific" with the mosquito nets and thatched roof. Furnishings are basic, with 2 or 3 beds and a dresser. The toilet/cold-shower block is outside, past the open-air kitchen and dinette. Rates are NZ$25/40, sgl/dbl.

The newer unit is good for couples, w/double bed, kitchen, shower/WC, and veranda. Rates are NZ$35/50, sgl/dbl.

You can cook or order meals. Breakfast or lunch is NZ$5, and an absolutely enormous dinner---chicken, octopus, fish, taro, sweet potato, salad, chop suey, fruit, bread---is only NZ$9.

**Cove Lodge** (35-888/fax 35-094, or via Air Raro) is a large 2-br house on the north. Dr. Archie and Kura Guinea are also congenial hosts. He's a Scotsman, former national Medical Officer, and ham radio operator (ZK1CT). She organizes the *maire* cooperative.

There are 2 baths, and guests share a lounge, kitchen, and dining area. The water tank is on the roof, so you may get a warm shower in the late afternoon. Rates are NZ$28/44, sgl/dbl. You'll cook most of your meals, but sometimes Archie and Kura offer dinner for NZ$9.

As you've probably guessed, there are no restaurants. Small shops have packaged foods, honey and cold beer, but little produce. What locals don't use themselves is exported. Your hosts may know friends willing to sell some vegies.

The Purea's run the general store in Areora, **Wendy's Shop**, no relation to the burger places. It's open weekdays, 9am-4pm, and Fri/Sat evenings. **Aretoa Store**, on the left before you reach Areora, is next to the bakery---which is closed if there is no flour. Baguettes are then flown in from Rarotonga!

Kimiangatau has tiny "family shops," which sell basic items from a room in a private home. Ask for the closest one.

Mauke is a good place to include coconuts in your diet. Drink from the green ones, and eat the meat of the brown ones. Look for sprouted nuts on the beach, with sweet *uto* inside.

Try "Laurette's Coffee": add a teaspoon of instant coffee to a cup of coconut milk. No sweetener is necessary!

## GETTING AROUND
Your hosts will meet you at the airport. As a matter of fact, half the island will meet you at the airport!

Mauke is only 16 km (10 mi) around, so you can walk most places. Roads are mostly sand, and pretty flat. Tautara has a motorbike he rents for NZ$15. Archie has two pushbikes (NZ$5 each), and may rent out the old jeep.

My motorbike had no rearview mirror, but as Tautara explained, "there's no traffic, so there's never anyone behind you!" The headlight was out, so at night I used my flashlight.

## NIGHTLIFE
Mauke is one island where the term must be used *very* loosely. Occasionally there are dances, and on Friday there might be a volleyball game. Saturday is bingo night at the Catholic Church.

You may attend the Mauke version of the tumunu, called **The Syndicate**. There's no regular schedule, however, so you'll have to ask around about this.

### Nighttime Peace and Quiet
Like Aitutaki, dogs are prohibited. As one local said: "Only uncivilized people feed dogs instead of people."

At the stroke of midnight the generator stops, and Mauke becomes one of the most peaceful places on earth. The only sounds are the waves crashing on the distant reef, and the dull thuds of coconuts dropping on the nearby sand. The air is clear, and it would take months to count the stars.

## PRACTICALITIES
The **Post Office** in Kimiangatau is also the liquor store. Tautara can handle limited **currency exchange** at Wendy's Shop, but bring what you need. The small **hospital** where Archie works is north of Cove Lodge. **Electrical power** is on from 6am-midnight. Most locals speak English. On Mauke, use *meitaki ra-nui-nui* for "thank you very much!"

**Sunday** is a day of rest. Wear appropriate clothes if you attend **church services**, and always keep swimwear confined to the beach.

**Shopping**: A crafts center is opposite the rugby field, on the road south of Areora. It's sometimes open weekdays. Look for pandanus hats and mats, and excellent carvings, including the famous phallic canoe bailers. **Wendy's** may have T-shirts and some souvenirs.

## AROUND THE ISLAND

**Kimiangatau** was founded in 1904 by the breakaway *ariki*, and it remains mainly Catholic. **St. Mary's Church** and school face the triangular village green. Towards the landing sits the **Post Office Building**. It once housed the **jail**, but that section recently burned down. They'd get "about one prisoner a year, usually a drunk." Crime is obviously not a major problem on Mauke, and there are no immediate plans to rebuild it.

The passage at **Tanganui Landing** was enlarged by exploding old bombs in the reef until the new barge could squeeze through. Boats still have to "surf" in on large waves.

Flying fish (*maroro*) abound during certain lunar phases. Just 100 yds offshore the bottom drops to 12,000ft, and tuna are plentiful. See the local fishermen about buying one for dinner.

South of Tanganui, behind Tautura's home, is the **Marae O Rongo**, one of the three *maraes* on Mauke.

The **Hospital** and **Clinic** are up north, past Cove Lodge. Archie may show you around if he's not busy.

The house before the airport is the family home of **Julian Dashwood** (1899-1971). *Rakau* ("Wood") arrived in the 1930's after teaching in Istanbul, farming in South Africa and planting rubber in Malaya. He married a local and managed a small store here.

The talented writer was elected to government, and served as Minister of Public Works until he tired of politics in the 1960's. He spent the remainder of his years in this little house in Kimiangatau, a portrait of Lenin said to be the prominent decoration in his living room. His books, written under the pen name Julian Hillas, include *South Seas Paradise* (1965), about his time on Mauke.

### Central Villages

At Kimiangatau's central triangle the coastal road continues south. Instead, take the inland fork through the *makatea*. The houses on the right are part of the tiny village called **Makatea**, which borders Areora. You'll pass the **power station** on your right, then **Mauke College** (high school), built in 1973. The college has an *Are Rau*, a one-room museum, open on some afternoons. Further on is the old **Ariki Palace**, across from the **Aretoa Shop**.

The locally-famous **fork-in-the-road sign** welcomes you to **Ngatiarua** on the left, and **Areora** and part of Makatea on your right. Let's turn right.

The **town hall** is on the left, as is **Wendy's Shop**, which also serves as the ANZ Bank. On the right are neat houses with orchids growing in old coconut husks, which retain moisture.

On the left is the highlight of the tour, the **Ziona CICC Church**, built in 1882. The origin of the divided church was covered in the History section, but you should also note the Chilean pesos inlaid in the pulpit railing.

Chilean money was used throughout the Pacific in the 1800's. When the British arrived in 1888 they tried to introduce sterling, but locals refused to accept it, as Tahitian traders required payment in pesos. It was not until 1901 that sterling finally replaced the peso. Trade and ties with New Zealand soon grew, and contacts with Tahiti began to diminish.

The road splits at the picturesque **Catholic Church**. The right fork passes the sometimes-open **Crafts Center** and the **old airstrip**, now a tiny cattle farm. Up the hill is the new **reservoir**, a favorite of the local ducks. **Marae Rangimanuka**, the *marae* of Chief Uke, is in the thick brush past the old runway.

Turn and head back towards town, but turn right just before the Catholic Church to reach the inland plantations. This **back plantation road** takes you by taro patches in the low swampy areas, then rises up past vegetable gardens, melon patches, and mango groves. This is the heartland of Mauke, and should not be missed.

The back plantation road splits in the center of the island. The main track to the right leads to the airport road and the coast, while the track to the left brings you past the whitewashed **Puarakura Marae**, still used for ceremonies. After you pass this *marae* you're soon back in Ngatiarua. Turn left to return to the fork-in-the-road sign.

## Caves
In Ngatiarua is a large open swimming cave, called **Vai Tango** (Water Goes Farther). Start by facing the fork-in-the-road sign, then bear left through

little Ngatiarua village. A short while after the houses end is a dirt road on the left. If you see lots of goats, you've got the right place. At the end of "Goat Road" is a foot trail down to the cave.

Vai Tango is a freshwater pool 50 feet long, 10 feet wide, and 12 feet deep. It's crystal clear, cool and refreshing, and there's not a mosquito in sight. It rises and falls with the tide, as it's connected to the sea through underground passages in the *makatea*. It's not salty, though, as it's too far from the coast. Local kids play in it after school and on Saturdays.

Vai Tango is easy to reach and close to town, but **Motuanga** is neither. This famous cave, also known as the "Cave of a Hundred Rooms," is hidden deep in the thick *makatea*. It's a twenty-minute walk past the end of a dirt road, southeast of the old airstrip. You'll need a guide to get there, and hopefully you can all get a ride to the trailhead.

Wear sneakers or walking shoes, as the *makatea* is sharp in some places. It's not really a strenuous hike, being more tedious than difficult.

You enter the cave by descending a narrow hole in the *makatea*, reminiscent of the start of the film *Journey to the Center of the Earth*. Bring your flashlight, as after the first cavern it becomes pitch black. After crawling on your belly through two sloped caves you finally come to an incredibly cool and clear pool of water, deep in the bottom of the third cave (Plate 32). It's very refreshing after the long hike and muddy descent.

There are supposedly one hundred rooms, but no one has gotten to all of them. They say the last one ends at the sea. To get to cave four we would have had to dive deep into the pool, then swim through an underwater passage of some unknown distance. Adventure is one thing, recklessness is another. We decided to wait until a scuba shop opens on Mauke.

An easier cave to find is **Moti**, which is near the trailhead to Motuanga. This large open cave is easily reached by crawling down vines and a makeshift ladder, but the brackish water is not very inviting.

On the north side of the island are three other water caves, **Vai Ou, Vai Totoro**, and **Vai Potera**. You're better off using a guide to find these.

## Beaches and Sea Caves

The reef fronts the entire coastline, so there's no lagoon for swimming. There are, however, some nice sandy beaches, mostly on the west and south. The north and northeast coasts are pretty rocky, but they also have some scattered patches of sand.

The best spots for a saltwater dip are the usual **bathtub beaches** (reef holes) and some **sea caves** at the base of the coastal cliffs.

Starting from Kimiangatau, we'll head south and go counter-clockwise around the island. Tracks through the *makatea* lead to lots of beaches, and several large ones are easy to find.

Fifty yards south of the Tiare Holiday Cottages is a track to the nice beach at **Anaio**. In the reef are several bathtub beaches, and if you go left around the large rock outcrop---at low tide---you reach **Kopu Pooki** (Tummy Rock). This large sea cave is about the size of a motel pool, and very refreshing.

Continue south along the shore road to the small beach at **Tukume**, where an inland road meets the coast. You'll find other secluded beaches nearby, at the end of small tracks to the coast.

A little further south is one of the best beaches on the island, **Te Oneroa** (The Long Sand). There are two nice picnic shelters made of thatched coconut leaves, and you'll find some bathtub beaches and sea caves along the reef. This is a very popular picnic spot.

Near the island's southern tip is a grove of barringtonia (*utu*) trees and a small concrete blockhouse. Past these look for a double beach with a picnic shed, and a pit toilet across the road. The beach is called **Anaraura** (Many Caves), for the nearby sea caves.

The beach on your right as you face the sea has been nicknamed **Nixon's Beach** by the locals. Once on the beach, look to the left for the profile of the former US president, on the dark rock outcrop jutting into the water.

Finally, further up the east coast, before it gets real rocky, is a track to the beach at **Anaiti** (Little Cave). This is another of the peaceful little spots on a peaceful little island, where there's "plenty to do---mainly nothing!"

# MITIARO

Population:  249
Area:       8.6 sq.mi.

Mitiaro is the third of the *Nga-Pu-Toru* (The Three Roots). It's the flattest and economically poorest, with little arable land. The center has two brackish lakes and a swamp, and *makatea* covers the rest. Locals grow crops in "soil islands" in the swamps (Plate 31). The beaches are not for swimming, as the reef meets the shore, but reef holes and water caves are very refreshing.

Mitiaro is as low-key as you can get. Rarotonga will seem like a bustling metropolis after a few days here. Thoreau would have loved Mitiaro, as it comes complete with its own version of Walden Pond.

## Orientation

Mitiaro, like Atiu and Mauke, was once a volcano that sank to become a coral atoll. It was also thrust upward 100,000 years ago, but unlike the others, it only rose up about 20 feet. The coral ring still died, forming the harsh *makatea*, but the central lagoon barely rose above sea level, leaving a large swamp. The high spots became the soil islands.

Everyone lives in one settlement on the west coast, but it's technically four villages---**Atai, Auta, Mangerei** and **Takaue**, north to south. Each is only a block long, and it's hard to know exactly where one ends and the next begins. The government buildings are in the Takaue section, so the settlement is usually referred to by that name.

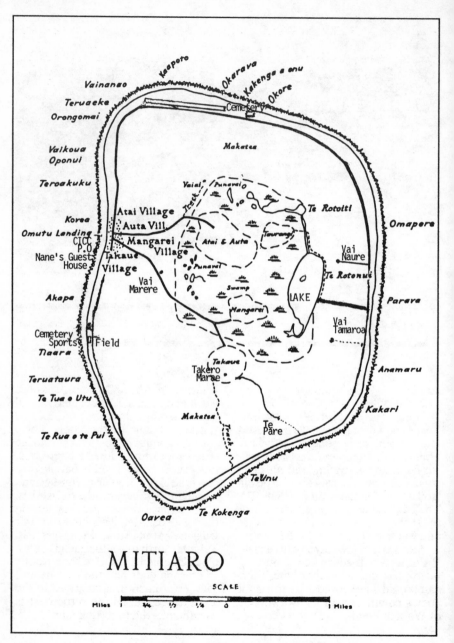

Vainanao
Kaapoto
Okarava
Kokenga a enu
Okore
Teruaeke
Cemetery
Orongomai
Vaikoua
Oponui
Makatea
Teroakuku
Vaiai
Punavaio
Te Rotoiti
Omapere
Atai Village
Track
Auta Vill
Korea
Omutu Landing
CICC
Mangarei
Atai & Auta
Taurangi
Vai
P.O.
Village
Naure
Nane's Guest
Takaue
Te Rotonui
House
Village
Punavai
Vai
Marere
Swamp
LAKE
Parava
Akapa
Mangarei
Vai
Tamaroa
Cemetery
Sports
Field
Tiaara
Takaue
Teruataura
Takero
Anamaru
Marae
Te Tua e Utu
Makatea
Te
Kakari
Te Rua e te Pui
Track
Pare
Te Unu
Oavea
Te Kokenga

# MITIARO

SCALE

Miles 1   3/4   1/2   1/4   0                    1 Miles

The villages were inland near the soil islands---"foodlands"---until the missionaries moved them to the coast. Locals still travel inland daily, on ancient coral roads, to tend their crops.

Locals recently completed the round-the-island-road, a task that took several years. The construction force is hard-working, but its numbers are limited on this lightly-populated island. New roads were also built through the *makatea* to two prime attractions: **Lake Rotonui**, and the **Vai Naure** water cave.

### Getting There
Air Raro flies 4 times weekly, for NZ$284/RT. Everyone is on a package, with Mauke and/or Atiu. If the plane stops either place make sure your bags are not unloaded. Always reconfirm routings on multi-island packages.

## HISTORY
Early history is entwined with Atiu, which conquered Mitiaro centuries ago. Atiuan chiefs appointed local chiefs to run their colonial districts.

The traditional name is **Nukuroa**, "Large Land," as the conquering Atiuans found it larger than their Mauke colony. The present name has been translated as "Face of the Ocean." Some think it comes from **Miti-Vai-Aro**, "drink the coconut milk," a reference to licking the blood of defeated Atiuans.

Two famous battles are memorialized. In the first, Atiuans were invited to a big feast. As the guests grated coconuts for dinner, they were all killed. All but **Maui**, an Atiuan chief saved by a part-Atiuan Mitiaroan. Maui returned home to recount the massacre.

Locals knew Atiuans would seek revenge, so a great fort, **Te Pare**, was built deep in the *makatea*. Sharp rocks surrounded it to protect from invaders.

Years later Maui's descendants, led by **Chief Rongomatane**, attacked Mitiaro, hoping to steal the beautiful daughter of **Chief Maaro** of Takaue.

The Atiuans were sighted off the coast, and everyone went to Te Pare. They knew it would take hours for the bare-footed Atiuans to reach the fort and scale the pointed rocks around it.

The Atiuans landed and devised an ingenious battle strategy. They laid their spears end-to-end in double rows on the *makatea*, and walked quickly inland, moving the spears as they advanced. When they reached the sharp rocks at Te Pare they quietly formed bridges over them with the spears, then suddenly attacked the surprised Mitiaroans.

As they battle raged, Chief Maaro realized their goal was to take his daughter. He ordered his sons to kill her, thinking this would end the fight. They refused. He then ordered his sons to kill *him*, so the Atiuans could not revel in eating a chief they had killed in battle. His sons did as he commanded, carrying him to **Takero Marae** for the sacrifice. Atiu won the battle and ruled the island until 1902, when New Zealand legally ended Atiu's control.

### European Contact
Rongomatane arrived with missionary **John Williams** on June 20, 1823, just a few years after the battle of Te Pare. It's not surprising locals quickly converted at Rongomatane's suggestion. Catholic missionaries later had some success, and today visiting officials must make two presentations---one at the CICC, and another at the Catholic hall.

### Mitiaro Today
The first thing you'll notice is the shyness of the people. Some misinterpret this as a dislike for tourists, but in fact

*Mitiaro* piere

locals are very friendly, and warm up quickly. They just don't get many visitors, and aren't sure how to act.

You'll see the elderly and the young, but not many in between. Most teenagers attend school on Atiu, Mauke, or Rarotonga, and few return to Mitiaro.

Things move slowly here. A three-week project to extend the runway took a bit longer, as the old backhoe broke down. A replacement part was finally located in England---a year later!

Many banana groves were recently damaged by hurricanes. Now arrowroot is popular, as it can be dried and stored for months. Taro, breadfruit, chilies, limes and sweet potato thrive in the foodlands. Sandalwood and medicinal *maire* vines grow in the *makatea*, but are not commercial crops. Beautiful pandanus handbags are exported to Raro.

Another export is *piere* (dried bananas). Ripe bananas are peeled, halved, and sun-dried for 5 days. Then they're wrapped in dried banana and pandanus leaves, and shipped off to Raro.

Goats, chickens and pigs are kept in medieval-looking coral pens in the *makatea*. Large coconut crabs, found in the outer *makatea*, are considered a delicacy. Crayfish are caught on the reef, and used for food or fish bait.

## WHERE TO STAY AND EAT

When it's open, visitors stay at **Nane Pokoati's Guesthouse** (36-107), also called **Nukuroa Guesthouse**. It's her home, and has a guest bedroom, enclosed veranda, kitchen, dining room, and shower/WC. Guests get the veranda or the bedroom; the latter is quieter in the morning. Water supplies are very low, so conserve on usage. Showers are cold in the morning, but the tank warms up in the afternoon.

Rates are only NZ$46/70, sgl/dbl, including all meals. The food is great: fish, chicken, vegetables and fruit. You can buy beer and liquor at the Post Office. Tiny shops are nearby, and visitors often supply dessert. Book via Air Raro, or call her direct.

Nane closes the house if she goes overseas, or takes time off to care for relatives. Always call in advance to see if she'll be there. If not, Air Raro or the CITA can arrange accommodation.

## GETTING AROUND

If you're expected, the big truck will meet you. If you're not, ride in on the flatbed cargo trailer, behind the tractor.

I wasn't expected, so I got the trailer. The pilot joked that I had paid for First Class, so they smiled and escorted me up front, onto the flour sacks!

You can walk most places, but a motorbike is handy. If you rent Nane's extra motorbike (NZ$10), she'll give you a free half-day tour. Nane can also check with her neighbor Metua, who may give a tour by truck for NZ$10.

29. Kids on Mitiaro are shy at first, but warm up quickly
30. Life on the outer islands is more traditional than on Rarotonga

31. Mitiaro: Lake Rotonui in the distance, with foodland "islands" in swamps to the right
32. Mauke: this cold and refreshing pool is deep inside Motuanga Cave.

*33. Mangaia: this CICC Church is in Ivirua, the most remote village in the Southern Cooks.*
*34. Mangaia: a villager walks through a spectacular "road cut" in the* makatea.

35. Rakahanga: lagoonside beach   36. Nassau: traditional thatched hut
37. Penrhyn: Omoka village at sunset   38. Pukapuka: relaxing in the afternoon
39. Tom Neale, the Hermit of Suwarrow   40. Manihiki: just another day in Paradise

## NIGHTLIFE
Weekend beach picnics may go all night. Nane has a VCR---start early, as the power stops at midnight! Dances are rare, but tourists once organized one, NZ$15 total for a band and hall!

## PRACTICALITIES
There's a small **medical clinic**, with resident nurse. Make **telephone calls** at Nane's or the Post Office. **Currency exchange** is limited, so bring funds from Raro. **Electrical power** is 6am-midnight.

Sunday is a day of rest. Dress appropriately if you attend church services. Avoid swimwear in the village. Ask before taking photos, as adults are very shy. Kids, however, will love it.

**Language:** Most people speak English. *Meitaki ranuinui* is "Thank you very much."

**Shopping:** Women in the *Nukuroa Vainetini* crafts group weave beautiful pandanus handbags. Woodcarvings, *kumete* (wood bowls), and pandanus mats may be available. Leis (*'eis*) with small yellow pandanus flowers aren't sold, but you might receive one as a gift.

## AROUND THE ISLAND
**Main Settlement:** Nane's is in **Takaue**, which is the south end of town. **Mangerei** is a block inland, at the **clinic** and **Public Works** depot. **Auta** is the dozen houses north of the CICC, and **Atai** is the few houses past Auta. **Taurangi** was the fifth inland village. The foodland is tended by the remaining families, but ---surprisingly for Mitiaro---their 2 or 3 houses are not considered a village.

The settlement is clean and neat, and Norfolk pines dot the town. Near modern houses sit thatched *kikau* huts, a rarity in the Southern Cooks. These are used by older kids, who still use the kitchen and facilities of the main house.

The white limestone **Cook Islands Christian Church (CICC)** has a hand-carved pulpit and multi-colored windows. Like other large buildings, it has rainwater pipes and a storage tank.

Nearby are the **Post Office** and **Government Office**. Pay NZ$5 for a "road permit" (donation for road maintenance) if you'll be using the roads to Lake Rotonui or Vai Naure cave.

The **Omutu Landing** was recently widened. It was so narrow only one boat could use it---now three can unload a waiting freighter. You can swim here, and snorkeling is good at dawn and dusk. Fishermen head out at night for tuna, barracuda, and snapper. If they're successful, you'll have fish for dinner.

### Cemeteries
The strangest sight for visitors has got to be the gravestone decorations: pots and pans, cups and saucers, and kitchen utensils! Follow the road south of Nane's for a mile, then turn right to the cemetery, before the sports field.

The custom relates to a belief that the spirits of the dead may come home for a meal, so their own cookware would be appropriate. It's hard not to pause at the small graves decorated with tiny cups and baby bottles.

There's a small cemetery on the north, past the airstrip. The graves are not as elaborate, but many are also decorated with utensils and cookware.

### Foodlands
Villages were once inland, near the soil islands called "foodlands." Roads from the coast were built hundreds of years ago by placing coral boulders in the swamp ten feet apart, then filling the space between with rocks and sand.

Three foodlands are on the north inland road, and two are on the south inland road. Take the latter, near Nane's.

**Takaue Foodland** is the largest. It's unique since it borders the *makatea*, but you must still pass through the swamp to reach it. There are nice picnic spots on the first fork to the right after the fruit groves. Continue to a large clearing, where locals often stop for lunch.

Tiny **Mangerei Foodland** is my favorite. Bear left at the fork in the middle of the swamp. It's very strange to be in a huge swamp, then suddenly see an oasis of palm trees ahead. You pass through arrowroot, banana, and other plantations, and it ends in a grove of shade tress, a nice spot for a picnic.

Return almost to town, but bear right near the pig corrals. The north inland road will soon be on your right.

**Atai** and **Auta Foodlands** share a large soil island with the small **Taurangi Foodland**. They are completely surrounded by the swamp. At the end of the road in the Taurangi section you reach the muddy trail to Lake Rotoiti, a twenty-minute slosh to the east.

### Caves

The closest cave is **Vai Marere**, a ten-minute walk on the south inland road. It's an open cave with a sulphur pool, good for relaxing or washing your hair.

Off the north inland road is a half-mile track to **Vai Ai**, the freshwater Sandalwood Cave. Mitiaro is one of the few islands in the Cooks where this valuable tree grows, but it's usually in the thick *makatea*. There are some trees near the cave, but you'll need Nane's help to find the larger groves.

Two open water caves are reached from the east coast. The most accessible is **Vai Naure**. This was once a tough hike through the *makatea*, but the new road makes it a five-minute ramble from the road entrance. Pay your NZ$5 at the PO for maintenance costs. The gate at the road entrance is usually unlocked. Jump in from the rocks, or carefully climb down into the freshwater pool.

The women make a *tere vai* ("journey to water") a few times each year, often when relatives visit in December. They pile into a truck and usually head to Vai Naure. After a wild trip of singing and dancing, the leader says a prayer and jumps in. Everyone follows, throwing coins, soap, and lucky charms.

Men can join them, but must travel in a separate truck so the ladies can get as wild as they like without interference.

Another open water cave is **Vai Tamaroa**, with 30' cliffs around it. It's a half-hour walk through the *makatea*, with some sandalwood on the way. Look for the Boys' Brigade "tombstone" marker at the trailhead on the east coast road, south of Lake Rotonui.

### Lakes

The two brackish lakes are famous for their tasty eels---*itiki*---and succulent freshwater prawns. **Rotonui** (Big Lake) is now easily reached by a road from the east. Previously you had to walk a mile through the *makatea*, or slosh through the mud from Taurangi Foodland. Make your NZ$5 donation at the PO for your road permit.

The shores around the lake are peat bogs, and if you jump up and down the earth moves easily. I'd think twice about a swim in the muddy, brackish water.

The lake is the site of an ambitious milkfish farming project, begun in 1984 under the United Nations Development Program. Nane can introduce you to the UNDP coordinator, who can show you around the project.

A boat tour and picnic on the small islet might be a good island fund-raiser. If tourism *really* grows, it might be the site for the future Mitiaro Sheraton!

The smaller of the lakes is named, appropriately, **Rotoiti** (Small Lake). Eels are also grown here, and a tilapia fish farm is planned. This is a tiny lake, and is best approached by the mud trail from Taurangi Foodland.

**Beaches**

South of town, past the cemetery, is the village sports ground. Head through it to the coast, and you'll come to a nice section of sandy beach, which runs all the way back to town. Its traditional name is **Tiaara Beach**, and some locals call it **Lovers' Beach**, or **Sunset Beach**.

The road is now complete around the south coast, and rough tracks in the *makatea* lead down to tiny beaches, some accessible only at low tide.

North of town, near the school, are tracks to the **Oponui** area and **Honeymoon Cave**, which is dry at low tide. At **Okore** is a small, but windy, beach.

**Te Pare and Takero Marae**

The ruins of **Te Pare** are in the *makatea*, near **Te Unu**. A few rocks show the site of the great fort. Nane can arrange a guide, and you must get permission to visit from the *ariki* of Takaue. The same applies to the **Takero Marae**, where Chief Maaro had himself sacrificed during the battle of Te Pare. Although it's close to the road in the Takaue Foodland, it's not well-marked, and you'll probably need a guide to find it.

The main fork in Takaue Foodland leads to a rough track in the *makatea*, which passes tiny caves before reaching the coastal road. This is a longer route to Te Pare. The right fork also leads to a *makatea* track to the coast.

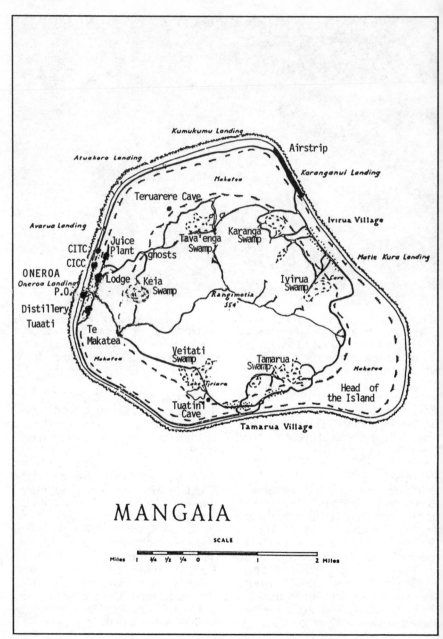

# MANGAIA

SCALE

Miles 1  ¾  ½  ¼  0                    1                              2 Miles

# MANGAIA

| | |
|---|---|
| Population: | 1105 |
| Area: | 20 sq.mi.(est.) |

Mysterious Mangaia is rarely visited by tourists. Perhaps it's the lackluster lodging, or the locals' undeserved reputation as "dour and unfriendly". Whatever the reason, be prepared for something quite unlike the other islands.

It's very rugged, with *makatea* up to 200' high and a mile wide. Rough roads go through spectacular cuts (Plate 34), and some areas have yet to be explored.

Mangaians are fiercely independent, partly due to isolation. It's 127 miles southeast of Rarotonga, and not on any trade routes. Legends are also part of daily life, and many locals won't go inland at night, fearing ghosts. Christians they are, but "Spirits in the Night" could be the island song.

So, come to Mangaia, but bring your walking shoes, compass, and an open mind. Yes, it's for the adventurous, but those that make it will probably enjoy it, and will certainly never forget it!

**Orientation**
Mangaia is the second largest island, but its exact size is unknown. Locals don't recognize the Land Court, and refuse to allow a survey. As one said:

"Once they survey it, they'll want to tell us who owns this piece and that piece. So we head 'em off at the pass, and don't even let 'em get started!"

The *makatea* surrounds a band of taro swamps, and reddish hills rise to **Rangimotia** (554ft, 169m). On the west is split-level **Oneroa**, half on the beach and half on the *makatea*. **Tamarua** lies 4 miles southeast, **Ivirua** 7 miles east.

**Getting There**
Air Raro makes the 50-minute flight Monday through Friday, for NZ$254 roundtrip. Virtually everyone is on a package, for usually 2 or 3 nights.

## HISTORY
Unlike the other islands, Mangaian legends do not include Polynesian discoverers. Mangaia was created directly from the spiritland of *Avaiki*.

Legends say the female spirit **Varima-te-Takere** (The Mud and the Bottom) plucked off a piece of her side and created **Vatea**, the half-man, half-fish father of gods and men. His son **Rongo** fathered three sons by his own daughter, **Tavake**. The sons, including **Rangi**, then took land from the spiritworld to create Mangaia.

Many historians acknowledge Rangi, but think he was a commoner from Rarotonga who led his followers to Mangaia, then created the netherworld legend to hide his classless origins.

The name comes from **Mangaia-Nui-Neneva**---"temporal power monstrously great"---an early title of the most powerful chief. Forty-two wars were fought over this title. Mangaia is also called **A'u A'u, Au Au** or **Ahu Ahu** ("terraced") for its layered *makatea*.

The mountains form six distinct watersheds (*puna*) each run by a *pava* (chief). After British annexation these became *kavana*, from "governor." The most powerful became the *ariki* (high chief), who ruled with help from the *kavana* and district elders. Now called the *Aronga Mana*, this council still rules the island.

**Chief Mautara** banned cannibalism a century before the missionaries came. He believed all Mangaians were related by blood, marriage, or custom, and it wasn't a proper way to treat relatives.

**European Contact**
**Captain Cook** sighted Mangaia on March 29, 1777. Tattooed warriors paddled out, knives secured in slit earlobes (page 12). Seeing a goat, one asked the Tahitian translator what kind of bird it was. Cook asked if they ate human flesh, and they responded "with a mixture of indignation and abhorrence."

Many say Cook didn't land due to the "dour and unfriendly" natives. In fact he feared the reefs, not the locals:

"But I saw, with regret, that the attempt (to land) could not be made... unless at the risk of having our boats filled with water, or staved to pieces."

This is not to say that visitors were welcomed. Missionary **John Williams** stopped in 1823, but did not leave teachers due to the ferocity of the locals. They did accept his gift of some pigs, however, the first on the island.

**Missionaries and Relocation**
Tahitian missionaries **Davida** and **Tiere** landed June 15, 1824. All contact was with Tahiti, until **Maretu** came from Rarotonga in 1839. His bible was in Rarotongan---similar to Mangaian---and became the choice of locals.

Maretu wanted one Christian coastal settlement, so **Tava'enga, Keia**, and **Veitatei** moved to the new village at Oneroa. **Tamarua** and **Ivirua** moved to their present sites, and **Karanga** later joined Ivirua. The locals no longer lived near their taro plantations.

**George Gill**, the first European missionary, arrived in 1845. The chiefs were pleased, as a foreign missionary was a sign of prestige. **William Wyatt Gill** (no relation) arrived in 1852, and stayed 25 years. His *Cook Islands Custom* (1892) describes many Mangaian rituals, including the unique *maninitori* wedding ceremony (see our page 13).

Missionaries had influence, but the Aronga Mana still ruled. They forbade migration to Rarotonga until 1872, and enforced all criminal punishments, including the death penalty.

## Mangaia Today

Pineapple was king in the 1970's and 1980's. A juice plant and distillery were built, and the potent *Mangaia Ara* pineapple liquor was exported. Prices then plunged due to South American competition, and shipping became erratic. In the end the bottom dropped out. No juice. No *Mangaia Ara*. No income.

What to do? Do what they've always done. Grow taro! Taro to the left, taro to the right, taro in the middle. Mangaian taro---*mamio*---is very tasty, and valued throughout the Pacific. Mangaia also exports papayas, and has an experimental vanilla plantation.

## WHERE TO STAY AND EAT

The basic **Mangaia Lodge** (reserve via Air Raro) is on the hill in Oneroa. A nice veranda serves as lounge/dining area, and WC/cold showers are out back. For NZ$35 you get a bed in a shared room, and all meals.

The lodge could use some work. The walls are paper thin, and mice inhabit the attic and sub-floors. At night the roosters crow on the hour, and the dogs bark on the half-hour. Bring earplugs.

In sharp contrast to the lodge itself is the host couple. Metu and Nane are very friendly, and really help out the few visitors that arrive. The food is excellent, with chicken and fish on the menu.

The **CITC**, past the sports field, has a moderate selection of goods. The **MTC Store** has cold beer. **Pokino's Shop** is also on the lower road. The **Post Office** sells beer and liquor, and there's a bakery and donut shop nearby.

## GETTING AROUND

You'll be met on arrival. There are no rentals, but Metu lent me his motorbike and refused to accept any payment. I finally convinced him to take NZ$10 for petrol. The roads are *very* slippery when wet. For an island tour, have Metu or Nane contact Maare and Diana Ngu.

A rough road leads inland to the taro swamps, and a newer road circles most of the island. It's a nice inland walk from Ivirua to Oneroa, but watch out for ghosts in Keia after dark.

## NIGHTLIFE

You're not here for the nightlife, but there may be a dance on the weekend. Local bands put on a good show, and everyone from Ivirua and Tamarua arrives in the local school bus.

## PRACTICALITIES

There's a small **hospital** near the lodge. The **Post Office** handles limited **currency exchange**. Dress appropriately if you attend the **Sunday services** (10am) at the Oneroa CICC. **Electrical power** is 6am-11pm (12pm Fri/Sat). Many locals leave their bedroom light switch on, and use it as their wake-up alarm at 6am. This has caused some interesting incidents, especially since the hospital does not have its own generator (page 39).

**Shopping:** Arrange to see the **Tava'-enga Young Women's Association**'s sculptures and herb pounders made from stalagmites. Ceremonial adzes are in overseas museums, but I didn't see any here. Look for necklaces made from black *pupu* snails, found on the *makatea* after a rain. Some are bleached yellow or white, and hundreds are then threaded together for one necklace. Go next door to the **Bamboo Workshop** to view crafts and woodcarving projects.

**Language:** English is used, but not as much as on other islands. "Thank you very much" is *Meitaki ngao* (nya-o).

## AROUND THE ISLAND

**Oneroa** (Long Sand) is the only split-level village in the Cooks. The lower area, with the CICC and Post Office, is Tava'enga 1, while the upper level, with the Hospital, Bamboo Workshop, Primary School and Lodge, is Tava'enga 2. A steep road through a spectacular cut in the *makatea* connects them.

Before the road cut was made in the 1950's, locals had to walk up and down ancient steps in the *makatea* to reach their taro patches. A set of steps faces the lodge, and leads down to the CITC.

Inland from Tava'enga 2 is Te Makatea village. In pre-missionary days outcasts had to live in the *makatea*, and this may have once been an outcast village.

North of the lodge is the **Primary School** and the old **South Seas Juice Plant**. If you head south past the tiny **Hospital** and cross the inland road, the idle **Mangaia Ara Distillery** is on the right. Down this road is another nice cut through the *makatea*.

In Tava'enga 1 is the impressive **CICC Church**, built in 1889. Its hand-cut beams were originally tied with coconut sennit cord. The bindings were replaced in 1988, leaving only Tamarua and Ivirua CICC's with sennit ties.

You can swim a bit at **Oneroa Landing**, or **Avarua Landing** to the north. Locals catch tuna close to shore, and whales go by in August and September.

Past Avarua Landing is **Atuakoro Landing**, and inland is the **four-story makatea**, visible from the air. Further on is the **airport**, built in 1978.

South of Oneroa is **Tuaati** ("Broken Sea"). Easterly winds wrap around the island and meet here. Captain Cook approached this area, but was put off by the rough seas. Sharp pinnacles of black, grey, and white *makatea* line the coastal road to Tamarua, while tracks lead to **bathtub beaches** in the reef.

### Inland From Oneroa

The heart of Mangaia is along the old inland road. Head inland past **Te Makatea**. A partly-hidden trail on the left leads down the *makatea* to old **Keia**, where the missionaries first started. The stone foundation of an 1840's wooden church is in the **Rupetau** area, near a *marae*, but you'll need a guide for these.

The road forks to **Rangimotia** on the left, and the **Mangaia Forestry Nursery** on the right. "Any Interested Person Is *Mostly* Welcome" weekdays, 7am-4pm. Further on is the **Veitatei swampland**.

**Lake Tiriara** is Mangaia's only year-round lake. It's 25' deep and home to tilapia and eels. The black spot on the high *makatea* wall is **Tuatini Cave** (Thousand Branches), a burial cave you can visit with a guide. One burial cave you can't yet visit is the legendary **Piriteumeume**, where the warm, dry air mummifies whole skeletons. Its location is still a mystery.

### Tamarua

This is split east and west, not up and down. It's on the inner edge of the *makatea*, so the ocean is not visible.

On the west side is **Tamarua CICC**, built by Maretu in 1840. The sennit bindings were repaired in 1988. Chief Parima was the first *ariki* to convert, and Tamarua was the most important village until George Gill arrived in Oneroa in 1845.

A trail at the CICC leads to the large **Tamarua swamp**. The gravel road to the **primary school** and coast marks the centerline of town.

*Canoes hauled cargo to and from freighters until recent years.*

East Tamarua has an odd feeling to it. It's pretty far inland, in the middle of nowhere. One gets the impression it hasn't changed in a hundred years. It's close to the taro swamps, so it may have been the first district of the new village.

### Polynesia's Romeo and Juliet

Near the CICC is the **Rock of Oimara**, a limestone pillar 12' high. Its hollow center has a hole in one side. Legends say Oimara loved beautiful Tavero, but their tribes fought and he was banned from town. He snuck in each night and hid in the rock. Tavero fed him through the hole, and they spoke quietly.

One night she was seen talking to the rock and putting food through the hole. When she left, the chief sent warriors to the rock, and soon spears were aimed down at Oimara. He cried out Tavero's name, then met his death.

### Tamarua to Ivirua

There's an inland road between the villages, but none along the coast, and for good reason. It's extremely rugged four-story *makatea*, where little grows and no one goes. It may be the most remote spot in the entire country.

Mangaia loosely resembles a manta ray, with head to the southeast, fin tips on the north and south, and flat tail at Oneroa. Locals call this remote section the "Head of the Island," and Oneroa the "Tail of the Island." Few people ever venture to the head of the island.

### Ivirua Area

Perched on the sea side of the *makatea*, **Ivirua** has fine ocean views. It's a lovely place, despite being at the ends of the earth, Cook Islands-wise. Technically it's Ivirua on the south and **Karanga** on the north, but it's all called Ivirua.

**Ivirua CICC** is almost as old as Tamarua CICC, and just as beautiful (Plate 33). The original sennit bindings still connect the beams. Note the old concrete water tank, typical of Mangaia, where rainwater supplies the villages. The tiny **Sigma Shop** on the north end of town is the last outpost of commerce in the Cooks.

The inland road on the south side of town goes through an impressive *makatea* cut to **Ivirua swamp**, the only one that never dries up. This area is quite beautiful, with tropical gardens everywhere. Soon you're smack in the middle of the **Karanga swamp**, the last outpost of "the heathens," as the non-converts were called. When you reach the main track ahead turn left, towards Oneroa.

### Ivirua To Oneroa
This is also quite pretty, as streams and shade trees line the track. Small lakes on the right are home to tasty eels, and on the left is a track up Rangimotia.

Near the lakes is a circular track on the right through **Tava'enga swamp**, site of an old village. A trail leads up the *makatea* to **Te Rua Rere**, "the flying hole" cave. The reference is probably to its entrance, a hole in the *makatea* 20' deep, reached by climbing down branches and vines. The cave goes horizontally, and a window in the side offers views of the inland areas. A low cave leads into chambers with skeletons, stalagmites and stalactites. George Tuara (34-105) guides you to the cave entrance, and his son takes you from there. Cost is NZ$15 per person.

Back on the main road, fruit groves appear in the old **Keia** district. You can reach the **Keia swamp** on a track to the left. The main road heads up the *makatea* to Oneroa, where tracks to the right go to Tava'enga 2 and the lodge.

### Rangimotia and Across the Island
There are good views from **Rangimotia**, a moderately strenuous hike. I tried Metu's motorbike, but had to push it up most of the hill. It's not a day I'd want to repeat. A trail bike might make it. Bring munchies, and maybe a compass.

From the lodge, go inland past Te Makatea. Bear left at the fork. At the next fork, left takes you to the Keia swamp, right takes you up Rangimotia.

Take a break at the weather station below the summit. When you reach the highest knobs pick one out and call it Rangimotia. The peak isn't obvious, and three or four seem the same height.

Head due east on the "main" road, to end up near Tamarua. Head north to end up at the lakes west of Ivirua. If you get lost---like I did---aim for church roofs, or shacks near tended taro swamps, which have tracks to the road.

### Spirits in the Night
Aside from taro and caves, Mangaia is famous for its ghosts. William Wyatt Gill wrote of the locals' belief in spirits, and in 1921 Charles Nordhoff wrote:

"More than any other island folk they live in the past, for ghosts walk on Ahu Ahu, and the living commune nightly with the old dead who lie in the *marae*."

His friend's Mangaian mother-in-law went into trances to talk with Rakamoana---a woman who had been dead for twenty-eight generations and was buried in a *marae* in old Keia.

Writer Ron Syme recounted his own evening in old Keia, when an invisible evil force approached him as he walked home. A similar presence at the same spot was described to him by an American visitor, who was delayed in old Keia at sundown after his bike blew a tire.

Well, I'm not superstitious, but you won't catch me in old Keia after dark!

# PALMERSTON

Population:   49
Area:        0.8 sq.mi.

Tiny and remote Palmerston has an identity crisis. It's geographically in the Southern Group, but so far from Rarotonga---310 miles---many think it's in the Northern Group. It's a coral atoll, like most northern islands, which only adds to the confusion.

It's also the only island with a culture more European than Polynesian. All the islanders are descended from Englishman William Marsters (pictured above) and his three Polynesian wives, who settled on the uninhabited island in 1863. *Olde* English is the daily language.

The highest point is only twenty feet above sea level, and hurricanes wash across the six islets and thirty sand cays every decade or so.

## HISTORY

Although graves indicate earlier settlement, the atoll was uninhabited when **Captain Cook** passed by on June 16, 1774. He named it for Lord Palmerston, First Lord of the Admiralty. Cook returned on April 13, 1777, and went ashore to gather swamp grass and coconuts for his cattle. This is the only record of Cook himself setting foot in the country that now bears his name.

Missionaries and traders later stopped for coconuts, and the well-traveled Tahitians once thought of banishing criminals to the atoll.

The *Merchant of Tahiti* rescued four starving white men in 1850. In exchange, they gave the captain whatever "claims" they had to the island. He passed these on to his boss, John Brander, a Scottish trader living in Tahiti.

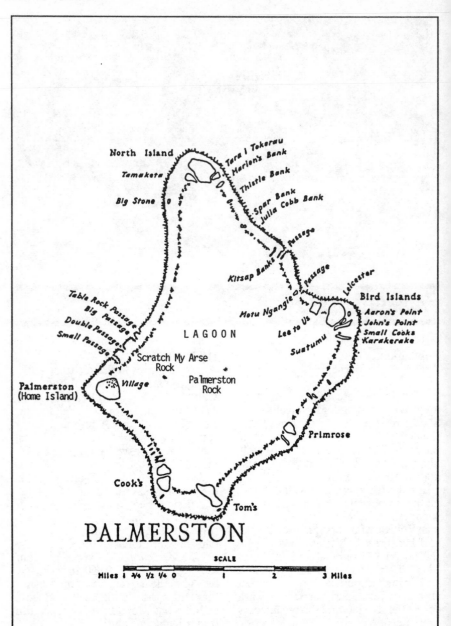

North Island

Tamaketa

Big Stone

Tara I Tokerau

Marion's Bank

Thistle Bank

Spar Bank
Julia Cobb Bank

Passage

Kitsap Banks

Table Rock Passage
Big Passage
Double Passage
Small Passage

LAGOON

Leicester

Motu Ngangie
Lee to Us

Suatumu

Bird Islands

Aaron's Point
John's Point
Small Cooks
Karakerake

Scratch My Arse
Rock

Palmerston
Rock

Palmerston
(Home Island)

Village

Primrose

Cook's

Tom's

# PALMERSTON

SCALE

Miles 1  ¾  ½  ¼  0          1          2          3 Miles

Brander arranged for a Mr. Sweet to live there and collect *beche-de-mer* (sea slugs), considered an aphrodisiac in the Orient. Sweet soon tired of atoll life, and Brander sought a replacement.

## The Father of Palmerston

Born in 1821, Englishman **William Marsters** moved to the islands and married a Penrhyn girl. He also married her cousin, and the family was living on Manuae when Brander's *Aorai* came by for provisions. Marsters accepted the caretaker position on Palmerston, and landed there with his two wives and several children on July 8, 1863.

A Portuguese seaman and his native wife soon joined them, but the couple quarrelled and he left on the next ship. Marsters then agreed to make the woman his third wife. She was, coincidentally, a cousin of his first two wives.

Marsters also had a fourth Palmerston wife. Their only child was a daughter, who married a Penrhyn man and moved to that island. When wife four passed away that branch no longer had local members, and thus has no land.

Marsters had 17 children and 54 grandchildren, and died in 1899. When his youngest daughter passed away in 1973 there were over 1000 Marsters, many in Rarotonga and New Zealand. Less than 50 remain on Palmerston, but all Marsters consider it their homeland.

Each of the three branches has a section of the main island for houses and crops, and parts of the other islets.

Marsters forbade marriage within each branch, and raised his children on a discipline of school and hard work. Later in life he asked the London Missionary Society to place a minister on the island. Penrhyn missionary **Akarongo** was relocated here, and served as teacher and minister for some years.

Britain annexed Palmerston in 1891, but the Tahitian traders challenged this. The court ruled they had abandoned shipping services and their claims had expired. Marsters was given the lease, which was renewed until 1954, when the family was granted full ownership.

Aside from being a prolific patriarch, Marsters was an accomplished carpenter and seaman. The main house was built from shipwreck timbers, as was the combination school/church building.

**Hurricanes** have devastated the low-lying island. In 1883 almost 200,000 coconut palms planted the past 20 years were destroyed. All but the main house and church washed away in 1914, and again in 1923. But the hurricane of 1926 is remembered as "the big blow."

On March 21 the winds reached 100mph, and huge waves broke over the houses. Everyone retreated to "the mountain," a 20' high sand mound.

By morning only the main house, with 18"-thick beams buried 14' in the sand, was intact. The church lay 200 yds away. It was slowly pushed to its original spot, using coconut log rollers, to connect it to the concrete rainwater storage tank, which hadn't moved an inch!

One person had died, and most of the palms were gone. New seedlings were shipped in, but it was decided the atoll could not support its 115 residents. Many tearfully moved to other islands.

A 1935 hurricane washed away two islets---leaving the present six---and destroyed all the trees planted in 1926.

In 1936 trade routes changed, and no ship visited until 1939, when legendary Captain Andy Thomson---born in Brooklyn, NY----added the island to the route of his *Tiare Taporo*.

Nine sandbanks are named for the **shipwrecks** on them. Palmerston's low profile is a hazard, but it was incorrectly charted until 1969. Until then maps were based on Cook's original 1774 charts, which proved to be ten miles off. That's not bad, considering he had no help from navigation satellites!

The *Yankee* visited in 1961. It wasn't wrecked here, saving that distinction for Rarotonga, three years later. Professor Ron Crocombe studied the unique land tenure system, and Roger Malcolm, of the Atiu Motel, was based here during a study of the earth's magnetic field.

## Palmerston Today

The settlement is on **Home Island**. The three branches have separate plots of land, but the twenty or so houses are essentially in one village. The main house and CICC Church face the coral road to the beach, and a small radio shack is nearby. Since 1939 it's been the only link with the outside world.

The church was built from the timbers of the French vessel *La Tour D'Auvergne*, wrecked in 1913. An old ship's bell announces Sunday services.

There's no jail, but each branch has an honorary policemen. The eldest of the clan handles the few official duties on *Parnati*, as it's called in Rarotongan.

Thousands of palm and pandanus trees thrive, and copra is exported. Breadfruit, papaya and banana groves are well-tended. Arrowroot, sweet potatoes and Pukapukan taro are cultivated. Mosquito-eating *gambusia* fish are stocked in taro patches, and chickens and pigs are kept in the village.

The lagoon has crayfish, giant clams, and lots of **parrotfish**, which are dried and shipped to Rarotonga. Fishing is good near **Palmerston Rock** and **Scratch My Arse Rock**. (Never let it be said William Marsters lacked a sense of humor.) *Maito* (black surgeonfish) are eaten locally, or dried for export.

**Sea turtles** nest on the reef, and are caught on moonlit nights in underwater caves. Giant tuna are caught offshore. Thousands of **red-tailed tropicbirds** (*tavake* or "bosun birds") nest on the islets, and their feathers are sold on Rarotonga for traditional costumes.

Two reef passes reach depths of five feet, but all ships anchor west of Home Island, and transfer cargo by small boat.

Shipping is still a big problem. Freighters stop every few months, but their schedules are erratic. This makes it difficult to plan a large harvest of crayfish, which spoil quickly if not refrigerated. Shortages of fuel and supplies are taken in stride, but the islanders send out the S.O.S. when the cigarettes run out!

Transport is a problem after the Constitution Celebrations. Ships make the outer-island pickup, but it's costly to return only weeks later. Folks from Palmerston may wait three months to return home, but they admit they enjoy the videos during their stay on Raro!

A new solar-electric system is planned. Twelve houses and the church will get power for refrigeration, lights, and water pumps---and some VCR's!

They may even get a modern phone system. One resident joked that the phone book would have only one letter ---"M" for Marsters!

Sports are very popular, with the families divided into only two---not three---teams. Reflecting the sense of humor common to other islanders, the **Warriors** always fight it out with the **Peacemakers**, in volleyball, cricket, darts, cards and ping pong.

## Getting There

The Waterfront Commission has freighter schedules, and skippers can assist with shore arrangements.

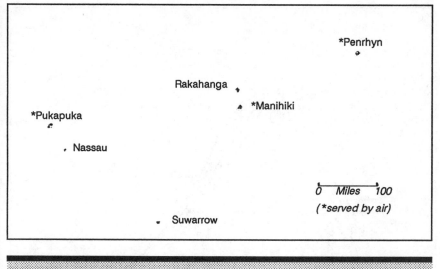

## THE NORTHERN GROUP

These remote islands are the "stuff that dreams are made of." Islets encircle turquoise lagoons, while coconut palms fringe pristine beaches. The weather is warm, fish are plentiful, and troubles seem far away.

But reality adds some twists. Hurricanes rage every decade or so, and fruit, vegetables, fresh water, petrol and medical care are limited. Despite these problems, the simple lifestyle allows reflection on what's important in life, and what isn't.

Until 1915 the "Cook Islands" meant the Southern Group. These were the "Penrhyn Islands" or "Manihiki Group," the latter still used in ham radio.

Until recently the US claimed Manihiki, Rakahanga, Penrhyn and Pukapuka, based on its 1858 Guano Act, which covered any island where US ships had mined guano (bird dung).

These claims were "technically" reaffirmed until 1965, when it was brought to light that none of these islands have, or ever had, guano deposits! A 1983 treaty finally relinquished all claims, but some maps still indicate "US/NZ."

**Manihiki** has a thriving black pearl industry, while **Penrhyn** produces natural white pearls. Both have weekly flights. **Rakahanga**, Manihiki's sister, still relies on fishing and agriculture.

**Pukapuka** and its tiny suburb of **Nassau** are closer to Samoa than Rarotonga, and their language and customs reflect this. A new airstrip on Pukapuka now allows easier access to both islands. Remote **Suwarrow**, once home to hermit Tom Neale, is now a National Park.

Freighters stop at all the islands of the Northern Group except little Suwarrow---the loneliest island in the South Pacific.

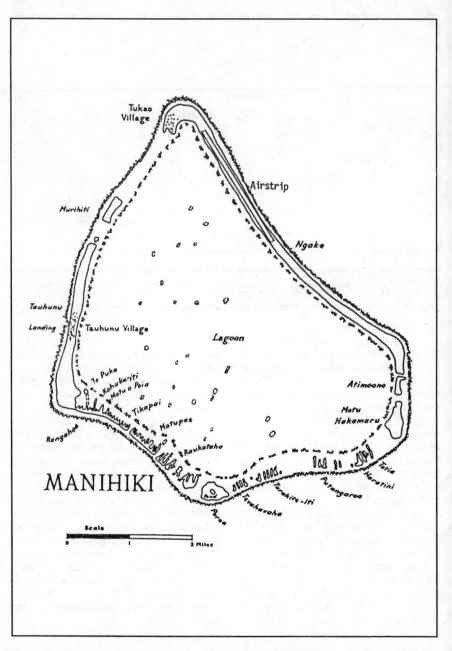

Tukao Village

Airstrip

Murihiti

Ngake

Tauhunu
Landing    Tauhunu Village    Lagoon

Te Puka    Atimoono
Kohakariti
Motu o Poia    Motu
Tikapai    Hakamaru

Rangahoi    Motupae

Raukotaha

MANIHIKI    Totio
Haretini
Putangaroa
Tevahavaha    Tarakite-iti
Porea

Scale
0    1    2 Miles

# MANIHIKI

Population:  666
Area:  2.1 sq.mi.

Lying more than 750 miles north of Rarotonga, Manihiki is comprised of dozens of small islets surrounding a triangular lagoon. Two dozen more sit in the center of the lagoon, a rarity in the South Pacific. The main village of Tauhunu is on the west, and smaller Tukao is on the north, near the airstrip.

The economy was traditionally based on copra, pearlshell, and subsistence fishing and agriculture. This all changed in the 1980's with the establishment of a large-scale pearl farming industry, which has brought some measure of wealth to the island.

## History

Manihiki was originally the little sister of Rakahanga, and was only inhabited a few months each year, when food ran low on Rakahanga. Although only 25 miles separate the islands, the currents are dangerous, and many lives were lost on these passages. Despite these dangers, no permanent settlement was established on Manihiki until after the missionaries arrived.

The first non-Polynesian discoverer was **Captain Patrickson** in the American ship *Good Hope*, on October 12, 1822. He named it Humphrey Island. Whalers and traders later called it Great Ganges Island, Gland Island, Sarah Scott Island, or Pescado Island.

The current name is short for *Manu-hiki*---from the canoe *Rua Manu* ("two birds") carried ("*hiki*") ashore. It's definitely more melodic than Gland Island!

In 1849 William Gill dropped off Polynesian missionaries **Tairi** from Rarotonga and **Apolo** from Aitutaki. They had some success, and convinced locals to start a permanent settlement.

Famed missionary **Maretu** arrived in 1854, and converted most of the remaining population. Within a year stone churches had been built in both villages.

The beauty of Manihiki women was known throughout the Pacific, and Peruvians, Tahitians and others came seeking wives. One writer said the ladies "had but one desire: to become the mistresses of Europeans." While this goal has clearly disappeared, most would agree that their beauty has not.

In 1869 "blackbirder" Bully Hayes convinced many locals to work for him on Rakahanga. After boarding the ship they were kidnapped to the Fiji sugar cane fields, and few made it back home.

Manihikians are legendary pearlshell divers, going down seventy-five feet in the clear lagoon. Some, however, go too deep, and become paralyzed when they suffer the "bends" on their ascent.

## Pearl Cultivation 101

When an oyster gets a foreign body in its shell, it covers it with a thin secretion of nacre and attempts to eject it. If it's not ejected, another layer of nacre is added, and on and on. The tiny impurity, coated with nacre, becomes a pearl.

In culturing pearls, a tiny piece of Mississippi River mussel shell is surgically inserted into the sexual organ of the oyster. If not placed properly it will be ejected, or unevenly coated. The oyster sits in the lagoon for eighteen months. It's cleaned regularly, and kept at the proper depth by floats.

When it's pulled up the lips are separated and a pearl pops out. Or, nothing pops out. The success rate is 50%, higher than Tahiti, but size, shape, color and nacre quality vary. Much depends on care while in the lagoon.

In the 1980's Tekake Williams and Tahitian merchant Yves Tchen-Pan began experimenting with black pearls. By 1987 the first group was successfully harvested. Thirty-two pearl farms are now spread around the lagoon, many off the tiny *motus* in the center. Family operations have from 1,000-75,000 oysters, while the Island Council cooperative has 300,000. The 1990 auction of 6000 pearls netted US$1 million, and annual sales could top US$2 million.

Pearl farming has halted the exodus of young adults to Rarotonga and New Zealand, and others have returned to seek their fortune. Manihiki's population has doubled in the past 5 years.

## Manihiki Today

The main village of **Tauhunu** is on the west. You'll find shops, a post office, radio station, a small hospital, primary school, CICC Church, and government offices. A coral road runs through town and down the center of the islet. The landing was recently widened, but it's still too shallow for yachts to enter the lagoon.

Smaller **Tukao** sits on the north end of **Ngake** islet, on the east side of the lagoon. The airstrip is south of the village. Another CICC Church, a primary school, the Veravera Meeting Hall, a few shops and a new library round out the tiny village. Ngake has several good taro patches, created by slowly filling coral holes with leaves, vegetable matter and bits of soil.

## Practicalities

Flights are once or twice a week on **Air Rarotonga** (22-888) for NZ$1000/RT. Some stop at Penrhyn, and most stop at Aitutaki. Package trips are available that visit Manihiki, Penrhyn and Pukapuka. Most visitors stay at a guest house in Tauhunu, but this must be arranged in advance through Air Rarotonga. Manihikians are very outgoing, and you'll meet lots of people pretty quickly. Bring snorkeling gear, a hat, sunglasses, suntan lotion, towel, toiletries, camera and film, and fishing supplies as gifts.

## Other Attractions

Though pearls have grabbed the headlines, Manihiki has other attractions. The women weave fine mats and baskets, and their bleached white *rito* hats are popular on Rarotonga. The lagoon offers excellent snorkeling in the coral gardens near the southern *motus*. The pond on Porea serves as a fish farm, with thousands bred yearly.

A sweet-tasting variety of coconut, *nu mangaro*, grows on the small islets. The meat is eaten raw or baked, or chopped and fermented into a potent palm toddy. On a southern *motu* was a famous seven-headed coconut palm, but only four heads remain. The rare *kakavai-maui* tern, found only on Manihiki and Rakahanga, nests on small *motus*.

The beauty of the Manihiki women is still a major attraction, despite the competition from pearls. Even on Rarotonga one notices the exotically-different look of some Island Night dancers, and inevitably they're from Manihiki or Rakahanga.

Their features may partly result from the island's popularity with early Spanish and South American traders.

A friend from Mauke, who knew many Manihikians, recounted the fol-

*Manihikian bride—1870's*

lowing story after I remarked that Manihikians looked a little different than most other Cook Islanders:

"A few years ago I visited America with a dance group from Mauke. We went to Los Angeles, and took a bus tour of the city. We went through a section of town they said was settled by immigrants from the South, so we figured we might see some people from the South Pacific.

"All the shop signs were in a foreign language we did not recognize. But we immediately recognized the people as being from Manihiki! And I felt so stupid. Even though my Manihiki friends knew I was going to Los Angeles, none had given me the names of any of their relatives living there!"

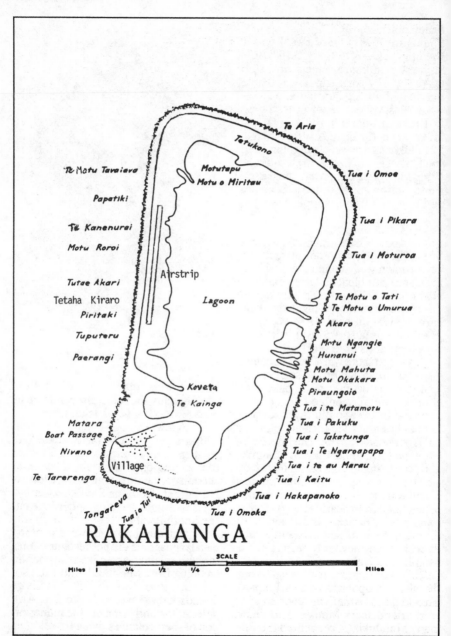

Te Motu Tavaiava
Papatiki
Te Kanenurei
Motu Roroi
Tutae Akari
Tetaha Kiraro
Piritaki
Tuputeru
Paerangi
Matara
Boat Passage
Nivano
Te Tarerenga

Te Aria
Tetukono
Motutapu
Motu o Miritau
Tua i Omoe
Tua i Pikara
Tua i Moturoa
Airstrip
Lagoon
Te Motu o Tati
Te Motu o Umurua
Akaro
Motu Ngangie
Hunanui
Motu Mahuta
Motu Okakara
Piraungoio
Tua i te Matamotu
Tua i Pakuku
Tua i Takatunga
Tua i Te Ngaroapapa
Tua i te au Marau
Tua i Kaitu
Tua i Hakapanoko
Koveta
Te Kainga
Village
Tongareva    Tua i o Tui    Tua i Omoka

# RAKAHANGA

SCALE

Miles | 1    1/4    1/2    1/4    0    1    Miles

# RAKAHANGA

Population:  262
Area:       1.6 sq.mi.

Low-lying Rakahanga is only 25 miles from Manihiki. It's roughly rectangular, a mile-and-a-half wide and three miles long. The lagoon is almost encircled by two low-lying J-shaped islands. If the Greenhouse Effect causes the sea level to rise, both of the islands would quickly become submerged, and Rakahanga would no longer exist.

The small settlement is in the southwest, near an occasionally-used airstrip. Ships anchor offshore, as there's no passage into the lagoon. The lagoon is not suitable for pearls, and the main export is copra. The land area is rela-tively large, allowing the production of a wide range of vegetables.

### History
Legends say Rakahanga was settled in the 14th century by **Huku**, who came from Rarotonga with his sister **Tapairu** and her husband **Toa**. Huku returned to Rarotonga, but the couple stayed. Toa and Tapairu produced four daughters, but since no one else ever came to visit the island, Toa had to marry his own daughters to keep the population from dying out.

The original village was on an islet in the southwest called **Te Kainga** ("The Home"). Two-story huts with sleeping lofts were common in the well-built village. The atoll supported some crops, but the population grew and food would occasionally run out. Everyone would then make the rough trip to Manihiki in their 70-foot, twin-hulled canoes. Currents were dangerous, and some villagers would be lost at sea. Months later the canoes returned to Rakahanga, often with more loss of life.

The first European discoverer was the Spanish **Captain Pedro Fernandez de Quiros**, on March 2, 1606. Although Pukapuka had been sighted by Mendana and Quiros in 1595, Rakahanga was the first island in the Cooks where Europeans actually went ashore.

As indicated in our main History section, Quiros was very impressed by both the ocean-going canoes and the beauty of the islanders. It was a friar on his ship who first called it "Isla de Gente Hermosa"---Island of Beautiful People.

No other Europeans visited for over two hundred years, until both a Russian and an American ship came by in 1820. The American captain called it Reirson's Island, which was used in early writings about the Pacific.

The missionaries that landed in Manihiki in 1849, **Tairi** and **Apolo**, soon arrived on Rakahanga. By 1852 they had convinced the Rakahangans to permanently move half their population to Manihiki. This would prevent food shortages on both islands, and save lives by reducing the number of inter-island voyages.

The missionary **Maretu** arrived in 1854, and persuaded the locals to move from small Te Kainga islet to the larger islet to the south, known as Rakahanga. Rather than build a new village they lifted up all 45 houses, a school and a wooden church, and carried them across the small channel to the new settlement, called **Matara** ("separated").

Maretu taught them to burn lime from coral, and the first stone structure, the LMS (later CICC) Church, was soon built.

One unusual feature of the new village was a tiny jail, built at the suggestion of the missionaries. Its use may have related to the forced break-up of polygamous marriages. Most Rakahangans, like other islanders, had several spouses.

Christian converts had to give up all but one spouse, and tensions ran high, especially among multiple husbands of the same local beauty. The jail was used to calm down husbands who found out they weren't number one, despite what might have been whispered to them on earlier moonlit nights.

Like other Northern Group islands, Rakahanga suffered from the misdeeds of the Peruvian "blackbirders" of 1862-63. About 100 of the 300 residents were persuaded, coerced or kidnapped onto slave ships, and few ever returned.

Recent history includes several shipwrecks, and at least three groups lost at sea on their way to Manihiki. One group of seven was never found, and another group ended up on Pukapuka. One journey, where the locals drifted all the way to Vanuatu, is detailed in *The Man Who Refused To Die*.

The most unusual shipwreck in the Cooks is the expedition raft *Tahiti Nui III*. It had successfully drifted from Tahiti to South America and back, proving migration was possible in ancient times. On August 30, 1958 the large raft was smashed to bits on the reef at Rakahanga, killing the expedition's leader, the famous French navigator Eric de Bisschop. The story of the expedition is told in Bengt Danielsson's *From Raft to Raft*.

## Rakahanga Today

The easiest way to get to Rakahanga is to fly to Manihiki, then take the 3-hour trip on the inter-island motor launch. New ship-to-shore radios have been installed to make the journey safer.

The little settlement at Matara, also called **Nivano**, has a tiny wharf and boat landing. The CICC Church, primary school, a couple of shops and some government offices sit among well-made houses in this sleepy town. Locals are more reserved than their Manihikian cousins, but most warm up quickly.

Cemeteries reflect the custom of erecting tiny huts over graves, where possessions of the deceased are placed to help them in the world beyond.

The lagoon may not produce pearls, but it has lots of huge coconut crabs, which make a tasty dinner. The fishing on the outer reef is good, and flying fish (*maroro*) are dried and eaten as a delicacy. Large sea turtles are caught on the outer reefs, and gamefish are plentiful in the offshore waters. A tuna competition is held in January, with boats often bringing in 200 fish a day.

Large breadfruit trees, of a variety that is sweet and productive year-round, line the village paths. Sweet *nu mangaro* coconut palms and pandanus trees round out the vegetation, and women weave fine mats, baskets, and beautiful *rito* hats from the leaf fibers.

The wide islets have fertile soil, and produce a variety of vegetables. None, however, is as famous or important as the coarse dry taro called *puraka*.

Although Manihiki is larger, the locals all preferred Rakahanga, since *puraka* could not be grown on the soil-poor islets of Manihiki. When the *puraka* ran out on Rakahanga they all sailed to Manihiki and its fish-laden lagoon. A few months later the *puraka*

*Rakahanga dancers at Constitution Celebrations*

would be ready to harvest again, so everyone returned to Rakahanga.

While *puraka* is enjoyed by Rakahangans, it has a bland, starchy taste that does not appeal to most foreigners. One European who had lived on Rakahanga passed on his favorite recipe:

"Cut up the *puraka* into small chunks, about the size of your thumb. Put them in a pot of boiling water, along with a coral rock about as big as your hand, and cover the pot. Cook it all for three hours, adding some salt and pepper every hour or so.

"When the three hours are done, drain away the water, throw away the *puraka*, and eat the rock. It will still have more flavor than the *puraka*!"

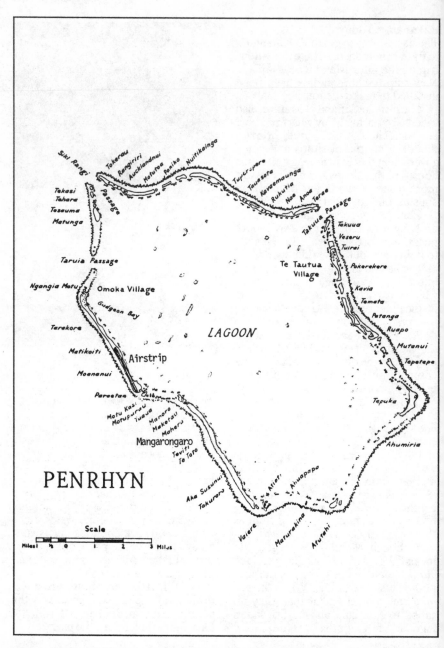

PENRHYN

# PENRHYN

Population:   503
Area:        4 sq.mi.

Penrhyn is the largest atoll in the Cooks, and one of the largest in the Pacific. It's seven miles wide and fifteen miles long, and Te Tautua village on the east is barely visible from the main village of Omoka on the west.

At 850 miles from Rarotonga, it's the most distant island from the capital. Its closest neighbors are Rakahanga and Manihiki, 200 miles southwest.

Despite its isolation, Penrhyn has been a center of commercial activity ever since the whalers and traders discovered its two main assets: numerous pearlshells and an excellent harbor. The former brought the traders, and the latter brought everyone, as harbors are few and far between in this part of the Pacific.

At only 9 degrees below the equator it can get pretty hot, but this is moderated by cooler sea breezes. It's safely north of the hurricane belt, but for the same reason it has periods of low rainfall and occasional droughts. The droughts reduce the production of copra, its traditional export, but this has become less of a problem now that pearl farming is growing as a source of revenue.

### History
Legends say it was fished from the sea by **Vatea**, using flesh from his thigh as bait. Early Polynesian settlers named

it **Tongareva**, "south of the empty space," since open ocean lies to the north. This is still a popular name, as is, to a lesser extent, **Mangarongaro**, derived from the sweet *nu mangaro* coconuts found on some of the islets.

The latest name comes from the *Lady Penrhyn*, whose **Captain Lever** sighted the island on August 8, 1788. The vessel had carried prisoners from England to Australia, and passed by the island on its way home.

Whalers, traders and beachcombers visited next, including **William Marsters**, the future Father of Palmerston. He stayed long enough in 1850 to marry the chief's daughter, and also married her cousin. His third wife was from Penrhyn as well.

The real influx of European visitors began as a result of the shipwreck of the *Chatham*, on January 6, 1853. Trader **E. H. Lamont** and others survived, and were graciously adopted by local families, despite the islanders' warlike reputation. He enjoyed his 18-month stay, and married three local ladies.

After Lamont was "saved" by a passing ship, he penned the small classic *Wild Life Among the Pacific Islanders*. In it he mentioned the deep lagoon and the abundance of pearlshell, and from then on traders always made it a point to stop at Penrhyn.

Missionaries arrived soon after the traders. The islanders quickly converted, and gave the mission almost complete control over their lives.

This proved costly in 1862, when the four native missionaries "sold" their congregations to Peruvian blackbirders for five dollars a head. Three of the missionaries and their wives were to go with the group to South America, and serve as interpreters and overseers for $100 per month. It's not clear if they knew it would be a one-way trip, or if they were also duped by the blackbirders. Out of 500 Penrhyn islanders, 412 were convinced to board the ships. Most never returned from the mines of Peru. From then on Penrhyn was known as **The Island of The Four Evangelists**.

The missionaries had consolidated seven villages into four, each with a minister. After the blackbirders treachery only the present two remained.

The decimated population slowly grew, but epidemics in the early 1900's took another toll. Leprosy hit, and a leper colony was set up on a *motu* near Omoka. In 1926 most lepers were moved to a new hospital in Fiji.

The next population increase began November 8, 1942, when 1000 American servicemen arrived to build an airstrip to defend the mid-Pacific. The 10,000-foot airstrip was built, but fighting didn't reach this area. The GI's left on September 30, 1946. The wreck of a bomber is still scavenged for metal for combs, fish hooks, and other uses.

When atomic bomb testing began in the North Pacific in the 1950's, both the British and Americans used the island for refueling and storing supplies.

Captain **Viggo Rasmussen** skippered the schooner *Tiare Taporo*, and he later settled here. He passed away in 1947, but many relatives remain. A son served as Chief Administrative Officer (CAO).

**Penrhyn Today**
The main village of **Omoka** is on **Moananui** island, on the west of the lagoon. There's a small hospital, primary school, radio station, church, shops and government offices. A road runs through the village and continues two miles south, to the airstrip.

Yachts can enter the lagoon through three passages, but most use the twenty-foot-deep **Taruia Passage** north of Omoka. Omoka has a small wharf, and a larger one is planned for the patrol boat *Te Kukupa*, which may move here to monitor foreign fishing boats.

**Te Tautua** is seven miles east, on the smaller but more fertile **Pokerekere**. The population is half that of Omoka, but there's a primary school, church, and post office, which sells unique Penrhyn Island stamps. Pokerekere produces papaya, breadfruit, and bananas. Goods are transported between Te Tautua and Omoka by sailing cutter and motor launch.

On one islet is **Te Papa-O-Sokoau**, a rock wall three feet high and forty feet long. Sokoau was the beautiful but unfaithful wife of a jealous husband, who killed her and then built the wall. It was either a *marae* to honor the place of her death, or a fortress for his own protection from the authorities.

In addition to the larger islets that almost encircle the lagoon, there are dozens of small sand cays in the center. The coral is colorful, and there are enough tropical fish to please any snorkeler. There are also lots of sharks, but most apparently are harmless. A small mackerel-type fish called *koperu* is often caught by using partially-chewed coconut meat as chum to attract them to the surface.

Copra is still exported, and fine woven *rito* hats fetch high prices on Rarotonga. Mother-of-pearl jewelry and pearlshell also bring in revenue.

Their natural white pearls are sold on Rarotonga, but the big money would be in a Manihiki-style cultured black pearl industry. This was planned in the early 1990's, but some local opposition led to the proposal being put on hold until details of lagoon use and ownership could be worked out.

E.H. Lamont

Singing and dancing are popular pastimes, and a local home-brew is a favorite beverage. The birthrate is one of the highest in the country, and the population of Omoka is growing so fast that some families are building houses in outlying areas of the *motu*. Could this be the start of the "suburbanization" of the Cook Islands?!?

**Practicalities**

There are weekly flights on **Air Rarotonga** (22-888), with stops at Aitutaki in one direction. Fares are NZ$1100 roundtrip. Air Raro also has some package tours that stop in Penrhyn for a day or two. Ships visit every few months on a swing through the Northern Group. Contact the Waterfront Commission on Rarotonga for current schedules.

No special visitor accommodations are available, but you can arrange to stay with a local family when you make your air or ship reservations. Bring extra food and your snorkeling gear.

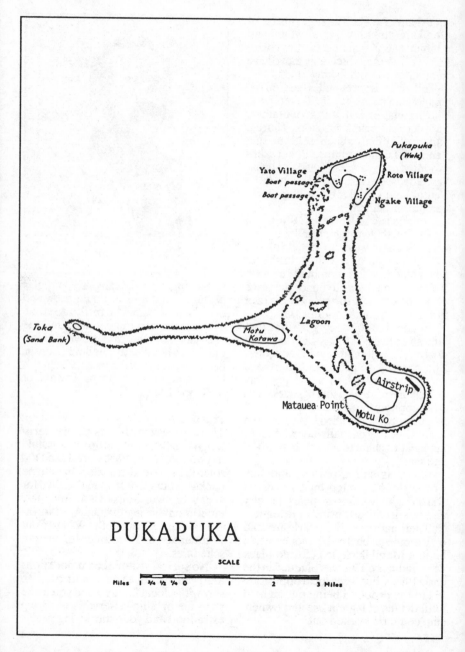

Pukapuka
(Wale)

Yato Village

Boat passage

Boat passage

Roto Village

Ngake Village

Toka
(Sand Bank)

Motu
Kotawa

Lagoon

Airstrip

Matauea Point

Motu Ko

PUKAPUKA

SCALE

Miles  1  ¾  ½  ¼  0          1          2          3 Miles

# PUKAPUKA

Population:  780
Area:       1.9 sq.mi.

Of all the islands, none has quite the reputation for romance as Pukapuka. Asked to name its main asset, other islanders all say "the beautiful girls!" It's closer to Samoa than Rarotonga, and the customs and language reflect this.

In the 1920's Robert Dean Frisbie's relatives and friends berated him:

"Young man, you are wasting your life! Here you are, nearing thirty, with nothing accomplished, no plans, no bank account! You must reform! It is your duty to help keep the Wheels of Industry moving! Be efficient!"

He sought a place beyond reach of "the faintest echo from the noisy clamor of the civilized world." He found it.

Pukapuka, for better or worse, entered the modern era when the airstrip opened in 1994. The 820-mile trip from Rarotonga is now a 5-hour flight, not a 5-day voyage. As one local said, their constant "feelings of fear" of medical emergencies and cyclones are gone, as help is only a few hours away. It has yet to be seen whether the disadvantages of progress are similarly close at hand.

### Early History
Samoans and Tongans arrived about 1300 AD. The first settler, **Riki**, called

it *Te Ulu o te Watu*---The Head of the Rock. The present name comes from the *puka* (laurel) trees, or means "little hills." In 1550 a tidal wave killed all but 2 women and 9 men. It was repopulated by, one writer said, "a communal effort."

**Captain Mendana** of Spain sighted it August 20, 1595, marking European discovery of the Cooks. On June 21, 1765, **Commodore Byron** in the *Dolphin* noted huge reef swells, and named it **Danger Island**, still seen on maps. Missionaries didn't arrive until 1857, making it the last island to convert.

In 1863, blackbirders kidnapped 140 people, a third of the population. The mission ship *John Williams* visited the next year, but was wrecked on the reef.

Mendana saw four islets, but hurricanes had reduced one to a sand bank by Frisbie's arrival. Frisbie's 1924 charts were official maps until a 1975 survey.

**Robert Dean Frisbie**
Born in Cleveland, Ohio in 1896, Frisbie was inspired by Stevenson and Melville. He moved to the islands, hoping to pen the classic South Seas novel. In 1924 he was hired to run a shop here.

He learned the language, married, and wrote stories of an island where romance was commonplace and premarital sex a virtue. These appeared in *Atlantic Monthly*, and later as *The Book of Puka-Puka*. His novel *Mister Moonlight's Island* was good, but not a classic. His *Island of Desire* included more tales, and coined its current nickname.

Frisbie died in 1948, and is buried in Rarotonga. His friend James Michener helped daughter "Johnny" publish *Miss Ulysses From Pukapuka* and *The Frisbies of the South Seas*. Michener wrote of Frisbie in *Return To Paradise*, as did James Norman Hall in *The Forgotten One*. Also set in Pukapuka are Beagle-

hole's *Island of Danger*, and *The Raft*, about US airmen drifting here in WWII.

**Pukapuka Today**
Everyone lives on **Pukapuka**, also called **Wale** (Wah-lay), meaning House. **Motu Ko** and **Motu Kotawa** are food reserves.

Villages are aptly named. On the windy east is **Ngake** (Windward); in the middle is **Roto** (Central); and on the calm west is **Yato** (Leeward), near the two landings. A coral road---The Main Road---connects the villages, and a 6' high concrete causeway spans an inlet.

Most homes have block or limestone walls and thatched roofs. All large buildings have rainwater catchment systems. Wale has a clinic, school, PO, radio station, government offices, shops and 3 churches. About 75% of locals are CICC members, 15% are Catholic, and 10% Seventh Day Adventists. The Catholic Church has cowrie-shell motifs by the Dutch priest, Father Benetio.

**Communal Economy**
Work, copra profits and food are equally divided among the villages. Laws are also communally enforced. If a bird is killed out of season, or crabs or coconuts taken early, small but humiliating fines are imposed. For worse offenses, the person is treated as a child until sincere remorse is shown. He may not speak at meetings, and is given a child's food and wages. Most atone quickly.

Each village owns one island. Roto owns **Wale**, and controls taro production. A taro patch was created over the years by adding bits of soil and vegetation to a coral pit. By custom, only women tend this plot. It was destroyed in a 1990 hurricane, and seedlings had to be parachuted in to restore the crop.

Coconuts are started on Wale, then transplanted to Ko and Kotawa. Copra is the main export, but is often threatened by coconut termites. Dried fish and uto make up the balance of exports.

Ngake owns **Motu Ko**, the largest islet, which produces the most copra. Frisbie often stayed at Matauea Point, where tradewinds lessen mosquitoes. The new airstrip is along the coast.

Small but fertile **Motu Kotawa** ("Frigatebird Island") is owned by Yato. Papaya and banana trees thrive, while thousands of birds supply valuable eggs.

Lagoon depths reach 60', and pearl and trochus cultivation are planned. Clams, flying fish, parrotfish, and sea turtles are caught offshore and near **Toka** sand bank. A few chickens and pigs round out the diet.

Locals also fish at **Tema Reef**, 20 miles away. The reef is only 3' below the surface, and few ships pass at night. Several rusting hulls attest to its danger.

Pukapukans are skilled boatbuilders, and a traditional sennit-lashed canoe is on display at the museum in Rarotonga. Women weave wide-brimmed *rito* hats, and fine mats and baskets.

### Daily Life

Cricket, volleyball, coconut-husking contests, canoe races and singing are popular. Friday is a day for socializing, with dances in the evening. Sunday is a day of rest, with all-day services. At sunset Sabbath ends, and card games and ukuleles begin.

Population density is high, and many locals emigrate to Pue village on Rarotonga. One expatriate teacher observed that "sex is very casual here---often the number one recreation." Nine out of ten kids are born out of wedlock.

"Ping pong" is a type of group date, where a man and a woman each invites a "team" of four friends to the beach, where couples pair off if they so desire.

*Pukapukan soul traps*

The "Christmas Games" are allegedly for "cleaning, cooking, and dancing," usually by unattached residents. First the women move one village west for a week. After New Year's the men move one village east for a week. When the "chores" are finished, all return home.

### Practicalities

Air Raro flies every week or two, for NZ$1100/RT. Package tours stop overnight. Ships are a lot cheaper, but it's 5 days each way, and schedules are erratic; check with the Waterfront Commission. Arrange lodging with your transport.

Although most locals know some English, it is rarely spoken. Here are a few basics to get you started:

Hello (How are you?)---*Pewea*
I'm fine---*Ko lelei wua*
Thank you---*Ata wai wolo*

# NASSAU

Population:    103
Area:         0.5 sq.mi.

Tiny palm-covered Nassau is unusual for the Northern Group, as it's the only island without a lagoon. A treacherous reef encircles this "suburb" of Puka-puka, which lies 55 miles to the north.

Until recently there was no permanent population, as Pukapukans only visited to harvest copra. There is little contact with the outside world, and Nassau is probably the most traditional island in the country.

It will be easier to reach now that Pukapuka has an airstrip, but landings are still dangerous since there's no boat passage. The freighter *Manuvai* ran aground in 1988, with some loss of life.

## History

Archaeologists document early Polynesian visits, as do Pukapukan oral histories. An early Pukapukan caretaker was Ngalewu, and it was called **Te Nuku-O-Ngalewu** (Land of Ngalewu). When it later became uninhabited, Pukapukans called it **Motu Ngaongao** (Lonely Island).

The European discoverer may have been **Captain Coutance** in 1803. It was not mapped until March, 1835, by **Captain John Sampson**, in the American whaler *Nassau*. Missionary William Wyatt Gill visited in 1862 and 1881.

In 1873 American **John Ellacott** started a copra plantation. He registered his claim with the US Consul in Tahiti, and hired Pukapukan harvesters.

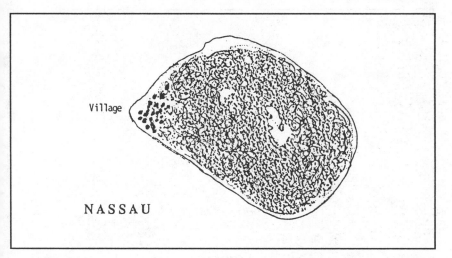

Village

NASSAU

Ellacott later sold out, and foreign companies owned it until 1945, when New Zealand bought it for 2000 pounds sterling. The Pukapukans cut enough copra to match that price, and on June 2, 1951, bought it from New Zealand.

**Nassau Today**
The village is on the northwest, where the reef is narrow and small boats land if seas are favorable. Most houses are thatched, and a school, radio station and clinic complete the village.

Nassau has solar-electrical panels to supply refrigerators, freezers, lights, a washing machine and water pumps.

This 30'-high island is a small Garden of Eden. In addition to its numerous coconut palms, inland are rich taro swamps, fruit groves, and a freshwater spring. Fish and shellfish are caught off the reef. The food supply is better than on crowded Pukapuka, so most Nassauans don't mind the isolation.

They also don't seem to mind the surreptitious visits of Asian fishing boats, which stop without registering with the central government. These visits, never openly acknowledged by locals, are reflected by Korean fishing floats, plastic Japanese jewelry worn by young ladies, and the Asian features of many village children.

Every July, 40,000 taro plants are taken to Pukapuka, during their annual visit. One year the taro was cut and ready, but the freighter couldn't find Nassau and continued on to Samoa. Americans Bob and Chandace Richardson, obviously Beach Boys fans, sailed their 40-foot *Ba-Ba-Barann* to the rescue, and took the taro to Pukapuka before it rotted on Nassau.

**Last One Off, Turn Out The Lights!**
In July a ship picks everyone up, stops at Pukapuka, and continues to Rarotonga for the Constitution Celebrations. Two months later the ship reverses the route, and Nassauans head home.

During this period all the buildings are closed up, and the island is absolutely deserted. And the last one off turns out the (solar powered) lights!

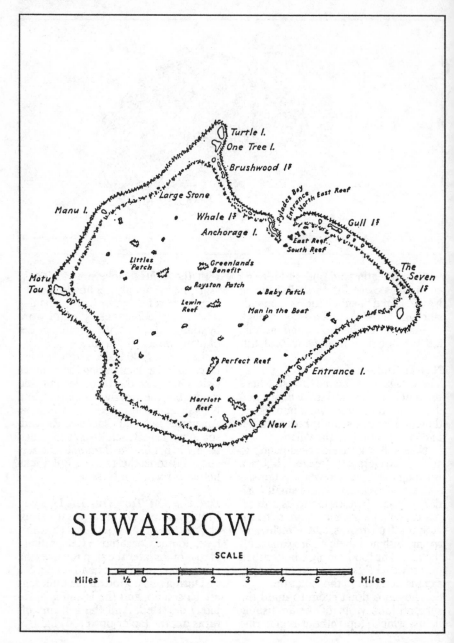

# SUWARROW

SCALE

Miles 1 ½ 0 1 2 3 4 5 6 Miles

| ISLAND | Population 1961 | Distance and Direction from Rarotonga Miles | | POSITION | CLIMATOLOGICAL DATA | | EXTREMES | | Area in Acres |
|---|---|---|---|---|---|---|---|---|---|
| | | | | | Rainfall in inches | Mean Temp. Deg. F. | Maximum Deg. F. | Minimum Deg. F. | |
| RAROTONGA | 8,676 | - | - | 21°12'06"S 159°46'33"W | 83 | 74 | 92 | 48 | 16,602 |
| AITUTAKI | 2,582 | 140 | N | 18°51'45"S 159°48'10"W | 78 | 78 | 96 | 55 | 4,461 |
| MANGAIA | 1,877 | 110 | ESE | 21°54'30"S 157°58' W | 77 | - | - | - | 12,800 |
| ATIU | 1,266 | 116 | NEbyE | 19°58'45"S 158°08'00"W | 83 | - | - | - | 6,654 |
| MAUKE | 785 | 150 | ENE | 20°08'30"S 157°21'20"W | 76 | - | - | - | 4,552 |
| MITIARO | 307 | 142 | NEbyE | 19°51' S 157°43' W | 76 | - | - | - | 5,500 |
| MANUAE (Hervey Is.) | 18 | 124 | NNE | 19°15'43"S 158°57'43"W | - | - | - | - | 1,524 |
| TAKUTEA | | 118 | NE | 19°48'35"S 158°18' W | - | - | - | - | 302 |
| MANIHIKI | 1,006 | 650 | NbyW | 10°25'20"S 161°01' W | - | - | - | - | 1344 |
| PUKAPUKA | 718 | 715 | NWbyN | 10°53' S 165°49' W | - | - | - | - | 300 |
| PENRHYN | 628 | 737 | NbyE | 8°59'45"S 157°58'50"W | 95 | 82 | 96 | 65 | 2432 |
| PALMERSTON | 86 | 270 | NW | 18°04' S 163°10' W | 109 | 82 | 99 | 67 | 500 |
| RAKAHANGA | 319 | 674 | NbyW | 10°02'30"S 161°05'30"W | 71 | 83 | 94 | 72 | 1000 |
| NASSAU | 109 | 673 | NWbyN | 11°33'20"S 165°25' W | 83 | - | - | - | 300 |
| SUWARROW | 1 | .513 | NNW | 13°14'40"S 163°06'15"W | 92 | - | - | - | 100 |

# SUWARROW

Population: 10
Area: 0.2 sq.mi.

Little Suwarrow is one of the loneliest islands in the world. Its nearest neighbors are Manihiki and Nassau, 200 miles north, and tiny Palmerston, 330 miles south. It's 590 miles, and a dozen light years, from Rarotonga.

The beautiful lagoon could fully enclose Rarotonga, but the five islets total only 100 acres. Like Penrhyn, it has a large lagoon passage, and yachts often seek protection in its sheltered waters.

It's home to a million seabirds, thousands of coconut crabs, and hundreds of sharks. And 10 people.

That's high for Suwarrow, people-wise, as it's always been uninhabited ---except for 1952-1977, when Tom Neale, the Hermit of Suwarrow, lived here alone. Official reference charts listed Suwarrow as:
"Population: 1".

Now it's a National Park, and a caretaker and his family reside year-round. Its history includes castaways, hurricanes, shipwrecks and buried treasure.

## History

It was sighted September 28, 1814, by the Russian **Captain Lazarev**, in the *Suvarov*. He named the uninhabited island, but didn't register a claim as he was too busy supplying Russian settlers in Alaska. Cold War politics surely would have been different in the Pacific if Lazarev had perfected his claim.

Archaeologists confirm earlier Polynesian and European visits. Spanish galleons were wrecked in the 1740's, and an 1855 salvage operation found a buried chest with US$15,000 worth of old coins. In 1874, Mexican coins worth US$2,400 were uncovered. Suwarrow is still popular with treasure hunters.

Britain took over in 1889 and renamed it Suwarrow. Robert Louis Stevenson visited the next year, and observed "some beachcombers, pearl divers, traders and castaways."

Lever Brothers leased it to establish a pearlshell industry, but the market dropped and the lease was abandoned. The A. B. Donald Company tried harvesting copra in the 1930's, but a termite infestation hit and the crop was ruined.

Suwarrow served as a temporary home to Palmerston Islanders in 1935, after a tidal wave hit their atoll. When World War II began, New Zealand set up a coastwatchers' base.

## Gone With The Wind?
In early 1942 Robert Dean Frisbie and his family came from Pukapuka for a short visit. They were soon joined by New Zealand surveyors preparing a seaplane base, and two seamen on a trading vessel seeking shelter from an impending storm.

On February 22, 1942, one of the worst hurricanes on record hit low-lying Suwarrow. Waves crashed over the island day and night, and Frisbie tied himself and his children to tall *tamanu* (mahogany) trees to avoid being swept out to sea. A series of forty-foot waves finally bombarded the island with huge coral boulders, and much of Suwarrow was washed into the ocean.

Everyone miraculously survived, and were rescued a few weeks later. Frisbie recounted the horrendous storm in his *Island of Desire*. Suwarrow was totally replanted the following year, before it could erode into a reef.

## The Hermit of Suwarrow
New Zealander Tom Neale was born in 1902. He was a sailor by trade, and dreamed of living alone on a tropical island. He read of Suwarrow in Frisbie's book, and his ship stopped there in 1945. It was love at first sight.

He saved enough for tools and supplies, but the government refused to allow him to live there, as evacuation would be costly if he were seriously ill or injured. In 1952 he finally received permission, and on October 7, 1952, he became a modern Robinson Crusoe.

For 15 of the next 25 years he lived alone, tending his garden and chickens, and catching fish and coconut crabs. He repaired the coastwatchers' shack, and built a "summer home" on Motu Tou. He wore a thin strip of *pareu* cloth, but would put on shorts when yachts came by every six months or so.

In 1966 a friend helped him publish *An Island To Oneself*. Neale was appointed Postmaster of Suwarrow in 1969, and stayed until 1977, when he returned to Rarotonga due to stomach cancer. He died that year, and is buried in the RSA Cemetery on Rarotonga.

Tom Neale was in the hospital when I met him in 1977. Still feisty, he complained that the government had agreed to look after his things, but friends had told him many items were gone.

Tom passed away a few months later, shortly before Suwarrow was declared a National Park. The caretaker now looks after Tom's things, which serve as a monument to his life on Suwarrow.

Englishman Michael Swift had a similar dream, and stayed there in 1965 and 1966 while Tom was on Rarotonga. Swift considered returning in 1970, but when he found out Tom had returned he changed his mind, figuring it wasn't big enough for both of them! These and other Suwarrow stories are in *Sisters in the Sun*, by Helm and Percival (1973).

## Suwarrow Today
Facing the large passage is **Anchorage Island**, where the caretaker lives. Yachts anchor in the lagoon, then

register with him. There's a small jetty where he ties up the outboard boat used in his duties. The coastwatchers' shack serves as his family's home, and there's a cookhouse and bathhouse out back.

**Motu Tou** is the other large islet, with lots of palms and lots of coconut crabs. Tom learned quickly that crabs find fingers and toes a tempting night-time snack, so he built his bed high above the beach at his "summer home."

The large lagoon is filled with sharks, but they didn't bother Tom unless he was fishing. They always wanted to share his catch.

Suwarrow is one of the most important breeding sites for seabirds in the entire Pacific. A million sooty terns (*tara*) nest on its islets, along with thousands of frigatebirds, boobies and red-tailed tropicbirds. It was originally declared a bird sanctuary by New Zealand in 1939, but little was done until 1978 to insure the protection of its avian inhabitants.

The lagoon ranges in depth from 30-180 feet, and there are plans to start a pearl-farming project. The US has given the government a large research grant for pearl-farming surveys of Suwarrow and other atolls in the Northern Group.

Pearlshells are plentiful in the southwestern part of the lagoon, near Motu Tou. Divers from Manihiki and Penrhyn stop by once or twice a year to harvest the largest ones. An automatic weather monitoring station is being built to help predict the movement of hurricanes as they pass through the Northern Group.

## Practicalities

Tourists need a permit to visit Suwarrow, and stays are limited to 31 days. In practice, passing yachts can stay for up to three days, after registering with the

*Tom Neale's classic on Suwarrow*

caretaker. Visits to islets other than Anchorage Island are not allowed without approval of the caretaker, who must accompany all such visits. The patrol boat *Te Kukupa* has been sent up in the past to evict yachts that have overstayed their welcome.

## Life On A Tropical Island

Tom Neale lived the South Seas life that others dream about, although I'm not sure most would want to do it alone. Maybe his words, from *An Island To Oneself*, will help us understand why the dream lives on:

"I chose to live in the Pacific islands because life there moves at the sort of pace which you feel God must have had in mind originally, when He made the sun to keep us warm, and provided the fruits of the earth for the taking."

# GLOSSARY

**ara metua**---ancient coral road that once circled inland Rarotonga; much of it is still in use today

**ariki**---high chief of a tribe

**atoll**---low-lying ring of coral islets (*motus*) surrounding a lagoon

**bush beer**---home-brewed orange beer, now found on Atiu at a tumunu

**CICC**---Cook Islands Christian Church; Protestant sect succeeding LMS

**copra**---dried coconut meat, used in oils, soaps and perfumes

**'ei**---Rarotongan word for "lei"; necklace of flowers or shells

**eke**---octopus

**ika mata**---marinated raw fish

**kava**---mildly narcotic drink made from root of the pepper plant; banned by missionaries, no longer used in Cooks

**kopeka**---rare swift found only in one cave on Atiu

**koutu**---ancient open-air royal court

**LMS**---London Missionary Society; first missionaries in Cooks, in 1821

**maire**---medicinal plant of Mauke

**makatea**---ring of dead coral on Atiu, Mauke, Mitiaro and Mangaia

**Maori**---"indigenous to," referring to natives of Cook Islands

**marae**---sacred open-air religious site

**maroro**---flying fish

**mataiapo**---chief of a major lineage

**moko**---gecko; small lizard that eats *namus* (mosquitoes)

**motu**---islet

**namu**---mosquito

**Nga-Pu-Toru**---The "Three Roots," refers to Atiu, Mauke and Mitiaro

**nita**---papaya, also called pawpaw

**pandanus**---sword-leafed tree, used for roofing material, baskets, etc.

**Papa'a**---foreigner, European, or their language

**pareu**---colorful wrap-around sarong

**pate**---wooden slit-drum

**poke**---arrowroot pudding, made with bananas, papayas, or other fruit

**rangatira**---sub-chief of a lineage

**rito**---young inner leaf of coconut palm, used in making hats

**rukau**---leafy top of taro, rumored to be an aphrodisiac

**sennit**---coconut-fiber cord; used in canoes, found in churches on Mangaia

**tangaroa**---phallic male god of the sea, fishermen, fertility, etc.

**taro**---starchy tuber; a popular food in the Cook Islands

**tivaevae**---colorful patchwork quilt

**tumunu**---on Atiu: the hollowed-out coconut trunk where bush beer is brewed; the huts where one drinks the beer; or the tradition of drinking bush beer

**umukai**---an island-style feast, from *umu* (earth oven) and *kai* (food)

**uto**---sweet chiffon-like center of a sprouted coconut

# RECOMMENDED READING

*An Island To Oneself*---Tom Neale's classic about his life alone on Suwarrow; Fontana Silver Fern (1975)

*Atiu, An Island Community*---excellent locally-authored chapters on history, customs, etc.; USP (1984)

*The Book of Pukapuka*---Robert Dean Frisbie's 1929 stories from Atlantic Monthly; reprinted by Mutual Publishing of Honolulu. Also *Island of Desire* (1944)---Frisbie's tales of Suwarrow and Pukapuka; *Mr. Moonlight's Desire* (1939)---Frisbie's novel of the South Seas; *Miss Ulysses From Pukapuka* (1948) and *The Frisbies of the South Seas* (1959)---daughter "Johnny" Frisbie's stories of her father, and her life in the Cooks

*Cannibals and Converts*---the writings of Maretu, cannibal-turned-missionary; with translation and background by Marjorie Crocombe; USP (1983)

*The Cook Islands, 1820-1950*---academic-style history, with economy, government, politics; Richard Gilson; Victoria Univ. Press/USP (1980)

*Cook Islands Cookbook*---local dishes that you can prepare at home, by Taiora Matenga-Smith; Rarotonga (1990)

*Cook Islands Custom* (1892, reprinted by USP 1979) and *From Darkness To Light in Polynesia* (1894, reprinted by USP 1984) by missionary William Wyatt Gill---customs of Rarotonga, Mangaia and other islands from 1852-1892

*Discoverers of The Cook Islands and the Names They Gave*---A.M.J. Kloosterman; concise, thoroughly researched history; CI Library and Museum (1976)

*Doctor to the Islands*---Tom Davis' life before politics; Little Brown (1954); also his autobiographical *Island Boy*, and *Vaka* (1992), about early voyagers;

*The Flame Tree Cookbook*---recipes by Sue Carruthers from her award-winning restaurant; Rarotonga (1993)

*Gems From The Coral Islands*---Missionary William Gill's stories of early customs; (1856, reprinted by USP)

*History of Rarotonga Up To 1853*---early traditions and history of the main island; Taira Rere; Rarotonga (1991)

*Isles of the Frigate Bird* (Michael Joseph, 1975) and *The Lagoon Is Lonely Now* (Millwood, 1978)---the late Ron Syme's stories of the Cooks, 1950's to 1970's;

*Land Tenure in the Cook Islands*---study by expert Ron Crocombe; Oxford University Press, Melbourne (1969)

*The Man Who Refused To Die*---Barry Wynne's true story of 7 Manihiki men adrift for 64 days; Souvenir Press

*The Pareu Book*---Color photos of how-to-wear this versatile wraparound; Lynnsay Rongokea Francis; (1992)

*Rarotonga*---beautiful color photos by James Siers; Millwood Press (1977)

*Sir Albert Henry*---biography of first Premier of the Cook Islands; Kathleen Hancock; Methuen (1979)

*Sisters in the Sun*---interesting history and stories of Palmerston and Suwarrow; A.S. Helm and W.H. Percival; Robert Hale & Co. (1973)

*Slavers in Paradise: The Peruvian Labour Trade in Polynesia, 1862-1864*---decimation of Northern Cooks by blackbirders; H.E. Maude; USP (1981)

*South Seas Paradise*---Julian Dashwood's life on Mauke, written under pen name Julian Hillas; London (1964)

*Tivaevae*---the art and styles of local hand-sewn quilts; Lynnsay Rongokea Francis; Rarotonga (1992)

*Years of the Pooh Bah*---Dick Scott; the highly informative and entertaining account of the colonial era; CITC Rarotonga (1991)

*They Came For Sandalwood*---Goodenough's visit to Rarotonga in 1814; Marjorie Crocombe; Suva (1979)

**Language Publications:**
*Say It In Rarotongan*; the basics, with good vocabulary list; Mana Strickland; Pacific Publications (1979)

*Learning Rarotongan Maori*; everyday conversation, prepared for Peace Corps volunteers; Makiuti Tongia; CI Ministry of Cultural Development (1991)

*Conversational Maori*; for the serious student; Taira Rere; Rarotonga (1988)

*A Dictionary of the Maori Language of Rarotonga*--Stephen Savage (460pp)

**South Pacific and Oceania:**
*Exploring Tropical Isles and Seas*---Frederic Martini; excellent scientific look at tropical fish, plants, reefs, ocean environment; Prentice-Hall (1984)

*Faery Lands of the South Seas*---1921 classic by James Norman Hall and Charles Nordhoff, who later wrote Mutiny on the Bounty. Includes chapters on the Cooks; Garden City Pub.

*In Search of Paradise--The Nordhoff-Hall Story*---Paul Briand's biography of Mutiny on the Bounty authors, who traveled to Cooks and around Pacific; Mutual Publishing of Honolulu (1966)

*Lost Paradise--The Exploration of The Pacific*---Ian Cameron; excellent history, with beautiful color plates of Polynesian and European discoverers; Salem House (1987)

*Pacific Islands Yearbook*---the complete almanac/reference book of the islands; updated every 3-4 years (not yearly); Angus & Robertson

*South Pacific--An Introduction*---culture, land, politics, by authority Ron Crocombe; Longman Paul (1987)

*Voyages of Discovery*---Captain Cook and other early voyagers, by Lynne Withey; Univ. of Calif. Press (1989)

**Regional Guidebook:**
*South Pacific Handbook*---David Stanley; the most practical and comprehensive guide to travel in Polynesia and Melanesia. Includes moderate and upmarket hotels, in addition to backpackers' accommodations; Moon Publications (Box 3040, Chico, California 95927); Fifth edition, 1993

# INDEX

(Maps in **boldface**)

Solution to puzzle on page 176

We hope you've enjoyed our guidebook. If you complete the crossword puzzle below, consider yourself a knowledgeable "Cook Islands Companion".

## READY FOR RARO!

### ACROSS

1. Take some time ___, you need a vacation!
4. ___ metua, old inland road
7. Horse feed
11. Black pearls are ___ favorite souvenir
12. Cleverness
13. Train track
14. *Thank you very much!*
17. ___ Rangi Passage, Penrhyn
18. Tummy Rock beach, Mauke
19. Missionary implement
21. ___takitaki, Cave of the Kopeka, Atiu
22. Motel division
23. ___iami, uninhabited international airport, Aitutaki
24. You'll bring one home
27. *Sleep*
28. Anagram of Len
29. Definitely not a Polynesian hut!
30. Umukai centerpiece
31. Senior ladies
32. Not Raro weather!
35. *Islet*
36. Cook Islands' airline
40. Got up
41. *Octopus*
42. *Earth oven*
43. Unwelcome guests
44. Sun, in Spain
45. Storage (abbr.)

### DOWN

1. Electrical unit
2. Entrance charge
3. The "Pukapuka man"
4. Don't stay ___ all night on an overseas flight
5. Pukapuka's Adam
6. She has beach bungalows on Raro
7. Kia ___ ! (*Hello!*)
8. Top grade, four times
9. ___kaveka village, center of the South Beach area
10. Anagram of also
15. Pinball no-no
16. *Spiritual power*
19. ___ a ride; hitchhike
20. Portof___ Restaurant
21. The legend of ___, Atiu
23. Coral's buddy (abbr.)
24. *Bush beer schools*, Atiu
25. Mangaia ___, pineapple liqueur
26. Abbrev. of "not tonight, sweetie"
28. *Papaya*
29. Pukapukan village
30. French dads
31. Paradise Inn or Kii Kii
32. Girl's name
33. Animal definitely not in the Cooks!
34. Former
35. *Gecko*
37. You should have one for your lodging (abbr.)
38. Official world time (abbr.)
39. ___. 4, 1965, Independence Day

(Copyright © 1994, E.R.Smith)

(Solution on page 170)